OVERCOMING A MYSTERIOUS CONDITION

Don Shetterly

Mind Body Thoughts Publishing
www.MindBodyThoughts.com

Don Shetterly/Mind Body Thoughts Publishing
https://www.MindBodyThoughts.com

Disclaimer: This book is not intended as a substitute for the medical advice of physicians. The reader should regularly consult a physician in matters relating to his/her health and particularly with respect to any symptoms that may require diagnosis or medical attention. Do not use this information to diagnose or develop a treatment plan for a health problem or disease without consulting a qualified health care provider. References are provided for informational purposes only and do not constitute endorsement of any websites or other sources. Readers should be aware that the websites listed in this book may change. This is my recollection of events as they happened. They are my be-lief and opinion based upon my experiences as I recall them. I have endeav-ored to be factual in all things written. My intent is to provide the context for overcoming a mysterious condition.

Editing by Jeff Lemlich
Book Cover Graphics by Aiden Bailey
Cover photo by Yuriy Bogdanov on Unsplash

Overcoming A Mysterious Condition/ Don Shetterly. -- 1st ed.
ISBN-13: 978-1-7329270-0-1
ISBN-10: 1-7329270-0-6

To the ones that helped me realize unconditional love does exist.

To the ones that helped me find my way home.

To the ones that helped me when I struggled to find my way.

I thank you all from the innermost depths of my heart.

This book goes out to all those who have unexplained symptoms and pain while struggling to find answers and healing.

Table Of Contents

Foreword By Dr. Paul Canali.. vii
About Conversion Disorder ix
1. How Did I Heal?..1
2. The Missing Body 9
3. The Early Days 17
4. I Never Accepted My Condition 41
5. Relaxation 53
6. Notice, Sense, Feel... 63
7. Survival Mode... 75
8. Coming Out Of Survival Mode 87
9. Stress Impacts The Body 105
10. Fear 119
11. Into The Unconscious Mind 133
12. Numbing And Avoiding... 145
13. The Magic Pill... 157
14. Avoiding Healing 169
15. Loving That Negative Pleasure.................................... 177
16. Dealing With Our Insecurities 187
17. My Experience With Anger.. 199
18. Healing Is Hard Work 225
19. The Little Steps In Healing.. 237
20. What Has Worked For Me... 243
Additional Resources 253
Index 255
Chapter Quote Sources 261
About The Author.. 263

Foreword By Dr. Paul Canali

Dr. Paul Canali is the founder of Unified Therapy ™ at Evolutionary Healing Institute in Miami, Florida. Dr. Canali has created a new model for healing and treating chronic pain, anxiety, PTSD, toxic stress, and trauma in the body.

One of the greatest mysteries of all time is how the mind can change the body. Sigmund Freud and Jean-Martin Charcot -- both medical doctors and neurologists -- would get together and have long, drawn-out discussions on how to solve this mystery. The very birth of psychotherapy and even mental health came from these doctors, with their limited understanding, meeting at the Pitié-Salpêtrière teaching hospital in Paris. They were trying to comprehend how hurtful and traumatic events from an individual's past could be converted into real-time physical symptoms, often mimicking neurological diseases.

When Don Shetterly came into my life, I realized that he had a wealth of information trapped within his body. Don had experienced chronic pain, seizures, and had been paralyzed, after years of physical abuse and torture. The question was, could his symptoms and his early life experiences be related? How could one have anything to do with the other? How did it work in his brain and body? Could there be potentially thousands, or maybe millions of Don's out there suffering and often misdiagnosed?

I think of another patient, 19-year-old Brittany, who had an extensive history of emergency room visits. After multiple diagnoses from various specialists, and years of pain and suffering, she found herself at the Mayo Clinic, blind in one eye, addicted to pain medication, and suffering from one of the most severe types of chronic pain -- trigeminal neuralgia. Amazingly, during her examination at the Mayo Clinic, the blindness shifted from one eye to the other. She was diagnosed with conversion disorder, also known as functional neurological disorder (FND). She was told there was nothing they can do.

I remember when Brittany's eyesight came back, and the terrible trigeminal pain went away. Instead of anxiety and depression, there was peace and hopefulness. But what amazes me even more was that I fully expected her to have to go to a detox program to get off her pain medication. That was not needed. Maybe, just maybe what I thought about the opiate receptor in the brain and addiction was not true at that moment. Human beings have an innate sense of plasticity to recover and heal.

Early childhood environments can shape the brain and the body, for better or worse. The Centers for Disease Control now recommends that every physician in America administer the ACE study (Adverse Childhood Experiences), which measures early trauma and stress by allowing individuals to answer a series of questions. It's a fact that many chronic diseases in adulthood are determined decades earlier by toxic, stressful environments, which change the brain pathways in children and can set them up for a lifetime of physical and emotional illness. This is what happened to Don.

Through the years Don has been an incredible teacher for me. He helped me to see this amazing brain-body connection and to perfect the ability to biohack, that is gain accessibility into the unconscious mind. A big part of coming back from this mysterious condition is developing the skill to move energy, to move emotion, to move anxiety, to move pain, to hold on to pleasant feelings and release negative ones. Happiness is a pathway, just as pain is a pathway or anxiety is a pathway. It is a physical pathway in the brain and body that can be biohacked. The brain can be accessed, and it is possible to repair these neurodevelopmental scars.

I believe that Don Shetterly has a living, breathing source of knowledge in his body. Don helps us gain new insights into human disease and suffering, and the mystery of the human condition. Until humanity begins to understand that what we do to each other has a much bigger impact than any of us could ever imagine, we will never get out of this state of perpetual suffering.

This book isn't just about the mysterious condition. It's something much greater, something intergenerational. The book contains knowledge. It contains a key that can open a doorway of understanding that is missing in all of us.

Dr. Paul Canali, DC
www.EvolutionaryHealingInstitute.com

About Conversion Disorder

"Conversion disorder is a mysterious condition in which toxic stress can convert, within the body, what appears to be a neurological disorder. Traditionally it was thought only to mimic conditions – seizures, paralysis, sciatica, etc. – without any organic root cause. Now we realize we must broaden the definition to include other affected biological or body systems, whether digestive, the immune system, or maybe even cancer itself.

*The knowledge that this condition holds is so important because it holds the connection between adverse childhood experiences and real-time physical conditions. It may be the very root of solving the mind body link." - **Dr. Paul Canali***

1. How Did I Heal?

"We are a result of the journey we have walked. Each day we have gives us the possibility of so much more." - **Don Shetterly**

One of the most common questions I get asked is, "How did you heal from conversion disorder?" I have asked this question of myself so many times because it was not a clear-cut path. However, it deserves a good answer.

There was no recipe or a step-by-step process that I followed. I didn't just fill in the color-by-number set hoping for a clear picture to appear. I was not following what everyone told me to do because the answers each person gave me varied greatly.

In many cases, I was hurting and going through deep pain. I was sitting in confusion, despair, and anxiety. There was nothing clear about the place I was at in my life. There was nothing that made sense at that moment, let alone allowed me to see the next moment.

Often, I see memes and platitudes that make it appear as if what we are facing can be solved in the blink of an eye or a statement on the screen. There is no reality to many of the things that are said and done these days. We are all so focused on not feeling all that is going on that we escape through things that offer nothing but empty space and pretty lights.

Yes, I know we claim we are doing anything but numbing. Numbing leads us to believe this. It helps us not see that which is painful and which challenges us to the core of our being.

It is in our desire to recognize the numbing that we move further ahead in our healing. Without the conscious awareness that we are numbing, we stay in the place we so badly want to escape from in life.

For years, I thought I was connected, happy, and aware, until my experience with conversion disorder. I found out that the opposite of what I thought and believed was true.

When life challenges us, it is not easy. I know that firsthand and yet I see so many trying to act as if it is. I see so many wishing that their lives could have nothing to do with the experiences they have lived through all these years. However, I know deep down that all the things I have faced in life have led me to this moment I am in currently.

Yes, it would be great if we could wave a magic wand and declare all of our past as being in the past, not impacting us at this moment. It would be so freeing and liberating for every human on this planet to do this. While I would love to say it is that way, I know far too well that overcoming experiences is more challenging than platitudes suggest.

In my own life, I put the happy smiles on my face. I shared only love with others while I harbored pain, agony, and anger deep within my cells. I was convinced, though, that this was what a good person does. It is how you act. You don't let others see you sweat or show weakness. You must act as you have it all under control. We're taught not to let others see our pain. Many times, we give more to others while ignoring how badly we need to heal and be there for ourselves.

As I write these words, I realize that so many would gasp and claim, "But oh you don't need to do all of this hard work. You are making things way too difficult. You just need to move on in life." Many only want to insert their favorite platitude or meme rather than work at truly waking up in life. As I wake up and see what is happening in this world, it is then that I once again realize just how asleep we are. I see it easily because I once lived that same life.

As I found out when I was paralyzed from a conversion disorder, what I thought I knew and what I exclaimed for all to hear was not what reality was. My life was so numb and disconnected that I had no way of knowing what an authentic life was. You would not have been able to convince me in those moments that I was living a lie. You would not have been able to convince me that I was numb and disconnected. In to-day's times, I see the same thing happening all across human civilization.

Most of us are living that lie, and we don't know it. Sure, we know how to say our prayers, do our mantras, meditate and play the game of being all-knowing, but we only fool ourselves. I say this from personal experience because I did this very same thing. It took me years to wake up and see the full breadth of my numbing and disconnect.

If you're reading this, you're most likely on a journey of searching and discovery. This book is for those who are searching and wanting more from life. This book is about seeking out that which we don't un-derstand and going beyond all that we know at this moment. While this book may challenge you (and I hope it does), my greater hope is that the challenges will give rise to a new birth within you that helps you understand far more than you can see at this moment.

Overcoming challenges in whatever form they have shown up in life is essential to becoming more than we are at this moment. Learning how to overcome challenges leads us to greater heights that may have seemed impossible before, but not now. When you overcome challenges, life looks different than it did before because now you see from a new awareness and consciousness.

When I came through the paralysis of conversion disorder, it was not easy. It was not simple. There was no one to tell me step-by-step what I should do to heal. To this day, doctors and medical facilities struggle to understand how to help someone heal from conversion disorder. I hope that we learn how to deal with this before it becomes a condition that engulfs the world.

I've seen more and more people now struggling with conversion disorder, and while some can overcome it and make progress, many are struggling to break free from its grasp. Many don't feel you can heal from it. Many are searching for the pretty neon lights when the answers are within us.

Is It Easy To Heal?

Is it easy to heal from something like conversion disorder or trauma or PTSD? Is it easy to conquer anxiety, depression or suicidal thoughts? Is it easy to have a life that we can live in joy and peace, rather than pain and heartbreak? No, it is not! I know that overcoming challenges is possible, even if it is not easy.

If you want to cast doubt on what I am saying, that is your choice, and you are free to do so. I cannot force you to change or do that which you don't want to do. Only you can offer your mind new information and then see how it applies to your life. You alone are in control of what you allow to come into your conscious thought because no one else can do that for you. People may show up to help share insights with you, but at the end of the day, what you do with your life is your choice.

We must recognize that our experiences in life impact our current moments of thought. They are sneaky and sly, trying not to let us see just how much impact they do have. It is up to us to become aware of them and then make a conscious choice to change what we have done to find something new.

I write this book from my experiences of what I used to heal my life. Many entered my path and helped hold a flashlight on my journey so that I could discover more. They helped me learn more about myself. They helped me see more in myself than I knew was there. I did not always recognize them when they were present, but I can see them more clearly now as I look back over my journey.

Even with all those that were there for me, I had to go in and allow myself to see what I did not see. I had to throw off the security blanket I held over myself. It required that I had to discard that which I thought was my foundation when in fact, it would become clear later that it was a foundation of sand.

I had to allow myself to go deep within, even when I was not sure of where the path was leading me. It was up to me to say, "What worked in the past is no longer working, and I need to find the truth that will help me walk forward and heal."

To heal, I had to challenge everything that I held dear to my heart. I had to evaluate every person in my life. What I thought was the truth would need to be evaluated to see if it was true or if I was following a charade that appeared as the holy grail.

In my search for healing, I found that many things were not as they appeared. I found that many of the teachings out there only led me part of the way to the next step. The more I discovered, the more I knew existed in the world. The more I knew existed, the more I could see.

When you find yourself on the floor because your legs can no longer hold you up, you will end up seeing life differently than what you thought it was. You are confronted with a view of existence that you did not have before this moment. It will be your choice at that time to learn from it or let it take over control of your life. That is what I was facing with conversion disorder.

In all my healing, I've learned that I had to challenge every core belief I held and everything that I knew. I could leave no stone unturned because to find myself and heal, I had to let go of it all. It was not some pie-in-the-sky concept that helped me through it. The difficulty of the situation helped me desire to move beyond where I was, let go, and look for the core truth that would help me. Overcoming challenges in life is not a quick fix.

Closing my eyes to horrors that I could not articulate, did not help me heal. Acting as if my life was one big happy picture served very little purpose. I not only had to confront the ugly truths in my life, but I had to allow myself to recognize their existence. In those moments, I often wanted to give up. It rocked my life to the core of my existence.

For me, healing was about going in and discovering my innermost self from the deepest part of all my existence. It was about not listening to everyone that thought they had the truth, but seeing if there were parts of truth in what they said that I could apply to my life and healing. Even in those moments where you think what others say is of no value, there is generally some nugget of truth. The trick becomes to find that nugget and discard the rest.

Far too many of us think we have life all figured out and that we know what reality is. Unfortunately, this is the opposite of what exists. Just like in conversion disorder, we are numb and disconnected from the mind and body. We don't see what we think we see and we don't know what we think we know.

We focus on what happens in the mind. We focus on positive affirmations and mantras. Often, we try to force our minds to think in a way that we believe helps us heal our lives. While all these things can be helpful, they often become a Band-Aid for a gushing wound. If we are not careful, they become a distraction.

We must travel into the core of our existence. Healing is more than making the mind think that we are much more than we are. The body is the keeper of the mind and the holder of our thoughts.

Experiences we have been through reside in the body and are held within our cells and are often hidden from conscious view. Until we go in and open these things up, we will only know they exist, not that they have a hold on our lives. The experiences we have been through not only hold the bad in but they also become the keys to unlock the greater truths found within us.

I have seen far too many healing modalities and spiritual concepts that miss this connection. Yes, they will give lip service to its understanding, but they do so at the expense of consciously becoming aware of what it is. They miss where it resides in the nervous system, cells, tissues, and body. They miss the connection between those and the brain.

All these moments that we go through are our own individual journeys. These moments are the challenges that we face. It is necessary for us to dig beneath each layer and discover more of the light within, but we must choose to travel there. The path we take will differ from others, but at the essence of it, we are walking towards the same questions and seeking the same answers.

We should not stop walking on our path. The going may get tough and difficult, but never stop moving. Even if you don't know where the path leads, keep putting one foot down in front of the other. Keep looking for the flashlights that help to illuminate the path ahead. Keep looking for the markers on the path. The overturned stones that you may notice are from those walking in front of you.

Core Truths I Learned

What I have shared in this book is not a recipe that you can apply to be completely cured in 30 days. Instead, it is a sharing of the concepts and things that I learned along my way which have helped me continue my journey of discovery. These are core truths that I have discovered, and when used as ingredients in a healing journey, you can create results that work for you.

I do not believe that healing is necessarily about coming to an endpoint. In my mind and view, it is more of coming to greater awareness and consciousness. Once we arrive at that moment, more will be opened to us, but it is a continual process of evolving and becoming more of who we are meant to be.

Never settle for where you have arrived. It is okay for you to stop and rest, but continually seek to know and understand more than you know today. Becoming human is about our continued growth through life in awareness and consciousness, not an arrival point.

The more you discover, the more you will know. The more you know, the more you will see. The more you see, the more you will have the opportunity to discover. Take all of it by the hand and welcome it into your life because the opposite only leads to further pain, despair, and hopelessness.

In my first book, Hope And Possibility Through Trauma, I shared some of my story and journey in how I found healing. It was the beginning stages of me finding my voice. Overcoming A Mysterious Condition uses my previous book as a launching pad.

May your life be changed as you continue reading this book. May the concepts that have helped resonate within my own life, help you in your life. I hope that you will take what I share and push it to the limits, offering your life so much more. May you challenge the concepts I have learned to see if they fit in your life, or perhaps you will end up discovering something more.

<u>Try This Exercise</u>

List the challenges you have faced in life and how you have used them to push you past the limits of what is possible.

2. The Missing Body

"Many people in pain have trained themselves to disconnect from their body experience in a defensive attempt to avoid feeling more pain." – Dr. Peter A. Levine, Ph.D.

I see the buzzwords of mind body thrown around these days. People have the jargon down, but they are often missing the true concept behind the words. mind body is more than a couple of words and is more than a concept.

It is great that everyone realizes healthy practices involve the mind. I'm ecstatic that people now recognize this. Several years ago, few spoke about this, let alone started to piece it together. It was barely a concept not that long ago.

Unfortunately, while the understanding and awareness have begun, there are far too many that have acted as authorities. In my view, they do not fully understand what it means. It is more than a set of views in the world about how you see your life. It is more than a bunch of platitudes of positive thinking or claiming the answers that everyone should live by in their lives.

Mind body is more than what many of us understand it to be. It is more than mindfulness. It is more than thinking something in your mind.

All these things are great, but they are just a part of the mind body connection. Unfortunately, we focus on the mind more than the body. Without the second half of the mind body phrase, you're missing an important connection. There is a reason that it has both the words mind and body. It is meant to include both parts, not just one.

The mind body connection begins with feeling in the body that allows us to connect deeper to the consciousness of the mind. Using the felt sense, we feel what is happening with the body, which provides the connection to the mind. It is then we begin to see with awareness so that we become more conscious about life. As we do this, all that we thought we could see and feel is realized from a new perspective.

While we may want to think we connect with the mind and body, we often don't understand the "body" side of things. The body side of things is where you stop and go inside your body to feel. It is where you go in and notice and sense all parts of your muscles, cells, tissues, organs, and brain. It is where you connect with your feelings, emotions, thoughts, and memory.

The mind body concept is the entire mind, body, spirit and all parts that you are aware of or fail to notice. It is your current consciousness and how you fit in with the world. It involves connecting deep within your heart with what is in your mind that shows up through your words, actions, and compassion. Also, it includes awareness of things that may exist, but you have not yet discovered. The nervous system is a big part of the mind body connection.

While we may think we understand this, I've seen time and time again that we do not. I'm not chastising anyone, but merely opening up the awareness. After all, we are all human. We all are trying to live in a body, and there was no owner's manual given to us when we were born.

Years ago, before being paralyzed from a conversion disorder, I thought I was in touch with both my mind and my body. However, I found out just how disconnected I was. I was walking around with my head in the clouds while thinking I saw everything on the ground.

Making The Mind Body Connection

When you stop to notice, sense, and feel, that's when you start to make the mind body connection. If you do this, you will discover things in your body that you did not realize were there, from aches and pains to all kinds of sensations and feelings. Good and bad, the mind body connection encompasses everything.

So many times, the full breadth of what we feel and sense in the body eludes us. We think we know it and in our current consciousness, that may very likely be a true observation. However, when you stop and notice, sense and feel, it is then that you give yourself the opportunity to see what else is there. At that moment, you have given yourself the possibility of that which you are not aware.

When you can connect with all that you sense and feel at any given moment in the body, you will find that there is a great awareness that is hiding from your consciousness. If you stay with what you sense and pick up, you then can focus your mind on it, as if it is a magnifying glass of discovery and awareness. It becomes a great power within you to change, heal, and find balance. The most important part, though, is that you must begin to feel this within the body because without that part, you're only working with the mind and forming an incomplete picture.

The more we become aware of that which we do not currently see, the more we can go further in life and accomplish things that we do not realize exist. Our awareness at that moment is based on what we see, not what we have held ourselves back from seeing. It is at this moment that we begin to come alive with so much possibility that even the most difficult challenges begin to take on new meaning. It is not just a thought process, but one that comes from deep within the memories of our physical cells.

The one detour we often take when we start to feel things is attempting to put them into a lockbox of what these feelings and sensations should be. They become what we perceive, not what they are. In the true mind body connection, there is no analysis needed. All that's needed is to focus on feeling and sensing and noticing. The lockbox exists because of what we have been taught and shown, even if we are not aware that these things are impacting our lives. It exists because of and despite our experiences or perception in life.

From the beginning of time, we have watched those around us in how they do things and what paths they take. We have noticed the things they didn't realize we saw and have used those to form the basis of our current lives. The way others close to us respond to situations and life's necessities becomes the lesson plans we mirror. From a young age, we have learned to mirror what others around us do in their lives and adopt it as the basis for ours.

Some things we witnessed and learned were helpful, while others were not. It is up to each one of us to challenge and relearn all that we hold dear in life. While these moments gave us the building blocks of the life we know, they may now be stumbling blocks into the truth for our lives. These concepts we learned can very easily become something that holds us back.

What we learn is worthy will stand the test of time, while learning what is no longer helpful to our lives will push us to let it go. Letting go is not easy for many people including myself, but as I continue to find each day, it allows much greater moments and beautiful gifts to find their way into my life.

This awareness is where we discover our mind body connection. It is where the missing body becomes one in our awareness and consciousness. It is life and the beginning of so much more possibility.

We all put boundaries up in life. We only let certain things in, and we keep other things out. It is part of the mind body connection and is critical to our survival. However, there are times that our boundaries get in the way of our growth. By putting walls up and never taking the opportunity to see beyond them, we limit ourselves. We limit all that is possible before us.

If we recognize the boundaries that are there and then question if they still serve a purpose, we are now in the driver's seat. We are one with the mind body connection. At this moment, we have a greater awareness which leads to a deeper consciousness.

When you begin to focus on the boundaries and walls that you have, where do they take you? What do you notice? Does fear come up or does the pain intensify? Does the act of noticing it become uncomfortable? Does your mind drift? Do you stop breathing or can you notice if you stop breathing?

These are just some of the questions that arise when you go into the mind body connection. It is connecting with all parts of your innermost self, not just the ones that have screamed so loudly that they finally get your attention. If you wait until the parts scream that loudly, the mind body connection is being silenced.

So often in life, we disregard the messages the body sends to us. We are more disconnected and numb than we may realize, so the messages try but never get through to us. The more we ignore the messages, the further harm and damage we inflict upon our bodies. The body is reaching out, but if no one is home, the messages pile up on our doorstep.

When I was in a healing session with Dr. Paul Canali, I noticed that my legs went back to the moment of paralysis. It was almost as if I was back in the moment of conversion disorder. He would instruct me to move my legs, and while my brain wanted to do that, nothing would happen.

I would try with all my mental power to say "legs move," but they would just sit there. The messages were not getting through to me. This concept is at the heart of somatization. We don't hear the messages of the body. The body is screaming, but we are unable to hear them.

Somatization is the ability of the brain to convert emotional and mental stressors into a physical condition.

There are so many things beyond our conscious thought and control that take place in the body. When we are not in touch with the mind body connection, this becomes nothing more than an academic exercise. It is like calling someone on your phone, but no one answers.

Far too often, we are so oblivious to what is truly going on that we go through our days on autopilot. Without truly feeling everything, we hold ourselves back. We limit our potential, and we suppress our natural healing ability in life.

If you are not aware there is an issue, how can you begin to deal with it? If you continue to ignore it, the potential energy that builds up in the body has no exit. As it builds up, it begins to impact other body systems. The more we ignore it, the more it builds until it gets our attention, one way or the other.

*Always, in order to change, we have to come to a new understanding of self and the world so that we can embrace new knowledge and have new experiences. - **Dr. Joe Dispenza, D.C., Breaking The Habit Of Being Yourself***

Do you realize just how complex the body is? With trillions of cells functioning in unison to help create your day, the brain orchestrates your experiences and current encounters in life. Our cells replicate and pass the information along, while sensing, feeling, absorbing and recording many input sources we take for granted. All of this happens without your conscious thought directing it or giving it one moment of concern to your current experiences. It all just happens in the blink of an eye, almost as if we have no control over it.

The Felt Sense

Connecting with the missing body is not about trying to write a story regarding what is coming up. It isn't about trying to say that if you feel this pain, it means this. Connecting is feeling and sensing. It is about noticing and observing.

The act of connecting what is going on within the body with what you feel is referred to as the "felt sense," as Dr. Paul Canali, creator of Unified Therapy™ at the Evolutionary Healing Institute, has taught in seminars.

The felt sense is such a powerful healer and connector of the mind body. It will tap into moments that you don't even notice until you permit yourself to see them. It is one that brings the mind and body together, so you can change the way you observe the missing body. However, we must allow ourselves to permit it to show up because it will not until we let it.

It is in that moment of the felt sense that we now can tap into a power greater than we've experienced before. It is at that point that we now have a connection to something that brings us into awareness and consciousness as we've never seen before. This moment is the essence of who we are. It is where the healing takes place in the body that seems almost magical.

The mind body connection is far more critical to our lives than we could have ever imagined. We speak as if we understand it, but at the same time, we hide from it. Most of the time we keep it just beyond our awareness and consciousness. We treat it as a stranger or at best an unwanted friend, but we go no further into the relationship between the mind and body.

It is more than lip service and trendy new age thoughts. It is more than acting like you're an authority on something while being disconnected in life. The mind body connection is in the essence of who we are. It is much more than a thought process or routine. The mind body connection is more than beliefs or regurgitated learning.

I've learned the hard way in my life through paralysis and conversion disorder that there is so much more to my body and my mind than I was aware. Even through considerable hours of counseling, bodywork, and healing, there was still a part that I had not discovered. I was still hiding behind what I thought healing and awareness were all about, not what they are.

In my life and the words I write in this book, I hope that others will begin to get a glimpse of what the mind body connection truly is and not just what they have heard. There is so much more within each one of us and the limitations we put on ourselves only hold us back. We must choose to throw off the chains that tie us down to permit ourselves to discover what exists. May you find your own missing body in the mind and body connection of your life.

In my own life, I have been taught many things. While my experiences were challenging and difficult, they became my teacher in helping me to understand more of this connection. Yes, I fought them, and yes, I ignored them. Yes, I acted as if I had life all together. In the long run, though, I had to choose to stay ignorant or allow myself to go in and make new discoveries. My life and survival depended on it. My existence required me to make this choice.

Try This Exercise

Take a moment wherever you are at to try this little experiment. The quieter and more comfortable of a space you can get, the better off you are. However, this will work in just about any place.

Sit or lie there with your eyes closed and just focus on your chest as you breathe. You may even want to place your hands over your chest area for a greater effect. How much does your chest rise? How quickly does it rise and fall? How shallow or deep does it go? If you notice and observe it, does it change? What can you notice when you do this?

Check out the companion CD to this book,

Mind Body Meditation Exercises.
The exercise on "Breathing" corresponds to this chapter.
https://MindBodyMeditationExercises.com

3. The Early Days

*"We have learned that trauma is not just an event that took place sometime in the past; it is also the imprint left by that experience on mind, brain, and body." - **Dr. Bessel van der Kolk, M.D.**

For a long time, I didn't know the name of the condition I had. Later, I would find out the paralysis was from a condition called conversion disorder. I did not have a clear idea of what this condition entailed because there were very few resources for me to research. Also, I was more concerned about trying to recover my life and keeping the paralysis from coming back.

Rather than dealing with life, I could have just sat there and said, "I'll get to it someday." It would have been easy to ignore it and push it aside like I had been doing for years. I could have just continued to numb and disconnect, acting as if everything was fine in life. Unfortunately, I saw in the hospital just how far that got me. I have since learned that sometimes life needs to get so overwhelming that it gets us to act.

Even in the early days, I could not articulate what I had been through in my life. Sure, I knew that a family member had done sexual things with me. I even had convinced myself at the time that all this was normal. Didn't all families do this? I did not see it as sexual abuse even though it was.

Wasn't it normal for a family member to show you the ropes on how to give blowjobs and masturbate? Wasn't it normal for a family member to coax you into his room quietly as to not disturb someone sleeping next to you or your parents in the other room? Everyone did that, right?

Those rides to school functions or church were horrible. He would pull off the main road into a field entrance or some remote spot, and I knew the routine. Get the paper towels or other things to clean up with and do what I knew I was supposed to do. Praise God in one breath while holding your silence for the required sexual acts you were about to do.

No, there was no written code. It had been taught to me by example and expectation. I knew what was expected and I knew the consequences if I did not fulfill my duties. If I didn't do as instructed, all hell would come down on me.

In some ways, I may have known something was wrong with what he did with me. However, I didn't know what was wrong. Being sheltered and withdrawn from the world through religious teachings and church while being taught these things from an early age left them feeling normal to me. It is too easy to think that I should have somehow known what was wrong or right.

Many people would wonder, why didn't I speak up or say something to another person? Well, to be honest – who could I trust? I was taught to fear everyone. I was taught to keep family secrets within the family, lest you want to end up like the family pets in their last moments. The physical violence I suffered through was the keeper of the silence. The threat of death in our pets was all the proof I needed.

Even if I would have confided in another person, I didn't realize in many ways what was done to me or what I was forced to do was wrong. It felt like just a part of life. I had no other way to evaluate it or understand it. I did not realize that not every kid went through this. Even though others would gasp at what happened, it felt normal to me, and it seemed normal. It was as much a part of life as feeding the chickens and the pets or going to school every day.

I'm not sure if anyone noticed that anything was wrong. Many probably noticed that I was shy and withdrawn. I appeared to be a well behaved little boy full of wonder, but the side of life that was supposed to stay hidden would in no way come out. There was too much at risk. There were too many threats made against us.

I remember hearing from my dad that if we told anyone about any discipline or anything that happened in the house, we would regret it. It was made clear to us that we were never supposed to say anything to anyone. Deep down, I knew that if the lives of my pets were not safe, mine too was not. I suffered physical beatings and punishment for the smallest things. If I got beat and kicked for putting the silverware away wrong in the drawer, imagine what would happen if I told anyone the things that went on within our house.

Even within the family, it would be many years later before I would find out about some of the stuff that others experienced. In my mind, I thought other family members had escaped some of the horrors I went through. I thought it had stopped with me. I tried to stop it by taking it and enduring it, so they wouldn't have to. Even though I wanted to believe it had stopped, it had not. Unfortunately, I was wrong. It happened before my very eyes, and yet I did not see it. It happened in the same house and yet I did not know.

I heard about the gay stuff and was taught that this was an abomination before God; that if you were gay, you were one of the worst, most despicable people there was on the planet. I didn't know what it meant to be gay. I just thought the sexual stuff I was forced to do in the family was normal stuff. So, gay must have been much worse than what I went through, or so I believed.

It would take me many years to sort through my sexuality and realize that it was so messed up in my early years, that I was robbed of normal experiences. I would not come to know until many years later, what true love and normal sexual behavior are between two people. I weep at the thought of how my body was used to gratify those that stole the innermost depths of my being while using love to force themselves on me.

You see, there was nothing normal about my life, but to me it was normal. I experienced stuff from such an early age, and in fact, it was so early, that I didn't know anything different. It took me a long time to realize that I never fully understood that being happy was normal. I just thought life was about enduring torture each day.

No, it wasn't just one family member that abused and molested me. It was also my father, a.k.a. the sperm donor as well. Okay, that's what I call my father. If you asked him about it today, he would tell you I was crazy and brainwashed. He would tell you, in his opinion, that I just let my feelings get the better of me. He would tell you that the doctors and psychiatrists planted these thoughts in my mind.

I was ostracized for daring to speak the truth. I was pushed aside as punishment because my parents believed I was telling my doctors, when I had not even raised the issue. My parents tried to control and manipulate me. They told others how screwed up I was and that I was brainwashed and had no clue what I was saying.

In the end, the hateful letters they would write to me were daily reminders of how you could never tell anyone. You had to keep it secret no matter what. As my mom later wrote to me, "We all have skeletons in the closet." I wish I understood the full breadth of this statement. I wish I understood what she meant.

The letters, in the end, got so toxic and hateful that I had anxiety attacks just going to my mailbox and getting my mail. It got so bad that I would wait forever to get the mail and when I went there, I would shake most of the way, hardly able to breathe. I'd sweat bullets for fear that there would be another letter to stab me once again in my heart. The letters continued for months.

Finally, I asked one of my best friends, Art, to take the letters and read them. I told him that if anything was important to let me know. After handing several of them over to him, I finally asked him one day if there was any news. I believe his response was "I threw them away." There was absolutely nothing good in them.

How can parents do this to their own flesh and blood? First off, how can they physically beat, emotionally manipulate and sexually abuse a son? I should make that plural as in sons because my siblings were not exempt. How can they do all of this and act like they have God's love in their heart? How can they act as if they love their kid? I don't understand how all of this can happen, and I was ostracized as the horrible person, daring to speak the truth.

These were my early days of healing. I was trying to get my life back together piece by piece. I had managed to get back to my job and function as normally as I could. My legs worked, but I dealt with depression and anxiety. I struggled to remember anything. Suicidal thoughts became the daily struggle. There were many ways I tried to cover it up by staying busy. The more things came together, the more I felt like a shell of a person I hardly knew.

My work suffered because my memory was so overtaken by all that I was trying to forget. I wanted to flee what was buried deep within me, but it was becoming harder and harder to do that. I wanted just to put my life back together, but I trusted no one, and I felt helpless and hopeless.

As I kept trying to progress in the job, I continued doing therapy after getting out of the hospital. It was helping, but most of it was group therapy, designed to help each participant deal with life. I had no coping skills, although I thought I always handled life. I didn't know how to interact with people for I feared they would just use and abuse me. As the days went by, I kept trying, and I kept fighting against the odds. No way did I want those that abused me to win. I wanted to be normal. I wanted to be a regular person, not that I understood in the least what that meant.

At the time, I was living in a house located in a rural area. I grew more and more scared of the darkness at night where I lived. Living alone in this big three-bedroom farmhouse with my cat, I was afraid. I didn't know what I was afraid of, but the darkness of the night made me so anxious.

It got to the point that I was leaving the lights on in the house 24 hours a day. I wasn't just leaving a couple of lights on; I was leaving the light on in every room of the house. I didn't care about the power bill because I was too afraid to turn them off. No door was left closed, not even the closets. I lived in complete fear of the dark and had no rational explanation at the time why that was.

I remember seeing a program on TV. While I don't recall the name of the movie, the subject matter of it sticks with me to this day. In the movie, I remember that the grandfather was playing a game with his granddaughter called "horsey." The storyline went that no one wanted to believe the little girl that the grandfather had done something she knew wasn't right. As the mother and siblings started to confront this horrible truth, it awakened memories within them. They struggled with the family secrets.

I got angry beyond measure watching the movie and had no idea why. How could no one believe the little girl? How could no one think this was wrong, I wondered? Attempting to put it out of my mind, I grew angrier at what I had watched on the TV. My anger got so intense that I wanted to punch my TV!

Shortly after that, sleeping became much more difficult. It didn't matter how exhausted I was or how hard I worked. My eyes were afraid to close. Even sleeping with all the lights on in the house, I didn't feel safe. I was afraid that something was lurking in the house at night and if I slept, I would not be able to defend myself or know it was happening. As I write this now, I'm filled with extreme fear just recalling this moment. I'd like to stop writing this book, but I know I need to tell this story. I must get through this moment.

I had arranged with my friend Art that if anything happened, 24 hours a day, I could call him. That one night – I'll never forget it. It is as if it happened yesterday. I'm shuddering with fear and shaking as I type this, this many years later.

All at once, around 2 AM, I woke up screaming. I screamed so loud. Fortunately, I had no neighbors close to my house. I was breathing so hard. My heart was racing wildly. I screamed. I was afraid and frightened out of my mind. However, I had no clue why.

There was no memory to detail. There was nothing readily available as to why I was screaming. It was complete and utter fear that brought out the guttural scream within me.

Getting the courage up, I reluctantly called my friend Art. I felt bad for waking him up, but I needed someone to talk to at that moment. I couldn't sleep. I couldn't think about calming down enough even to exist at that moment. Fortunately, he picked up the phone and let me talk.

There would be more of these moments. I would find myself screaming at night, not knowing why. Nothing made sense. I felt abnormal and crazy. Maybe my family was right. I was crazy.

Somehow, I functioned the next day after these all-night episodes, but my work suffered. I would mix up ordering the right vaccines for the farms I managed. My boss and the company vet figured out that I had screwed up and instead of understanding that I was having issues, they accused me of cheating and lying. They would not listen to me that it was an honest mistake. I was outcast from them as a failure, another reminder in my mind of just how screwed up I was.

After being put on probation, I finally had to take a leave of absence. The company had once been very supportive of me and my recovery from conversion disorder, but now things were different. I found out through the grapevine that I was on their hit list of people to fire. It didn't take long before I could not handle the anxiety that all of this brought on and I finally just quit my job.

It was too much to fight, and my boss was one of those people you couldn't trust. He proved that completely as he told his version of the facts to his boss. They believed him. They shoved me aside as someone they wanted nothing to do with and did not want. It didn't matter how much they liked me before. They saw the opportunity, and they railroaded me out the door. I'll never forget trying to stand up to them when the final evaluation was written in such a way that proved I was a terrible employee. Only six months earlier, I was one they praised in an evaluation.

So, I decided in my depressed and anxious state that after hearing Don Lapre and the 1-900 dateline money making system, I was going to work for myself. It was not the best decision I have ever made, but I was taken in by the charm and promises this guy made on TV. This decision would later bankrupt me and leave me within days of being homeless. Of course, many years after this I would learn that he was taken to court for his system and I believe he took his life before going to jail.

The next year or so was rough and bumpy. I would find myself very afraid of going outside my apartment, especially if there were people nearby. At a nearby gym in Hot Springs, Arkansas, I would find myself sexually assaulted in the locker room. I would have to endure my psychotic neighbor calling the cops on me in the middle of the night thinking I was window peeping on him, even though we all knew the raccoons in the woods near us would climb up and down the wood poles outside.

My life would come crashing down as I ran up heavy credit card debt trying to make a business go that was doomed from the start as it was based on a scam. In those final days, when I knew I had to move out of my apartment but had no place to go, I was overwhelmed. I felt helpless and hopeless. There was no one to rely on in my life. At that point, I was preparing to live in my car with my cat and all my belongings I could take with me.

Fortunately, things worked out, and I found a job at the last minute. I was able to go back to a former company I worked for just out of college. I would have to scheme and finagle my way through a financial mess to get myself and my belongings out to this new place in North Carolina. It wasn't an easy feat, especially with having to file bankruptcy in the middle of it all. My life felt like one big ruined mess. Healing and recovery took a backseat as I had no time for that. It was pure survival. I didn't know if I could make it through this. It felt like this might be the end for me.

It felt like I was escaping town. I left no forwarding address, other than to a post office box that I had a friend check. I didn't want anyone to find me. Most of all, I didn't want my parents to find me. I wanted to be left alone, in peace, and disappear from life.

For the first month of living in my new place, I barely had enough money to exist. I had bought many canned goods to eat, and those became my meals. The only money I could spend was on gas to get back and forth to the place where I worked. The food was optional because I had to be able to pay my rent and electricity. Everything else was a luxury.

After the mess I had come out of, the physical work of my job was a blessing to me. It helped me get my mind off everything. There were still issues with the bankruptcy to deal with, and so these moments would get very stressful. I was afraid that someone would find me. I was afraid that my parents would find me. All I wanted was a life of peace. Anxiety and depression felt like my only friends.

I stayed to myself and just worked. I distanced myself from everyone. I had the unique opportunity of working with farm animals, and so they became my friends. I would talk to them and pet them as if they were the only things that mattered. I kept busy because I didn't want to think about all the horrors I faced or the problems that needed my attention. It was all too much. It was more than I could deal with at that moment.

As time passed, I started to get back on my feet. I watched every penny I earned and diligently budgeted out my expenses. I began to deal with the financial nightmare, so I could put it to rest. Slowly but surely, I began to crawl out of the mess my life had become.

It is much easier to write these words of how I came through this than to fully grasp just how difficult it was at the time. Some days all I could do was just function and get through my day. In many ways, that was a monumental mountain to climb. Exhaustion was normal, and strength was in short supply. I kept trying to put one foot in front of the other and do a little each day. It was all I could ask of myself as I worked to make it through this difficult time in my life.

Then one day, out of the blue, I got a letter from my mom. Damn it, I thought! How did they find my address? To this day, I still don't know how they got it because I tried to make sure no one could find me. I knew I should have changed my name and at one point, I almost did. At that moment, I wanted absolutely nothing to do with any of my family. I felt so abused and hurt and shunned by my parents.

Letter Dated Feb 27, 1996

Don,

I don't know if this will get to you as this is the last address we have. Hopefully, it will.

Don, I think it's about time we all did something that is, for some, very hard to do, and that is forgive and let go of yesterday and go on with tomorrow. Dad & I have been miserable for too long, as well as you have also. We apologize for whatever wrong we may have done and hope you will accept it. Our yesterdays are gone, and we seemingly can do nothing about them, but we do have tomorrow!

We ended up getting into it with your brother, and things were said of which you already know about. We have written him also.

We never ever believed we would see this in our family, but I have found we're not alone.

Dad and I would like to work at a relationship again, but first it has to start out by being friends.

The past years have not been good to us or for us and we felt we had to write and apologize to clear things up. We love you and have missed you Don. Things may never be as they were but it is something that can be worked on. Everyone has a messy closet in their life, nobody is exempt.

So, we hope to hear from you. There is no need in rehashing what has gone on, but by just trying to mend hurts will be a first step.

As you probably heard, we sold the acreage and are renting, for the time being, a new duplex.

Well, Don, we hope to hear and if we don't, we will try to live with that also. Healing needs to start and hope you feel that way also.

So, until then I'll close for now.

Love

Dad and Mom

This letter had serious flaws in it, and while it may sound all warm and great on the surface, there was so much hidden from view that the true story is not told. When this letter arrived, I was just in the process of piecing my life together. It was not an easy time, and I wanted nothing to do with them. I knew I had stopped communication with them, but for me to survive, I had to make a clean break. I would not have made it otherwise.

When people want to move on and put everything behind them without addressing the elephant in the room, it is never a good thing. You cannot act as if these experiences did not happen, but this is the way my parents dealt with conflict.

Saying that you apologize for whatever wrong you might have done is a phrase I've heard a million times in my family. If you don't know what you did, what are you apologizing for is what I wonder.

Even though she assumed that I knew where they were living or that they had a conversation with my older brother, I was completely in the dark. I knew nothing about what was going on with the people in my family.

For clarification on this letter, my dad seldom wrote to me. He had never learned how to write well, and so he avoided it. However, the one thing that I noticed in my family was that my mom expressed my dad's feelings. He did not know how to express feelings and emotions, so my mom always wrote for him. Unfortunately, I doubt he was connected to his feelings and emotions as much as my mom was.

I also thought it was interesting that my mom talked about a messy closet. Did this mean she knew what my dad did? I wondered if it meant there was more than I was even aware of, but needless to say, the phrase causes me to have more questions than answers. Later on, my cousin would indicate that there was more that I did not know, but she would tell me nothing. Once again, the family secrets go to the grave.

I wanted to have a relationship with my mom. However, I knew there would be nothing without my dad's involvement. My parents did not act without the other. They were very dependent upon each other for their emotional needs and support in life. Later as I worked through my healing, I would see just how co-dependent they were.

To this day, I'm not sure if my mom truly knew what all my dad had done to me. I tried to call and confront him. I tried to write letters to him and her, but it is a question for which I will never have an answer. There is so much I had hoped that I could sit down and talk about with my mom, but a car accident took her life far too early for that to happen.

I never answered the letter. I put it aside for safekeeping and continued to piece my life back together. Today, I live with the grief of knowing my mom and I never got to have that last conversation. I have come to accept it more, but it still haunts me.

My focus became that of moving on and trying to figure out what made me tick and how to heal all the things that were draining my life. I excelled in my job and focused on that as the animals brought me support and love. Human contact was very difficult at the time and only brought on more anxiety for me.

My days would lead me to transfer to a different department in the company. At this point, I began working in the computer department which was a challenge, but I kept pushing myself. I enjoyed being able to focus on a challenge and the opportunity to learn something new. Getting my mind off the horrors I faced was a welcomed relief.

As time progressed, I would finally be able to buy a mobile home, giving me something permanent to call my own and saving so much on my monthly expenses. Things were beginning to progress along in my life. My healing and recovery had been put on hold, and the pain within was beginning to awaken once again.

I was back to having the screaming fits in the middle of the night. The sleepless nights were wearing on me. Sometimes, it felt like I could see my father standing at the foot of the bed, which freaked me out. These nightmares seemed as real as if they were actually happening.

I would wake up in the middle of the night with a swollen face and head almost as if someone tried to beat me with a club. It would require me to get up and put ice on it to get the swelling and pain to go down. These events happened frequently.

At first, I could not even tell what was going on. I would wake up screaming, "NO, NO, NO" in the middle of the night. I don't know if my neighbors could hear me or not, but if they could, they never said anything. My poor cat, Snuggles, who had always been there for me, tried to stay close and comfort me, but there was no comfort. It was pure torment.

Then the nightmare of the color purple started. At first, when the nightmare in my mind showed up, I would see the color purple. I would wake up in a sweat, screaming. It made no sense to me. How on earth could the color purple be that horrifying to me? I was perplexed and tired and felt overwhelmed by this nightmare.

I hid in my mobile home, only going out to go to work and the store. Otherwise, I trusted no one. I was too afraid to leave. Keeping myself hidden, I drew the curtains, so no one could see me as I huddled in the safety of my home. Visitors were not welcomed, and I never answered the door. I just kept myself hidden from everyone. I was afraid, but I did not know why.

For months these things continued repeating themselves over and over, from the screaming rages of fear to the physical pain and swelling. I was horrified by the color purple. Nothing in my life made sense.

I was agitated, tired, and angry. I felt alone and like there was nowhere to turn.

It was at this moment that I knew I needed to get help, but I was scared and frightened. I felt beaten down and worn out. I felt ashamed, anxious, and depressed. As I look back, the fears were there, but I didn't realize it.

The thought of reaching out to anyone went against everything I had known in my life. It felt far too risky. It felt beyond what I had the strength to do. I wanted to continue to hide in my four walls, never coming out. I did not want to deal with what was surfacing and showing up.

After all, who in their right mind screams out in the middle of the night from nightmares as if someone is in the room? Who wakes up in the middle of the night as if someone had just beaten them leaving their face swollen many sizes? Who in their right mind struggles with anxiety so bad that they are afraid to leave the house because the monsters might be lurking?

There was no safety, and there was no strength that I found. I just hid and numbed. I tried not to let anyone see it. My default mood to the world was where I put the smile on while I stuffed everything that I felt deep down inside of me. I didn't let anyone see me cry and I didn't let anyone see me suffer. Ignoring what was happening in my life was all I knew how to do.

It was my way of survival. If you showed weakness or fear, the monsters pounced. If you showed any emotion, you could be subject to a lot of pain and hurt and ridicule. I had learned to trust no one, and that was the only way I found any sense of safety in my life.

Once again, I dismissed the thought of seeking help. After all, who would I go to for help? The ones that initially were there for me were now a thousand miles away. Who would I trust? I did not know. I just knew that if I started to seek help, I would lose the safety and comfort of what I had come to know. Even though that safety that I knew was detrimental to life, it was familiar.

On Thanksgiving Day of that year, I was home all alone. No one had asked me to come over and spend the day with them. It was never easy spending a holiday with others because my heart ached and hurt so bad for what some of my family had done to me and how I had to walk away. It was just as difficult spending the day alone, knowing that all these other families were out there celebrating together and spending time with one another.

Thanksgiving had always been a special time of year because my mom went out of her way to cook these big meals. If we were lucky, we would have people over to the house. If we weren't lucky, we would have to spend it together as a family. While much of these days were great memories for me, the bad and horrible were mixed in together with the good.

I remember the time my dad thought we all needed to drink wine and I was only a kid. Here I had been taught that any alcohol consumption was very bad, and God would send the lightning bolts and plagues down to get you. He would punish you for even thinking about taking one drink is what the minister preached. Now, my father thought and in fact demanded that every one of us had wine. I did not want it. I tried to resist, but my dad started pouting and guilted me until I gave in and took a drink. What a happy Thanksgiving it was in my house. Here, have a little more stress just before you pray and eat, giving thanks to God.

Thanksgiving meant we got to watch the parades on TV and outside work was limited. Stress filled the air, and you just had to dodge the angry monsters in the house or those who wanted to hurt you. You tried to be available when needed, but out of the way so all hell didn't come down upon you.

The Thanksgiving holiday when I was alone in my mobile home was so significant to me. It was a day I longed to be with family, but I hated the rest of what had happened. It made me very sad. I was very depressed. Feeling all alone, I questioned why I would want to go on. It was a loneliness that was beyond belief. There is loneliness, and then there is what I was experiencing, and it ran so deep that nothing else existed at that moment.

As my anger and hurt and pain continued, it began to consume me. I saw life as desperation without hope. I saw hurt and pain only. Nothing else mattered. There was nothing that made me feel better. I wanted to hide. I was in so much anguish that every bit of life sucked at that moment.

My mind started to travel down into the lowly depths of the memories that had been trying to surface. Even though my mind was trying to protect me, it was also trying to bring things out and piece them together. I did not want that. I tried to run and hide from it. It would not leave. I could not escape it. I tried hard, but it still showed up.

Out of nowhere, the freaking purple color hit me like a ton of bricks crashing down on my head. It felt like I had been electrocuted into seeing the color purple. Why... why... why was I so haunted by this color? It made no sense. It seemed so silly and stupid. Why wasn't I normal like everyone else?

Then, the picture – the image of the picture showed up. It was like looking through a microscope and focusing on the image below. As I continued to focus, I saw the color purple. It was a purple bedspread from my parents' bed. My dad was at home recovering from an accident. Everyone had to congregate around his bed while he was recovering.

I felt my face shoved down into it. As the bastard shoved himself into me and raped me, I could not cry and scream out. I could only keep myself from suffocating. Tears at the moment he was raping me were not welcomed. They were forbidden and punishable by further beatings. You had to take being raped like a man!

The full force of that memory came into view, and at this moment, it is trying hard to overtake me. It is difficult to write about these things to this day, even many years after they took place. I must write it. This story must be told to help others and help myself heal.

As the memory flooded my mind and the images became so clear, it was then that all the anger and pain and horror of that moment came out in full force. I was pacing near my front door with anger boiling over from every ounce of my body. The force came through my arm and hand and the next thing I knew, my hand was hitting the door with all the force that could be gathered.

Pain filled my hand and my arm. My hand hurt so badly that all I could do was cry. At first, I wasn't sure if I could move my hand. It started to swell. I got scared that I had broken it. Oh, great I thought, now how would I explain that to anyone? I wanted no one to know these secrets for I was ashamed of them. Even if my hand hurt, it would just have to hurt.

I went into a fog where I didn't care what else happened. I don't even remember the rest of the day. I just wanted to die. I wanted all of this to go away and to never enter my mind again. Begging these memories, I implored them to leave me alone. How much more of this would I have to endure? How much longer? I hated every minute of it. I hated myself, and I hated all that was done to me.

My life was despair and depression and sadness. It grew by the minute. I knew nothing else at that moment. It hurt. I wanted to be angry, but I was too weary to care anymore. It wasn't worth it. Life wasn't worth it. In my mind, my life was just one screwed up moment after another.

The next weeks leading up to Christmas only got worse. I wanted to die. I did not want to live. In fact, days before Christmas, I tried picking a fight with two guys much bigger than me in the grocery store parking lot. I was in a thousand different kinds of pain and had no one there for me. Even though I was alone, I wasn't ready to let anyone in my life.

Finally, with despair and depression and anxiety building each day, I found the name of a psychiatrist. It was a small town that I lived in so there was no one readily available in that town. I got the nerve to call him and made an appointment for him to come to the town and see me. It took every ounce of strength I could find to make that phone call.

I was scared to death. I knew that I had been through therapy, and I knew what to expect, but this time it was different. Was I ready to share these memories with anyone? I had been taught to stay silent. There were consequences of speaking out as my pets had found by receiving the ultimate punishment – death!

I went to the appointment, and he seemed nice enough, but he was a man. I was afraid of men, but I didn't understand why. Even though I tried to be open and share what was going on, I felt like I was holding back, and I was. I was not about to let out these secrets.

Unfortunately, this psychiatrist said he would put me in touch with his son who would be a better fit for me after the holidays were over. I didn't want to go to another person that I didn't know and explain all of this again. Telling anyone these secrets was excruciatingly difficult and having to do this again was overwhelming. It didn't matter because weeks passed, and nothing happened. The psychiatrist never followed through on his word. He let me down. If someone is begging for help, don't make a promise that you will contact them and then not follow through. You end up inflicting more pain on them and pushing them deeper into despair.

Finally, long after the holidays were over, I got an envelope in the mail from the psychiatrist. I was hopeful that it was something to get this process going. When I opened the envelope, it was nothing but a bill. The psychiatrist couldn't remember to follow through, but he could remember to send a bill. I was furious. His behavior was unprofessional and hurtful to me. In my mind, I said enough was enough, and I would find a way to live with the pain and the nightmares.

I continued to get by in life and to keep living a lie to everyone. It was all I knew to do. It was all I could do. The depression and anxiety worsened each day. Despair felt like my only friend. I had no other friends. I went to my job, to the store and home. That became my life, and it was difficult enough accomplishing that much in a day.

Sleep was not easy. I woke up with nightmares constantly. I kept seeing the color purple and the actions that played over and over in my mind. No matter what, the horror would not stop. It was like a loop playing over with no exit or off button.

Little by little, day by day I was sinking lower and lower. In my mind, there was no reason to keep going. I wanted my life to end. So, as a result, I started to look for ways to kill myself.

My mind concocted a plan where if I walked across the roads at the right time it would be all over. I wanted to find a foolproof way that would work, and it would be over quickly. Every time I tried, the cars somehow managed to avoid me. The cars either stopped or swerved. It made me angry and furious. It didn't matter if I stood in the middle of the road because somehow something was protecting me.

Working in a building where a lot of trucks passed by, I thought this would be my opportunity to get things over with and end it once and for all. It would be the perfect thing in my mind to have a truck be the one that ran over me. That would send a message to the monster who drove his truck for a living. I'd show him. I figured a truck would be enough to make sure I accomplished this.

However, the same thing happened. No matter what my timing of walking out into the road was or how slowly I walked or if I stopped in the middle of the road, something was protecting me. The trucks managed to either slow down or stop. No one knew what I was trying to do, but I knew.

Finally, in frustration, I knew that I needed to talk to someone, but once again who would that be? I could no longer live with the pain I felt in my life. The last psychiatrist just left me hanging by myself for dead. He didn't care. I wasn't about to let anyone I knew in on my secret that I was actively trying to kill myself. I didn't want anyone to know about this horrible secret of shame inside of me.

Somehow, I managed to find a place called the Baptist Counseling Center in Wilmington, NC. I would often drive by there, and so I would see the place along the road. I got up the nerve to make an appointment, not knowing what to expect this time. I just knew that if I couldn't be successful at ending my life, I needed someone to help me get through this. At this point, I was so tired of trying to run from it.

My body and my mind were worn out, exhausted, depressed, and full of despair. I just wanted this over. I wanted to live a normal life like everyone else.

Fortunately, this time, I met a wonderful therapist and counselor by the name of Emma Wallace. She is tops in my book, and she helped me get my life back. I will forever be grateful for her love and compassion and just being there for me as I walked through the difficult moments of my healing. It was not an easy road dealing with this, and many times I questioned why I was even doing it.

When I first went to her, I'm sure I was about as quiet as could be. I know I was a challenge to her because I could not speak of what happened. If I spoke about it and the monsters found out, they would come after me. They would destroy me, just like my pets. I couldn't risk that.

I lived 1400 miles away from them but lived in fear that they would find me. I had gone to great lengths to keep my whereabouts a secret. I didn't trust them. They only brought pain into my life, and I could not deal with any of them. These people were like a toxic poison in my mind.

I still remember one discussion Emma and I had about my fear of the monsters finding out I was seeing her. She asked me, "Do they know where you live?" No! "Do they know you are coming down here to see me?" No! Then she said, "They don't know, and I will never tell them what we discuss." While I understood what she was saying to me, I didn't feel safe. I had never felt safe in my life. Trusting another person with these secrets was almost too much for me. It meant I had to venture out into the unknown.

From as far back as my memory goes, there was no safe place. There were no safe moments. Life was about ducking the blows every second of the day. They would come out of nowhere for the most insignificant of things. You usually had no idea when it would happen, but you could bank on that you knew it would happen.

Not to mention all the horrible sexual things done to me that I was forced to participate in by the monsters. These began at least by the time I was five years old, or that was my earliest recollection. Life was about pain and horror. It was not about safety. I didn't know what it meant to trust anyone or feel safe.

I kept to myself for the most part, except where I played the role of working in my job. I was personable and happy to most, and I could get along with anyone. While I could connect with others, I did not let anyone inside the walls I had built. I kept my heart guarded. No one knew I wanted to kill myself so badly. No one knew of the pain I struggled with inside and how much I hid from everyone. I felt so alone, but no one knew or had a clue. If they did, they never spoke about it with me.

In my life, I had become a master at showing one thing to the world and hiding everything else. My mom was the same way. I remember her going to work and being so sick, but no one knew it. Most would have never gotten out of bed if they felt the way she did. Maybe I learned how to hide things from her, or maybe it was a combination along with learning how to hide all the pain in life.

No matter how difficult it got, I kept going to therapy. One of the things that helped was an exercise my therapist did with me to create a family tree. It was not just a regular family tree because we focused on "traits" and "behaviors" of my family members. There is so much about my family tree that I do not know. There are far too many secrets in it. However, as we went through this exercise, I could see a lot of patterns and how they fit into my life. It helped me to build a framework of piecing things together.

Often my therapist would suggest exercises and activities that I could do. Usually, I had a million excuses why each one would not work. In those days, I was full of excuses. I am sure I drove my therapist crazy at times. She was patient and resourceful though, trying to find something else that would connect with me.

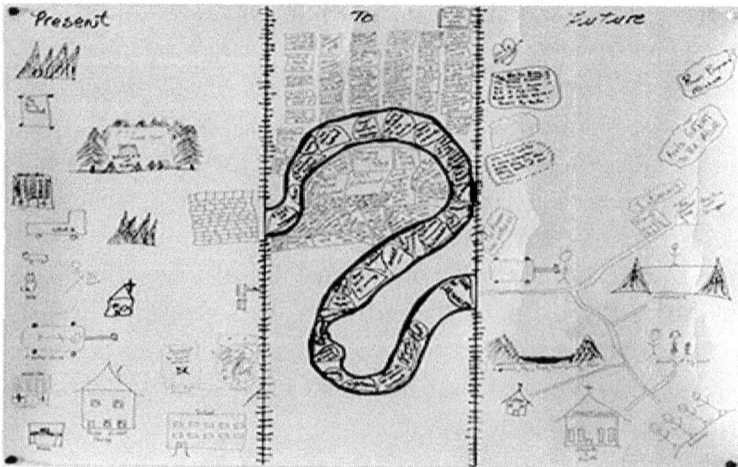

One of the ideas she had ended up being something that became helpful in my healing. In this exercise, I bought a large poster board from the store. Drawing a path or walkway down the middle, I separated it into three sections.

On the left was the present moment where I saw myself. On the right was what I wanted in my life at that moment. In the center was the pathway with drawings of boulders in it as I identified them.

As I began to identify things in my life that I discovered, I would add them to the appropriate section of this poster board. It hung on my wall, so I could see it daily to help me realize the progress I was making and to keep me focused.

In those early days, it was easy to get discouraged and think I was not making as much progress as I was. It helped me to see my progress visually, and I would show it to my therapist. In those days, it was difficult for me to voice things in my healing journey and so this poster board became a conversation starter. It was just easier sometimes to write or draw about what I was experiencing and share that. Physical conversations were just not easy because I was very afraid of telling my secrets. Voicing what was bothering me was difficult because it felt like I had no voice.

Each day, I was struggling to function and keep myself alive. I was dealing with the beginning part of coming to terms with what had happened to me. It was not easy, and it was exhausting.

The struggle was difficult on the best days and almost impossible on my bad days. I sometimes didn't think I would make it and I was not sure that I wanted to make it. Much of what it meant to heal was difficult for me to grasp in those days.

One thing that did help was writing. One poem of mine, "Show Me Your Face," which is published in my book, *A Journey Through Words,* helped give me a voice during the nightmares.

Show Me Your Face

By Don Shetterly

Where are you, I'm asking?
Why do you hide your face tonight?
I know you are there

For I feel your surprise
But why, tell me why
Do you hide your face tonight?

I feel so all alone
The pain it comes and goes
Always asking why
Because you are hiding tonight?
Your shadow lurks in the quiet, peaceful time
But why do you hide your face tonight?

The pain within me grows
The thoughts have grown so cold
I don't know where to turn,
Nor do I see your face to burn!
Your presence consumes me
But why do you hide your face tonight?

I can strike the keys
I can raise the band
I can lift the sky
But you still hide from me tonight!
What will it take, how much must I face?
Before you show your face tonight?

Wake up you dreadful thing
I no longer wish you to be my king!
You haunt me all night long
And rob me of my most precious time.
Why can't you leave
Why can't you find another home?

I have struggled for years to reclaim my life
I have fought the good fight
But now I am too tired and weary to fight
Please, I beg you leave me alone
Let me live in peace
And show me your face tonight!

Since I was going to a Christian counseling center, my therapist kept trying to get me to go to the church she and her husband attended. While I wasn't necessarily opposed to it, I didn't want to go to any church. There were too many memories starting to connect with me on what happened in my past. The church played a major role in the abuse I suffered in my life. After all, much of what had been done to me was because God told the monster to do it to me. He was showing me how much he loved me is what I remember the monster telling me.

I went to the Baptist Counseling Center because I was so afraid that a therapist or psychologist would put bad things into my mind. I had this drilled into my head by my parents. They told me that psychologists and psychiatrists brainwash you and put these bad ideas in your mind, blaming your parents. So, going to a Baptist Counseling Center, I thought I was safe. I am thankful my therapist didn't overly push religion on me. I remember asking her not to do this.

She kept trying many times to get me to go to a men's retreat with her husband. It was the last place I wanted to go, especially being around other men. I saw them as people who would abuse me and hurt me. To me, there was no safety in it. She kept bringing it up gently, and I kept avoiding the issues, dodging any response but not telling her why. I know she was working to find a way for me to have some positive male interaction, but it was too frightening to even consider doing.

Then, I found an organization called VOICES which stood for Victims Of Incest Can Emerge Survivors. They had a conference coming up, and I thought that this would be the best way to get my therapist off my back about going to a men's retreat. I can see it as comical now, but at the time, it was frustrating to me. I realize that I needed to learn how to have normal relationships with men, but I was just not ready at that point. Fortunately, VOICES was pretty much an organization with women in it and very few men. At that time, men were not as out in the open about being abused.

I still can't believe I signed up and flew to Chicago for this conference. If it hadn't been for my therapist pushing me to go to a men's retreat and me doing this out of spite, I would have never gone. I would have stayed in my own little shell and hid from the world. The frustrating ordeal I went through with my therapist on this was the best thing that could have happened to me at the time, even if it didn't feel that way at that moment. In life, I've learned that sometimes the uncomfortable places become the best moments of life and healing.

As I signed up for this and bought my airplane tickets and booked the hotel, it began to dawn on me just what I had done. The anxiety was real, and I began to doubt if I could do this. I began to feel as if I was not strong enough. I was venturing into something so unknown that I wasn't sure if I could do it. However, I had already bought the tickets, paid for the conference, and booked the hotel. I could not back out now because there would have been too much money lost.

I had written several poems at this point, and I saw that they had an art show for survivors. In those days, I had no clue what that meant. I didn't see myself as being someone that could do art or could write. However, I thought that maybe I could write out a couple of my poems and let them hang them up. After all, what's the worst thing that could happen, I thought? Maybe they would reject them or laugh at me, but I was determined to do this. It was a major step out of my comfort zone. A close friend at the time that was skilled in graphic design helped take a couple of my poems and make them into beautiful masterpieces.

Fortunately, I had contact with the lady that was organizing the art show via email before I went, and she was more than happy to have me bring my poems. When I got to the conference, she was the first person that I met, and that helped so very much. I was so frightened and scared to be there that it took every ounce of strength I had to get my legs to walk in the front door.

I remember well that first VOICES conference I attended. Ellen Bass, the author of The Courage To Heal, gave the keynote address. I can't quite recall what she said, but it was unlike anything I had ever heard before. I remember all of us as a group singing, "How Could Anyone," a song by Shaina Noll. I had not heard this song, but I fell in love with it immediately.

The entire conference was a life-changing event for me. It felt like a place where I was safe and wanted. I felt like I could explore and learn more about myself as well as learn how to heal. Some moments were very triggering, and some moments just helped me feel like I had found a group of people that understood. When you find a community where you feel like you belong, it helps so much in healing your life. Isolation is difficult, and while it is hard to step out of the comfort zone, it is the only way I found I could heal my life.

As the years went by, I got involved with VOICES and started writing their male survivor column. I would come to know author Mike Lew and be able to interview him for an article. Mike Lew has written some wonderful books for male survivors of child abuse. I would meet other people that would become some of the first survivors of child abuse that I truly got to know. There would also be heartbreak in those years, but it provided a fertile ground for me to supercharge my healing. It became a safety net for me to learn to trust again.

Sadly, VOICES is no longer around. The funding dried up, and so they are no longer in operation. In those days, there were no support groups online. The internet was in its infancy, and so places like VOICES provided much-needed hope for me. However, if I would not have taken that giant leap of faith and stepped out of my comfort zone, I'm not sure I would have progressed along in my healing as I did.

One of the biggest things I've observed while looking back at my life is how I took big steps into the unknown. Yes, I had to push past the anxiety and fear and despair. It required me to fight to take steps beyond depression and suicide. I had to push myself no matter how hard that became. I had to get back up after falling down many times.

If I had just let myself stay in those moments and succumb to the fears I faced, I wouldn't have made it. I know it isn't easy to do this. I have had to fight the odds so many times, but every time I said "I'm going to do it," I found myself reclaiming more of my life. Finding greater peace and healing than I had ever experienced before became the prize. Even while doing that, most of the time I thought I did not have the strength to make it through the moments I was facing.

Healing is not about some mindset where you're struggling one day and healed tomorrow. It is a series of steps progressing along to becoming aware of who you are and letting go of the things that no longer serve you. It is about pushing into the fear so that you reclaim the power that the fear holds over you. It is about becoming connected to your body, rather than living in numbness and being disconnected from life.

I could have just lied down and given up many times. I tried hard to do that, but something kept me going. There was something deep inside of me that would not let me stop. It was a force and a will to do this no matter what, even in those moments when all hope had vanished.

No one would have thought any less of me if I had just given up. Most people would have said, I'm not surprised. My path has not been easy. I've had to do so much of it alone, and I've had to do it even when some instrumental people in my healing chose to break my heart and treat me with disrespect.

I had to do it when certain members of my family turned their back on me, and I was left all alone to pick up the pieces and continue another day. I had to find my life when everything that I had been taught about life itself, including God and religion, meant nothing to me because it had become a source of pain, rather than something positive.

There is so much I could write about my early days, but it would be a never-ending chapter. As I continue in this book, the concepts will further display other aspects of my life and my healing that got me through from one moment to the next.

The story continues, but it shifts and changes as it progresses. As you continue to read, all the parts should begin to fit together and form a more visible outline of all that I did to heal the trauma in my life. Through my example, I hope that you can take the nuggets that I learned and apply them to your healing.

For me to focus on telling you all the horrible details of my story would limit the possibility of this book. It would become too difficult for most people to read. In fact, I'm not sure I could write all the details without being triggered and overcome with deep pain. Yes, there are many details to my story, but I choose to focus on my healing path through them.

Try This Exercise

How has the story of your life and the challenges you've faced impacted you physically, mentally, emotionally, and spiritually?

In what ways have they brought you to the point where you are?

How has your own story of challenges shown up in your body?

4. I Never Accepted My Condition

*"Trauma victims cannot recover until they become familiar with and befriend the sensations in their bodies." - **Dr. Bessel van der Kolk, M.D.***

A few years before I started to regain my life, I first had to conquer conversion disorder. As I started to come front and center with what paralysis meant to me, I wondered – could I ever make it? Could I go on? Did I want to go on?

I mean, everything was horrendously difficult for me. The odds were against me. There was not one bright spot in a day. Every human activity that we take for granted had now become something that I needed help to do. From eating to walking to bathing and going to the bathroom, I was not able to do anything for myself. My body could not balance itself, let alone stand or move around. I had very little control of my arms and exhaustion came very quickly when trying to do anything. The pseudo-seizures happened without notice, and I was at the mercy of them.

The humiliation I felt is beyond the words that I can even begin to write. The most basic of needs and daily life were now beyond my reach and control. There was nothing that was normal. When you have no choice but to ask for help from those that hurt you, it is one of the most degrading parts of human existence.

I had no control over what my body did. Everything failed, and if it didn't fail, it went into the pseudoseizures that would last for what seemed to be an eternity. Struggling to stay awake, I would fall asleep repeatedly, only to wake up and then long to sleep again.

There was no energy to function, and I felt like I was lost in a fog that would never lift. I could hear voices around me, but it was difficult to connect and hear what they were saying. I knew there were familiar people around me, but I felt trapped in my own little bubble. It was like I was witnessing my life from the outside looking in. Even though I was there, I felt disconnected and not present. It was almost like no one was home.

Doctor visits became the norm for my days, but doctors were not sure how to treat me, and so once again they would send me home.

Initially, the doctors diagnosed me with multiple sclerosis, which later turned out to be incorrect.

My parents had come to where I was living to take care of me, and at that moment, there was no end in sight. No one knew what to do, and no one had answers.

One day the pseudoseizures got so bad that I think I frightened my parents. They called 9-1-1, and the ambulance came to get me. I remember very little of what happened when it arrived other than feeling like someone cared about me. In the ambulance on the way to the hospital, I was frightened. I still remember seeing nothing but the clouds in the blue sky through the window of the ambulance. Everyone knew there was something wrong with me, but no one knew how to fix it. In many ways, I was on a runaway rollercoaster. Even with people trying to help me, I felt all alone and empty inside.

The tests continued and life at that moment was about existing, not getting better. I felt so alone and untouchable. So badly did I want someone to come up and tell me it was going to be all right. Even if they didn't know, I needed encouragement and support. These things I did not get. Should I fault my parents for it? It is probably not right to blame them since they were trying to take care of me.

However, as with most things in our society, we support from a distance when someone needs a touch or a supportive word. Humans react to touch and support. Sometimes that ear that listens or that softly spoken word of support from the love in our hearts can do so much for someone. You may not know how to help them, but in moments like what I was experiencing, I just needed to feel like I was not alone. I needed to know that someone was there for me. It had to be more than people staring at me in disbelief and fear. It needed to be a touch and a supportive word. In those moments, I needed that more than ever.

When I was finally admitted to the hospital, I remember lying in the hospital bed with my mind wandering all over the place. I wanted to cry, but the tears were not there. I wanted to scream out, but my voice could not form enough words or sounds to do this. Even though I wanted to escape the hell I was in, I could not find the way. It felt to me like I was trapped within myself with no way out.

My mind still somewhat worked, but it did so on a limited basis. Thoughts came and went, without me realizing the reality of what my mind was comprehending. I kept coming back to one recurring thought: I'm so tired of my life right now and I'm ready to give up. There was no way I could go on like this and no way I wanted to go on the way that I was.

As my mind wandered down this progression, it was like, "Why don't I just give up? Why can't I just die? I want to escape from this moment. There is no point. There is no hope." In my mind, I felt there was nothing anyone could do for me.

As the days went by, I remember staring up at the ceiling of my hospital room which was about all I could do. I started to wonder, "Is this all my life is going to be? I'm going to be a vegetable lying in this bed for the rest of my life. My God, I'm only 26."

How awful, I thought, that this is where my life had taken me. If only I could turn back the hands of time and somehow change this. If only I didn't have to rely on everyone taking care of me. All I wanted was to talk, move, and walk like I once could. That's all I wanted. It had not been that long ago that all the typical things I would do in a day were normal to me. Now, they were no longer part of my life.

When you're at this moment, it is a very hard reality of where your life is. There does not seem to be any hope or chance that things will change. You scoff at the thought that you can get better. You ridicule those that think you should pray or think positive thoughts or follow their latest advice. It all seems hopeless. It seems like a worthless and ridiculous point to even attempt to try.

Many times, people come up with advice that does not fit the moment. I know they mean well, but so often the responses and steps people tell you to take come from their mind, not from their heart. They have good intentions. Yet it's just not a conscious connection that shows they are with you in the struggle. In the situation, like I was in, there were too few that had any clue how to help me climb out of the hole.

Thoughts and prayers may make you feel good that you are helping another individual. However, in the final moments of existence, these things can become hollow. If humans could learn to get out of their head and connect more with their heart, it would vastly help many in this world. I have seen this happen so many times in myself and others. The ones that connected deep from the heart and not the head were the ones that offered me the most help.

Is Anything Possible?

When you get to this point, there is no hope of anything positive coming out of this situation. You can't see any form of positivity. Your daily life turns into existing and trying to make it from one moment to the next. Even one single moment is a struggle. Trying to contemplate many moments together was far too overwhelming and difficult.

The doctors struggled to help me. Everything was a great effort, from getting my hands and arms to work so I could feed myself, to even sitting up or rolling over in bed. I felt nothing but hopelessness and despair. I was convinced that nothing good or helpful or positive could come out of this.

To others, it is easy to demand that an individual like me in this situation needs to reframe how they view life. At that moment though, life was about existing and hopefully making it through that one moment. Anything more than this was overwhelming stress for me. In those moments, I needed someone to be there and help me find stability on the difficult journey of my life. There were moments that I longed for a hug or a touch or just someone to sit with me. I was so afraid at that point that I'd never make it out of this situation alive.

The shift started to happen the day they were doing tests on me, and my body checked out of this world. The bright white light was drawing me near it, but for some reason, I could not go up there. I looked around at all the people working on me.

The little room I was in was small but crowded with many doctors and nurses. They were trying to bring me back to life. Why were they doing this, I wondered? I'm right here. Can't anyone see me? Don't they know I'm right here?

I watched, but I was drawn towards the white light. It was the brightest light I had ever seen, and I wasn't sure what it was. It felt warm and inviting. It felt full of love. There was a familiarity to it. It was all too confusing. I did not understand.

I kept hearing, "You must go back – it is not your time." "You must go back – it is not your time. You must go back – it is not your time." I wondered why must I go back? Why would anyone send me back because this felt so inviting and peaceful? Why am I even here? What is this and who is this? Who is talking?

The questions were floating in my mind, and yet somehow, I just knew that the voice or thoughts or whatever it was, told me that I have much more to accomplish and I will impact many lives. The world needed me in it, but I was distraught because I wanted to escape the hell in which I had been living.

As they were bringing me back to life, I still wasn't sure what had happened. Nothing in that moment made sense. I thought my mind was creating some fictional story and so I shoved it out of my mind as hard as I could. "Was I crazy? Was I delusional?" Surely this bright white light was a figment of my imagination.

As the doctors and nurses filed out of the room quickly, the ones left behind to finish up with me were very quiet. There was an eerie silence in the room. I asked one of them, what had happened. Reluctantly and making sure no one was listening, she said, "we thought we had lost you."

They took me back to my room, and I lied there wondering what was happening. I had no answers. In many ways, I didn't want to remember what had happened. I just longed for escaping this world, but something kept telling me, "It is not your time." It was not like I could verbally talk enough to explain or share this with anyone.

It would be years before I would begin to come to terms with this entire episode. I buried it so deeply that I never thought of it again for many years. To this day, I still struggle to talk about it because I'm afraid that others will think I'm crazy. I am afraid that I don't understand it fully either and so while I know what I saw and heard, there are so many unanswered questions. It is not something I can fully explain.

No Coincidence

The next day a psychiatrist came in and started to talk to me. It happened to be the same day that I took my first step in physical therapy. Talking and taking a step were not mere coincidences in my view. They were key points that happened at the same time. It was the moment that my mind and body made the connection between my current situation and what I needed to do to heal myself. Reaching out for help to begin dealing with life's experiences allowed me physically to take the first step.

I still remember trying to get the courage to get up out of that wheelchair and hang on to the walking exercise bars. No amount of words could convince me that first day that I could do that. Up until that point, my legs had failed me. Every attempt to use them resulted in me hitting the floor as quickly as gravity could pull me down.

We take walking for granted in life. Once we learn it as an infant, we know it will be there. When your legs fail you, it psychologically damages you to the point of no longer believing in your ability to do the simplest human action. When your legs and your balance are taken from you, life does not appear the same way as it once did. You not only lose physical mobility and balance in your body, but a basic function now becomes one you no longer trust.

That day in physical therapy I didn't think I could stand, let alone take a step. I doubted all that was real in my life. I doubted every muscle, fiber, and cell of my being. To me, I thought it was crazy of the physical therapist to believe that I could stand or even take a step. What were these fools thinking, I wondered?

The physical therapist kept encouraging me and pushing me and telling me that I could do this. I doubted it, but I was like, do I have to show this idiot that I cannot walk? I somehow knew I had to show myself. It wasn't as much about showing them as it was about me proving to myself what I could do. I believe the physical therapist understood that, but they had to get me to see that I could do more than I thought I could. At that moment, someone asking me to walk on water would have gotten the same reaction.

Those thoughts and moments would later help propel me further into my healing. As I said, it is no coincidence that the day I first took a step out of that wheelchair was the same day I reached out for help and talked to someone. To heal, I knew I had to choose to change and live and free myself from the hell I had been living through in life. It was not up to anyone else to do that for me. I was the one that was in control of this even if I could not understand it at that moment.

If you think that it is easy to do any of this in the condition I was in, let me tell you that I'm a strong person who has survived a lot, but I almost didn't come back from this point. I almost just laid down and died. The strength and courage and determination to do this were beyond what most humans have. Sometimes I still reflect on this, and I don't understand where I found the strength to come back as I did.

Later my doctor would explain to me that my brain was shutting down. It was trying to protect me but growing weary of the fight. I was at the point of not being able to remember my name. They would touch the bottom of my foot with a needle or sharp object, and I felt nothing. Eating and sitting up were monumental accomplishments for the day. I had no appetite and cared less if I ate. Walking was like asking me to leap over the moon.

My brain was struggling with whether to function or give up the fight. It was not a conscious thought process at this point. It was more of an unconscious struggle going on in the deep recesses of my brain. While I had ultimate control over my thoughts, the logical part of my brain had grown so weary that it scoffed at me to think I could get better. My brain told me that I had ignored myself for so long. Why should I try now to help you?

I'll never forget a therapist who told me later that if she could give me a shot of self-confidence in the arm, it would help me greatly. I didn't believe in myself at that point. Losing all control of your body essentially wipes away all confidence and trust you have in yourself to function as a human. I had been raised not to believe in myself even though my parents would not admit this.

I believe that the white light I had seen helped give me courage and strength and motivation. It was a pure determination for me to get better, even if I didn't fully understand or comprehend it at the time. In my darkest hour, it was there for me, showing me in no uncertain terms that I was not alone. My life did a major reboot that day, and the white light helped guide me through this point. I don't know how else to explain it.

You can call the white light whatever you want to call it. The labels mean nothing to me, as I see the white light in a different way than most people. What matters is what I felt and how it came to me at the moment I needed it, offering unconditional love, power and a source of all that is available. I don't put this white light into a paradigm box and belief system as many in the world would do. It is source energy and love. It is something greater than we know within ourselves. I believe it is that spark within us that continues no matter what happens. While some reading this may disagree and call it whatever label they identify with in their life, I am completely fine not to fit it inside a box with defined borders.

Years later, I would be in a healing session, and the experience of the white light would once again appear. As the healing session was coming to an end, my eyes again saw this bright white light. When it showed up, it surprised me.

At first, I thought that the individual had left the overhead fluorescent lights on, and so not realizing I still had my eyes closed, I asked them to turn the lights off. They told me that the lights were off except for one dim light in the corner of the room.

I was confused. How could this be? I wondered, "Where was this bright white light I was seeing coming from?" It was hurting my eyes. It didn't feel hurtful, but the brightness was more than I could stand. I thought in my mind that I've seen this somewhere before but could not recall where that was.

Getting up from the table, I knew that something had changed in that healing session, but I couldn't quantify it. I just felt it. My mind was curious about this bright white light. I didn't understand it, but the familiarity of it seemed comforting to me. It was almost as if it was reminding me of something that I had forgotten.

There would be other experiences with other people where I would once again see this bright white light in situations, especially in a darkened room. In time, I began to remember the connection to the day in the hospital. It has taken me a long time to write about these experiences.

I know without a shadow of a doubt that I do not walk this earth alone. I know that many angels surround me and are there to help me. I know that my life's journey has had to endure so much and while I thought I was all alone, I now see that I was not.

This entire part of my healing journey is so needed because to heal from what I have experienced takes all the courage and strength and determination to move forward. It is far too easy for me to want to give up and I struggle with that constantly. Many parts of my life and healing journey make no sense yet and are still in the process of unfolding. I'm learning to lean on my angels and the bright white light of love to continue finding my way forward, touching lives of other people as I go.

What I write here is important for me to share. I am not as concerned if anyone believes me or understands it as much as I need to share it. I'm sure individuals will filter the words I write into their belief systems, and I am not able to control that. We put too many limits on what we know to be true and how we see the truth. We like to put everything into one little box that makes us feel comfortable and safe, but often it keeps out the truth of what exists.

The reason this story comes into play here is because, in the moments of complete paralysis, feeling confused and lost, I began to discover that I had to find the way through this. No one had the answers for me. It was my journey alone and one that would be difficult to walk through, but to heal, I had to find my way by taking steps.

I never accepted my condition. Yes, I had doubts in the hospital and the moments when I wanted to give up, but I never accepted where I was at during this time. The doctors had very few answers. They hoped that in time with rest, I could manage a somewhat normal life.

However, I was not about to let the doctors win. I was not ready to stay paralyzed or be dependent upon others. I had things to do in life, and against all the odds, nothing was going to stand in my way. I was determined.

Yes, my body was weak. I could barely walk ten feet or sit up in bed. I could barely find a desire to eat or talk with anyone. Too much of the time, I struggled and wanted to be left alone. I could not accept where I was at that moment. There had to be more, or that's what I kept telling myself.

The Odds Were Stacked Against Me

The odds were stacked against me. No one thought I would ever return to work again. No one thought I'd have a normal life. They all expected me to be in a wheelchair or go through episodes where all of this would come back.

My brain fought hard to prove them wrong. My brain said, "No way, I'm pushing you hard, and you're going to have to choose to make it in life. What you've done to this point didn't get you where you need to go, so now it is time to change that and do what you need to do to heal."

Years of intense healing and memories surfacing would test these realizations to the limit. It would take all the effort and energy I could find to keep going at times. Sometimes I felt like it was no use, and sometimes I felt like giving up, but I knew that there was more of my life to come than I could see at that moment. Some days I still get to the place where I don't understand this fully, but these early experiences keep me pushing forward in my life.

I see far too often, people who have struggled for far too long, just give up. It pains me to see this because it connects deep within me. I know the point I got to and how much it took for me to come back to life. I know how difficult it was for me even to realize there was a life to come back to at that point. There was a point of no return that I almost crossed.

If I had just accepted what the doctors told me, I would have never walked again. I would have never been able to work again or do what I do today. I would have given up and accepted the status quo, thinking that was as good as it gets.

If I had just gone on and labeled my condition, I would have ended up living up to that label, but I was bound and determined to prove everyone wrong. I was going to show the doctors and everyone around me. I was going to show myself. To me, this is what you must do in healing. Prove to yourself that you can heal. It is the best revenge for those that have hurt us or situations that we could not control.

It is too easy to give up and say this is what I am, or this is the condition I have. That is just far too easy because, in all reality, it is not truly who you are. You are buried beneath this pile of horror and pain, confusion, despair, depression, and anxiety. You are buried beneath all of it. Yes, I know, that's not the popular thing to say, but I speak from my own experience.

We embrace the diagnosis to define our existence, while it is only meant to be a point of what has happened to us mentally and physically. I understand that putting what is happening to us in a named condition can be helpful, but at the same time, it can limit the distance we go.

Each one of us is so much more than where we are at this moment. It may feel like there is no way out. We may think that this is who we are and nothing more, but don't believe the lies you tell yourself. If I had believed my own lies, I would not be walking and talking and functioning like I am today.

It has taken me years to start finding the true self locked beneath my conscious awareness. If I would have accepted where I was years ago, I doubt I would have made it this far. I fought the odds, and I have conquered them. It wasn't because I gave in, but that I was propelled to find myself and move on through healing my life.

We are not the labels that society puts on us. The labels hurt us more than they help us. Every time you identify with that label, you're telling yourself that this is all I can be. The more your brain hears that and your consciousness takes it in, the more everything in your body does to prove that is true. It limits you to discover all that you are, buried deep below the symptoms you are experiencing.

I know what I am saying goes against conventional wisdom and what we teach to the masses, but I also know from firsthand experience how true it is. We've got so much more potential to find that place of healing within us than we know or understand. It may not even be a figment of our imagination at this point in life, but it does exist. All I can urge you to do is trust that it exists and don't give up until you find it in yourself.

A long time ago I had a therapist who urged me not to accept labels for myself. While I wanted to know what the situation I was facing was all about, I did not want it at the expense of holding myself back. Was that an easy thing to do? No, there was nothing easy about my healing.

It was difficult every step of the way, but without that word of advice, I would not have healed as much as I have.

We all go to the safety of answers that we think help us, but those same answers can limit us and hold us back. You want to look for the answers within you that help you find your true self deep inside of your mind and body. You are looking for the part of you that you have not discovered. It is inside you, but you must go the distance to find it. You must travel into the moments of difficulty to reclaim the energy that it holds as a prisoner in your body.

If we accept that the situation we are in is as far as we can go, then we limit our potential. We limit our healing, and we limit possibility. If you had told me when I was paralyzed that I would be walking again, I would have laughed in your face. I would not have believed you. It was a reality that did not exist in my mind at that moment.

I had to allow myself to trust that there was more and identify little things along the way to help me realize I was on the right path. Most of the time, the reality that existed was so difficult to see. I ignored it in disbelief because it didn't fit in with my current paradigm of how I viewed my healing. I needed to allow myself to conquer and go into the unknown, not hide from or ignore it. The more I stood in opposition to it, the less I could heal my life.

I'm here to say that our current awareness, reality, and consciousness are not who we are. These things are just the sum total of where we have traveled and what we know at this moment. You can either use that to remain where you are or let it propel you into possibilities and hope that you have not yet seen.

While I had some horrendous moments of abuse and traumatic experiences, my determination not to accept what I knew at the moment and find out everything about the edges of what I could barely see is what has helped me keep healing. The more I learn and discover, the more I find that I don't know. It is in that quest that I discover a new consciousness every day that I'm alive. It is where healing takes place.

I know others sometimes think that I don't know what someone is going through, or that I do not understand. However, I know far more about what it is to struggle to the point of death and come back. I know that my own beliefs, opinions, truths, and paradigms are not going to define my life. Each day I search for what is possible, not what I already discovered. There are days that this is more difficult than others, but no matter what, I don't give up!

Yes, it can be a difficult road, and it doesn't always happen overnight. It took me many years to get to the point of writing these words. I never gave up, although at times I almost did. I kept going by putting one foot in front of the other and working to free myself from the past that was trying to enslave me and control me.

Don't accept where you are now. Don't accept the labels that have helped you connect with others or that identify your situation. Throw that away and learn to discover the real and whole person inside of you – the one that comes from the pure love in this world.

Yes, I know your journey may be difficult. Yes, I know that no one truly understands what you have been through other than you, but don't let that hold you back. Don't let it define you because it is not you. Take the hammer and chisel and chip pieces off each day.

The journey many of us have had to walk may not be fair, and I sure can't explain why we have experienced what we have. I know that what I have learned and discovered is now bringing me to another dimension of my life that I had no clue existed. Let us walk our journeys together so that we discover more for each person individually and collectively.

Never forget that what you know to be true in your life today is not where tomorrow may lead. We are in charge of how much distance we travel. We make the choice each day of healing our lives in discovery or holding us back in pain and suffering.

Try This Exercise

Create and map out your journey this far in life. Take special note to describe, in whatever format works for you, all the things you have been through and all the mile markers you've walked past into where you are now. Focus on what you have accomplished, as much as what you have been through in your life. Do you get a better perspective of your overall life that you could use when your mind tries to convince you more is not possible?

5. Relaxation

*"We don't give ourselves the time we need to relax and let our minds rest, or to truly come down and experience a true state of peace within our lives." - **Don Shetterly***

Relaxation was one of the beginning steps of my journey out of conversion disorder. While I see it now as a beginning step, at the time it was a radical change in how I viewed life. Now, I know that there is so much more than relaxation, but I also recognize it was the beginning of discovery for me to understand so much more in my life.

When I first started out on this healing journey, I had no idea what relaxation was. Okay, I thought I knew what it was. I mean, the weekend would get here, and I'd take a few hours and kick back, watch some TV and chat with a friend. I might go out and wash my car, or if I felt adventurous, I'd take a walk in the park.

Sometimes, I'd have a beer with friends or go to a party. Maybe I'd go out to eat or take a nap. These were the things that I thought made up relaxation as a whole. I thought if I squeezed a few hours of them in at the end of a week, I was doing what I needed to do.

Relaxation was a foreign concept, and I had very little time for it. There was always some activity or work project to do. If it wasn't that, I was tending to my own to do list or helping a friend. I didn't give relaxation the importance it deserved.

I didn't even truly know what relaxation was. Most of us in this world don't have a clue these days. It is a superficial concept where on the surface, we make it appear we're chilling and relaxing, but we're about as far from that as a leap to the moon is. It becomes a surface level awareness of relaxation rather than a mind body healing connection. We are pretty good at fooling ourselves, like I was, that we relax and take time out to do what we need to do for our mind, body, and soul.

Shortly before I was paralyzed and ended up in the hospital, I was working a minimum of six days a week. My days started out early, leaving the house by 7 AM to start heading to my clients for routine visits. I'd get home around 8 PM, rush to find something to eat, and try to do paperwork as quickly as I could before it was time to go to bed. Often,

I'd have phone calls to return and people calling me all hours of the day and night.

On Sundays, I would go to church in the morning, usually take a couple of hours off in the afternoon and then hit the paperwork to catch up and be ready for Monday morning. There was never a slow moment. It was one thing after another. The job demanded the hours I worked.

Of course, while I had a tremendous amount of responsibility and work to complete, I was a perfectionist. I couldn't let anyone down, and I was hard on myself to make sure everything was done on time, including always meeting the demands of my boss and clients. I excelled at my job, but I was burning the candle at both ends.

After I had gone to the psychiatric hospital following the stay at the Baptist Health Medical Center, I spent the first weekend outside in a wheelchair listening to the birds and watching the trees sway in the wind. I felt the breeze on my face and the sun shining down on me. It had been a long time since I had done this. At that moment, it felt like I was in heaven.

The downtime was refreshing. I had not had this much downtime for so long. I had worked so many hours at the expense of my mind and body, that I barely knew what life was about or who I was or what was around me. Life was all about working and doing the best job I could for someone else. Relaxation and time resting were foreign concepts that I gave lip service to but did not know how to implement.

After lunch in the hospital, one of the activities they had was a guided relaxation reading. At the time, I didn't know what this was, but I thought, what the heck? What do I have to lose? Someone suggested it was a pretty good activity and after all, I had all the time to kill in the world. I was going nowhere fast.

So, I sat in on the first one. The therapist had us seated around the room in comfy chairs. They were playing some soft, gentle music in the background, which I loved. The entire time, they just read a guided meditation. It felt so good during the time of these guided relaxations.

As the reading continued, it would carry me to a peaceful place. At those moments, I was so relaxed and calm. It was moments of bliss and peace and calmness. I had never felt relaxation like this before as far as I could remember.

When the guided meditation finished, I felt more relaxed in my body than I had ever realized was possible. I would be there in a moment of no worry and as content as I could be, which is saying a lot since my life was so upside down at that point.

I tried to do this every day that I was in the hospital because I realized there was something to this relaxation concept. I had no idea how to go about it on my own, but I was bound and determined to reproduce this effect on my own long after I left there. It was a life-changing point for me, and it propelled me to start digging deeper and learning more about relaxation.

I cannot stress just how much of a life-changing event this was for me. While I did not realize that at the time, I knew deep inside that the effect it had on my body was something out of this world. That connection I can see clearly today, more than I could at that point which was just the starting point of discovery for me.

When I was growing up, relaxation was something you did at night in your sleep after the monsters retreated to their rooms. It was something you did in a church service on Sunday morning. I was fortunate enough to play the piano, and so those were moments of relaxation for me.

But the house I grew up in was anything but relaxing. It was bombs and land mines going off constantly as we walked on eggshells around the monster. It was trying to make sure you did everything perfectly so that you couldn't be blamed for something and become the outcast. Even if you do relaxing things all day long and you're in a toxic environment, nothing will be fully relaxing. Relaxation will be nothing more than a temporary, fleeting moment.

My home was not relaxing. It was anger and frustration, yelling and screaming, along with misdirected issues one after another. If my parents relaxed, it was when they took a nap on Sunday afternoon, screaming at us to be quiet and let them sleep. I didn't see them doing much in the way of relaxation. Yes, there were vacations and holiday weekends, but outside of that, it was chaos. Sometimes my mom would take a walk. No one modeled relaxation to me.

When I was in high school, I ended up in the hospital because of a nervous stomach. In order to get well, all the doctors and friends and those I looked up to told me not to worry about things. Of course, when I asked how you did that, they would give me inspirational thoughts and feel good things, but no concrete steps to take. One quoted the serenity prayer to me. One told me I just needed to learn how to stop worrying. No one I talked to even suggested that I learn how to relax.

Relaxation is such a misconfigured and unrecognizable concept in our society. We don't understand it, and we don't realize we're not doing it. We are so numb and disconnected from the body that relaxation seems like a boring thing to do. It is, to many, a waste of time and something those new age people do, but not for the masses.

Thinking like this could not be further from the truth. Sooner or later something wakes us up in life, and then we begin to rethink what it is we do. We treat our bodies and our minds as if they are infinite and we can just run them into the ground. We don't stop to think for a moment that we only have this one life and if we don't take care of ourselves, sooner or later it will catch up with us.

You might have made it a long way in life without anything bad happening to you. You might be thinking that you relax and wonder what I am suggesting. Maybe you are saying that you will get to relaxation one of these years. Maybe you will put it on your New Year's resolution list and know that when you retire, you'll have all the time you need to relax. We keep putting it off until tomorrow or the next year, expecting our bodies to just hang in there with us.

The Body Says Enough Is Enough

When the body has said enough is enough, we end up at the doctor's office begging for a pill to help us. We've pushed our bodies and minds too far, but we're so numb and disconnected we can't even see it. We've consumed far more of our mental and physical health than we realize and so physical ailments show up, and we are surprised.

Relaxation is not something you should put off, because it will bite you later if you do. It will slap you hard in life like someone hitting you upside your head with a two by four. Relaxation is something you need to begin implementing today and do every day that follows. If you cannot take a little time out to take care of yourself, your life is out of balance, and you're heading for a fall.

After the hospital, I started researching and reading about relaxation in every source I could find. I had no clue and wasn't sure what the steps were that I should take. The thing I knew was that I wanted to repeat what it was that I felt while I was sitting in the guided relaxation at the hospital. That feeling in my body and my mind is what I wanted to repeat, and so it led me on a journey which has taken me to the point I am at today. This feeling of being able to let go and relax in peace and calmness intrigued me to do it more.

Was it easy learning how to relax? NO! Let me repeat that in case you didn't understand my response. Was it easy learning how to relax? NO NO NO NO NO! NO, it was not. I stumbled many times. I fell down many times. I gave up many times, and I fought to convince myself that this was worth the journey. The thing that kept me going was that feeling I had in my body from the guided relaxations in the hospital. That's what kept me going. The feeling was so strong because it connected my mind and body together in such a powerful way, I could no longer ignore it. I could not ignore the peace and calmness I felt in those times.

For each person, relaxation is different. Some people like myself can take a walk or paint or create something, and find that relaxing. Others might go out and garden or jog. Some might relax while reading a newspaper, although today with the way the news is, that isn't as relaxing as it once was. There are many ways to relax.

What works for me in relaxation may not work for you. What I like to do is different than what you may like to do. So, you've got to find those things that make your heart sing and do them. Do what works, not what someone tells you that you should do that they claim works. You are not looking for things that numb your mind or your body that many people feel are relaxing. What I am talking about is beyond numbing ourselves which so many do every day.

Look for ways that relaxation involves connecting your entire mind and body. Find the ways that allow you to turn the mind off and focus on the breathing in your body or the emotions and feelings that you tend to disregard. Make it a mind and body effort, not just something that keeps you active. Look for the way that grounds you into your body, not just gives you a momentary high.

Relaxation should not be something that you leave until there is a free moment in your weekend. It should not wait for you to take your vacation once a year as if that's when you're supposed to catch up on your relaxation. It needs to be more than what we do in this world because as a civilization, we have failed at it.

Consider how our society is now constantly connected through cell phones, Facebook, Twitter, email, and text messages. We are a society that is 24 hour second by second news and a civilization that doesn't stop. We're making it hard for ourselves to relax and collectively we're screwing up everyone else in the world! Yes, if you aren't relaxed, it carries over into every person you meet or everything you do.

Finding Time To Relax

Find time in your day to relax. Don't tell me you have no time to do this because I know that lie that we tell ourselves. You must make time. It is that important. The more you learn to relax, the more your health will improve, and your mind and body will be conscious and connected. Remember, the more you put off relaxation, the sooner it will catch up with you. When it catches up to you, it will slap you so hard, you'll wish that you had given it to your mind and body long before now.

It doesn't have to be a long time every day. You can spend a few minutes in the morning, maybe a few at noon and a few in the evening. It doesn't have to be some elaborate thing you do. You just need to take time out of your day and do it.

When I worked in an office building, I'd take a few minutes out at lunch and sit in the sun, listen to the birds and feel the breeze on my face. Those precious minutes to me were like gold, and I would not have traded them for the world.

I have a hammock outside on my patio. If you don't have one, I urge you to get one. There is nothing like lying in a hammock and feeling supported enough just to let go. Most days if the weather is nice, I'll go out for 10, 15 minutes or sometimes longer. Those few moments of stopping and relaxing in a day are invigorating. I think I get much more accomplished after that. It helps to reduce fatigue and brain fog. It helps me get clear about what I need to accomplish. It allows my body to stop, drop, and chill.

Even sitting at your desk if you work in an office, you can take a few moments to focus on your breathing. Spend thirty seconds or one minute. Put your hands on your abdomen and follow your breath. Just focus on your breathing. Feel it rise and fall. Feel how deep it is. See how deep or shallow it is. See how far your breath goes through your body. If you just do that, you'll get some wonderful gifts out of it like clearness, peace, calmness, and joy. Go ahead – play with it and see what happens. No one even needs to know you are doing it. I've done it at my desk many times. I've done it standing in a checkout line at the store. Thirty seconds is a lot of time to enact major shifts in your mind and body.

Part of relaxation needs to be slowing down and just embracing silence and stillness and peacefulness, however that works for you. Taking a walk can be very relaxing if you allow yourself to go deep within and connect with everything around you. If you're constantly worrying about your day when you walk, you're probably not hitting the point you want. In those cases, up the exercise to push past all that noise and chatter.

One of the things I love to do is go to the park. As I walk I try to observe everything around me. Is the sun shining? Are the birds singing? Is the wind blowing? There are other things that I observe, from animals scurrying about to birds flying. I also observe the different colors of the leaves in the trees and grass and plants around me. In essence, I take everything in and observe it. Far too often I see people in the park that don't notice the little things, as they are too busy in their mind to stop. Turning off that logical brain and connecting with your body deep to the core is going to bring about healthy relaxation and a mind body connection. Put the phone down and observe what is happening around you.

Sometimes you can get an added benefit if you do some more physical activity by going into the stress or tension and then allowing yourself to drop down. The difference between the moment of activity and letting your body drop can multiply the impact of relaxation.

If your body is so over-the-top that you cannot stop and relax, you may need to seek out bodywork that helps you start removing the layers. The layers of toxic stress and past experiences in life often prevent us from going in and relaxing to find pure peace and contentment in life.

Sometimes we need to let go of our daily lives. I often have told my clients that they can leave all their worries right outside the door when coming in for a massage. They can choose if they wish to pick them up when they are done or just let them go. We all think that we must drag all this luggage around with us. All our issues in the day become our identity rather than just simply our issues. We can choose to let go or continue to carry them. After a time, they get heavy to lug around, and they drain our energy. It is your choice what you do with them, but either way, it will impact your mind and body.

Don't make relaxation only about reciting mantras or prayers that end up being nothing but words and emotions. They can help, but I urge you to connect deep within your body. Discover and learn how to feel the relaxation in your cells, tissues, muscles, and bones. What does that feel like in your body? How can you tell? If you allow your focus on relaxation to be more than what society teaches, you'll discover more than you realize existed.

We go through our day so disconnected and numb that our bodies are usually just along for the ride. It is when we stop and connect with them, feeling our breath, feeling all those painful parts and learning to feel the happy parts that we begin to be masters of our domain. Instead of our bodies reacting to what we throw at them, we now empower ourselves to harness the energy that we've been wasting on disconnecting and numbing. Believe me when I say that we waste a lot of our energy on trying to run away from life, rather than recharging by stopping, feeling, observing, and connecting.

All of this may sound radical. It may sound like new age mumbo-jumbo. It may go against all that you think is true. If it does, you will need to choose whether you're doing enough to take care of yourself, or if you're heading for disaster around the next bend. The choice is up to you. No one else can make it for you. Often, if we are not relaxing as we should be, we are too numb to see what is getting ready to attack the physical body and mind.

Many times, healthy behavior in life is not modeled to us, and so we end up believing what we've seen, not what is true. Don't believe everything you think is true. I say that because so much of what I thought held my life together was beliefs that had no basis and foundation. They did not get me through the rough moments of life, and to heal my life and reclaim it, I had to let go of everything I held dear. When I did that, I found what was true for me and what were just beliefs regurgitated throughout my life.

Relaxation connected to the body through breath, observation, feeling, and awareness can propel our consciousness into a realm we barely even know. There is so much more out there, but when we limit ourselves by not relaxing in our day, we inflict so much unnecessary pain and illness upon ourselves. It is up to us to make the choices we need to make.

Relaxation needs to work for you. Find something that works and do it. Don't make excuses. Don't get too busy for it. Look for what makes you jump to the moon and back. Look for those things that help you get to know your body more fully from a cellular level. If one thing doesn't work, try another. Find the activity that your body and your mind crave. You want to find the things that bring you to deep peace and calmness. These things are produced within the body, not introduced to the body.

Don't hide from emotions and pain in life, but embrace them and hug the daylights out of them so that you can reclaim all that these experiences are trying to take from you. These rough experiences are leading us to a deeper awareness of who we are and our relationship to everything in the world. We only have one body and one mind. If we think it is an endless physical entity, we are only fooling ourselves.

Make sure that you find the body based ways that help you connect deeper. What you know today is only a portion of what is out there for you to know. Don't stop the bus halfway on your journey. Go the distance and discover a little more of who you are and what makes you tick.

Embrace the journey of relaxation so that it helps you discover more fully the mind body connection. The more we do that, the more we come alive and can deal with life in a dramatically different way. The more we come alive, the more fully we can be there for others. So much can start just by implementing daily relaxation in your life. Why not give it a try? What do you have to lose?

Deep relaxation helps bring deep peace and calmness to your life. We need that so we can face the challenges in life and the stressors of our day. Without this calmness and peace, we're only passengers on life's journey.

Try This Exercise

Find a quiet place outdoors. It could be a backyard, a patio, walking trail, a lake, or a park. Look for a simple place where you can have as few distractions as possible and spend some time there. Focusing on your breathing, just allow yourself to settle into the place. Now observe all you can from the sounds you hear to the smells present. How many animals, birds, flowers, plants, trees can you see and notice? What shades of colors do you notice in the trees and sky? Observe and notice as much as you can while focusing on all the sounds around you. Realize that what you notice in the beginning as you sit down, may be a small part of what you notice as time goes. Relax into the sights, sounds, colors, and everything you observe as this pulls you into the bigger picture of life.

How does this shift what you feel in your body? Can you notice a difference in body tension or breathing? Does your body feel more peaceful? How can you identify a peaceful feeling in your body?

6. Notice, Sense, Feel

"What is split off, not felt, remains the same. When it is felt, it changes. A few moments of feeling it in your body allows it to change." - Dr. Eugene T. Gendlin, Ph.D.

As you notice, sense, and feel, you will realize that you feel more than you thought was possible. It will also surprise you how much you don't feel. It may be overwhelming and frightening at first. If you have many overwhelming challenges in life, ease into this slowly. Overwhelm is not a friend to the mind body connection or healing.

In fact, to supercharge the mind body connection, you want to go to the edge of your comfort zone and then back off. If you go into overwhelm or beyond the edge of the comfort zone, the body will search for safety and go into a defensive mode. The body will seek shelter, not awareness and healing. By going to the edge and backing off a little from that, you're giving the body permission to safely go deeper and further.

The body yearns to discover more, rather than retreat in fear. It is built into our biology. However, we hold discovery back in the body and mind. We do this by not recognizing how fear can help us push further while not overwhelming ourselves. Either we avoid fear while acting as if it does not exist or we embrace it as if it gives us life. Neither side of this is a healthy balance.

Most of us have been numb for a long time to all that we feel, sense, and connect to within a day. Even if we feel like we are highly sensitive, we are often still numb to the inner workings of life. It is in those moments that we need to negotiate through the muck to find freedom and power. Keep in mind that we are talking about the inner noticing, feeling, and sensing, not what you feel on the surface.

The body is very wise. It knows when there is safety and when there is not. You may or may not fully be aware of this, but make no mistake about it, the body knows more than we understand. The mind is constantly trying to interpret and make sense of all that the body knows. Conscious intelligence lies in the awareness between the body and the mind.

To strengthen this connection, one needs to go carefully into the realm of all that may be frightening, overwhelming, or too stressful. If you push the process too quickly, you will overwhelm the body. It will result in having to gain the body's trust back. If you become too fearful to go in, your body will get tired of waiting for you to connect with this consciousness. The more tired and reluctant the body gets, the more physical issues will build up to unhealthy levels.

Most of the time we think we must tackle everything before us in one fell swoop. We think that it is best to go in and get to the root of the problem in the first minute. I fully believe this is more harmful and damaging to human healing than just about anything we can do. I have witnessed it in my own body as I have healed and returned from paralysis.

Have you ever watched an athlete prepare for a major sporting event? Do they go and start their training by lifting 500 pounds the first day or running 20 miles? I would assume you would answer no to this question. It is not how athletes train.

Athletes prepare for major competitions by starting out small and building up. They will focus on nutrition, engagement, rest, and repetition. They will do a little bit and then repeat, always pushing themselves a little further, but not to the breaking point. If they go past the breaking point, then their bodies will need to go back to rest and repair, setting them back in their training.

In the mind body connection, it is the same way. You must ease into it. If you take a small part of what you are trying to accomplish and savor it, you'll experience the full effects much more. If you try to jump into the mind body connection all at one time, you will be overwhelmed, and there will be a good chance that will be the end of it. Most likely, you will end up letting everyone know just how ridiculous it is to connect with your mind and body.

Time and time again in healing sessions, I've learned that instead of going deep into things and pushing way too hard, I get further by going in just a little, then backing off. After giving myself a moment of pause and rest to assimilate all that had just transpired, I would go in a little more and then back off. Some people such as Dr. Paul Canali, Dr. Peter Levine, and Dr. Bessel Van Der Kolk call this the concept of pendulation.

Pendulation gets you further into healing and striving towards that connection to awareness. It is a process where you go in a little bit and then back out. Once you've caught your breath in the training process, you go in a little deeper but never to the point of overwhelm. You want to push yourself up into the edge of that boundary, but not go past it to the point of fear. Once fear has engaged, you've stopped the healing moment. When you go to the edge of discomfort, it is then that your mind and body feel empowered, not overwhelmed.

I've learned over the years that it is not in the hysterical moments of emotional release that I heal. It is the more subtle movements that are connected deep within me as I am in full consciousness of that moment. It is through pendulation and other techniques that I have learned how the subtle can be powerful and life-changing.

Healing is more than an emotional release. It is the connection to the deep moments of pain we have stored within us as we embrace the fear and pendulate from the edge of discomfort to a moment of ease and possibility. Many times in deep healing, there is an emotional release, but it comes as a result of letting go through the mind-body connection, not necessarily the emotions of the moment.

By allowing the body to take in a little at a time, it builds up trust and safety. It builds up the strength and empowerment that connects with the mind to say, "I think I can do this." It turns "I think I can do this" into "I can do it." The more you practice it, the more the body can work through and connect stronger with all parts of the mind.

Our bodies take the brunt of life's experiences, and even if you're not acutely aware of how much you have experienced, most likely it is there. Healing these experiences is like coaxing the body to attempt what may seem impossible while keeping the conversation going with the brain to allow it to happen. It is the merging of what the body holds within, so the conscious mind can catch up and sync up to all that is there.

When we've experienced trauma and stressful events, there is a disconnect between the body and the brain. To heal, we must sync those two things up, or we will stay numb and disconnected, only hoping that we can fully heal. When we sync these up, we are rewiring the brain with new possibility. It is easy to use the jargon of rewiring the brain, but to fully do this, we must find the body connection, not just a series of thoughts where we think we are rewiring the brain.

During paralysis, my mind and body were not talking together. The muscle tone was there for my legs to work. Functionally, the legs could move if someone assisted me. My mind could not get the message to my legs, and even though my legs wanted to listen to what the mind was saying, they could not understand. It was as if the body heard one language and the mind was talking a different language. There was such a disconnect that as hard as I tried in my mind, my physical body acted as if it was separate. Little did I realize at the time, to heal my life, I had to find a way to go in and turn this connection back on while letting go of everything standing in the way of it.

This mind body connection is critical to healing our lives. Every time we experience toxic stress, painful events, and trauma, we store a little bit more in the cells and tissues. The gunk of the cells and tissues continues to build up and weigh us down little by little. It begins to impact more and more body systems. We don't see it in real time and so when physical ailments, pains, and mental health issues arise, we do not see the connection between what we have experienced and what is currently showing up.

Issues In The Tissues

If we look deeply, we see that issues in the tissues are present. They arise when we fail to jackhammer the gunk out of our cells and tissues as we let it build up a little at a time. Experiences in life are more impactful when there is an emotion that connects to trauma, abuse, or other harmful moments of our past. The past moments multiply the effects many times over. Emotions cement what has happened deeper into the layers of life.

We've been taught from a toddler on up that we need to move on and get over it. We don't need to think about any one event or moment taking place. "Don't dwell on the past" is what we tell ourselves. That's what we are told and taught, and what we witness in our family and societal units. Unfortunately, this message is one that is extremely harmful. It is an unconscious message that propagates throughout every part of our society and culture. Families pass this on from one recipient to the next without even being aware of what they are doing.

Life's experiences and trauma take us from feeling, sensing, and being connected to the body, to the point of being disconnected from it. We become unaware of our internal mechanisms and structures to accommodate the message we were unconsciously taught. It is not about blame or what should have been, but understanding where we traveled and what we've experienced. The more we understand and are aware of this phenomenon, the more we can interact with it and give ourselves new possibilities. It is not a pie-in-the-sky concept. It is very real, and you can prove it to yourself. I have seen it in myself and many others.

I know we all live in a world where we get busy, and we've got a million things to do. We live sedentary lifestyles for the most part and consume far more food than we need (not to mention the poor quality food that we eat). Our lives become fantasy projected as reality. We get so wrapped up in life that we barely understand what life is because we've replaced it with things that matter little.

We react and pontificate all day long as if it is the normal thing to do while we miss the innermost workings of civilization. The things that truly matter are drowned out by the screaming of the day. We seek out medical attention rather than first going deep inside. Instead of seeking out more about what makes us part of a whole society that functions together, we stand opposed and blinded by our fears.

All of these things help us continue the disconnect between the mind and the body. It helps keep us in the dark, rather than bringing us into the power of the mind and body. We stay numb to all that there is because we're so wrapped up in pain and suffering that we miss the bigger picture of awareness and consciousness.

All too often, when we go in for bodywork, and we don't feel pain and muscle burn, we conclude that it is not effective. However, from what I have found, the more pressure needed to feel the pain, the more disconnected and numb we are. I remember having clients wanting me to push deeper and deeper and put more pressure when getting a massage. By that point, I was already a mile into their muscle. They could not feel it. No matter how much pressure I applied, they would not be able to feel it.

When we go from deep pressure and back off to more of a feel and sense mode, we will begin to connect with the body. When we get the body to invite us in, it is at that point where we have empowered it to connect with the mind. It is a point where the mind listens to the body. While this is a subtle difference, it is a very important and powerful one.

Humans don't always feel what we think we feel. After years of numbing and disconnect, the body becomes so shut down that there is no feeling. In conversion disorder, you don't realize that you are at this point and by the time you realize it, your body has learned to adapt in an unhealthy way to the stressors and challenges of the day. When I was in the hospital and paralyzed, they took a needle and tried to poke the bottom of my feet. Normally I would be very ticklish there, but I could not even recognize that they were doing this. I had shut off all feeling in my body.

Maladaptive Problem Solving

Maladaptive problem solving is another way to describe this concept. I first heard this term from Dr. Rochelle Caplan in a video I saw online of her discussing conversion disorder. This concept is about how we learn to deal with life experiences, stressors, and problems in ways that are not helpful. It is a quick fix that gets you nowhere, but as humans, we do it all the time. Often, it is how we survive that moment, but then we teach ourselves that this is how life functions for the rest of our lives.

> *When patients are faced with these stressful situations, the way they kind of problem solve is rather maladaptive. In other words, the way of problem solving is avoidance. Often, it is very difficult to make a conversion disorder diagnosis because other than the physical symptoms, these children and their parents deny any other problems. Everything else is fine. One actually has to get through this barrier that there are problems other than everything is fine. These kids continue to live their lives in a very maladaptive way and problem solve through the use of their body or problem solve in some other maladaptive way.*
> *– Dr. Rochelle Caplan, M.D. (Child Psychiatrist, UCLA Los Angeles) (Excerpt from the Annual Meeting of the ADAA 2016 – Anxiety and Depression Association Of America)*

When things got too tough for me as a kid, and they often did, I would get where I could not feel a thing. I would shut down and numb myself out. Now, no one could most likely tell that I did this. I could in no way show anything that bothered me or that I was angry with my father. If I did show any emotion, I either got labeled as a crybaby, or I would get beaten.

Sometimes I could not escape these things, and so once I could get away, I would go outside and look for something like a stick, rock, tool, or anything hard. I would take whatever I could find and start hitting myself over and over until it hurt so bad that I could begin feeling something. It was my way of dealing with the shutdown, anger, and sadness and all the other negative emotions that came up in me.

The best thing I could have done, most likely, was kick the living daylights out of my father. Unfortunately, I was too small for that. I could have told someone that I trusted, but I didn't trust anyone, and I knew that if I dared say a word, it could cost me my life or the life or our pets. There was no way out. There was no solution.

So, I learned to adapt in an unhealthy way to the experiences I was facing in life. While I was going through them, they seemed normal because they were all that I knew. I didn't know I was problem-solving in a maladaptive manner. I would have had no clue then, and it would take me many years of my life to figure that out.

How many times do people get sick while on vacation because their bodies are exhausted? When they were working long days, their body had no time to stop and recover. Once they stopped and gave the body a moment to catch up, the illness came on full force. How would their life be if they stopped and rested along the way?

How many times do people not feel neck or back pain while working, but the minute they lie down in their bed at night or sit in front of the TV, the pain comes on at full strength? While they are busy, they barely notice it, but when they stop, the body finally catches up to what they are feeling. Again, what would their life be if they focused on relaxation each day?

Trauma and the build-up of stress shut the body down. We learn unhealthy adaptation to stressors and challenges. The layers build up and little by little we feel less and less, to the point where we feel almost nothing at all. Yes, it may take significant pain in our lives to fully bring our attention back to the moment we are living in, but by then we've neglected and ignored so much in life. We've adapted to life in a way that is unhealthy and will only continue taking us down a road to the point of no return. It is maladaptive problem-solving within the body.

For someone such as myself that was so numb and disconnected, it took a great effort to go in and wake up. I was not feeling much at all, and I find I am not alone. You don't need to experience conversion disorder to see this. We all do it as humans. We numb and disconnect from feeling the body every day. Applying more pressure to get the body to feel is not the ideal way to turn numbing off and feeling back on.

If we try to force our way in, the body resists. If we allow the body to invite us in, then we've tapped into a power no one has ever seen. We do this by stopping and waiting and sensing and feeling. It may seem far too simple. It may be asking a lot of someone that can't sit still for two seconds, but it is one of the most powerful secrets in life that they forgot to tell us when we were born.

We think that meditation or a relaxing moment alone can solve our issues and will let us sense and feel. Unfortunately, if you don't connect the sensing and feeling with the meditation moment, you're swimming in water infested by sharks - only you can't see them. Stopping to sense and feel and notice what is going on in your body is one of the greatest things in life that you can practice. Meditation and relaxation will help get you to stop and notice, but if you don't fully feel in your body, it will only be a beginning point in your journey.

For someone suffering from survival mode as the result of trauma, stopping to sense and feel will be extremely difficult. As long as your life is full of so many horrible and frightening moments from your past, peace and rest and sensing will be foreign enemies to you. The more you can deal with these things as they happen and take back your life, the more you will be able to sense and feel. If your closet is full, you cannot put anything into it, but if you clean out the unwanted junk from your life's closet, then you can fill it with more peace and joy.

Stop, Sense, And Feel Exercise

Try this exercise and see if you can stop, sense, and feel. See what you notice. Maybe this exercise is too much. Maybe you can only do it for 30 seconds. Try it and see where you get. There is no failure in trying. There is no wrong way if you are exploring and learning. The steps you take are up to you, so take this moment and try the exercise to see if you can train yourself and push yourself inward. There is much more to you deep inside than you most likely know at this moment.

To stop and sense and feel, is just like how it sounds. Take a moment where you can minimize distractions and just allow yourself to feel safe and secure. It could be in your favorite chair or on a quiet park bench. It could be lying down in a hammock or on your bed. It doesn't matter where it is as long as you feel safe and secure and you're not going to get interrupted a million times.

Once you have found your spot, just sit or lie there. You don't have to do anything else for the first few moments or minutes. If you start thinking about everything you have to do, acknowledge that these thoughts are there and let them travel past you. Hey, they are what they are, and there is no sense in trying to fight them because you're trying to embrace all that you are at that moment.

If the thoughts continue, mentally ask them if they are necessary right now. Is there something that needs immediate attention, or could they wait for however long you want to take the downtime? You may also just mentally picture yourself taking all these concerns, cares, and thoughts and placing them outside your door so that you can pick them up after you are finished with your time of stopping and sensing.

They are there for a reason, and we should honor them. Maybe these thoughts are there to help you go deeper into yourself. You may not want to ignore your thoughts because they might hold a key that is crucial to this moment. If so, honor and respect these thoughts. Acknowledge and ask them what their purpose is, then wait and listen.

As you begin to quiet your mind, just allow yourself to be there. Allow yourself to surrender to that moment of nothingness. Begin to scan your body using your mind. Think of this process as taking a big magnifying glass and scanning every muscle and cell, arm and leg, tissue and bone. It is not a time for judgment. It is not a time for you to attempt to dictate what you will find. Neither is this a time for you to try to create what you should be feeling or what you are not feeling. It is not a time of chastisement as to how much you can or cannot feel. Neither is it a time of interpreting what you are feeling.

All you are trying to do at this moment is feel and sense. You want to notice everything about you from the smallest part to the largest part. You are allowing yourself to stop and rest, but consciously, you are scanning your body to see what you feel and sense.

If you don't feel anything the first time, don't give up. Some of us are so disconnected that it takes us a little while longer. Just continue to give yourself the moments of stopping and resting, sensing and feeling.

As you continue to do this, you may start noticing things within your body. Maybe a slight trembling or a nervous twitch. Maybe a little spot that seems painful or an area that feels hot or cold. There could be some stiffness you sense. You might feel a tingling sensation. All of these things are valid, so honor every one of them that comes along at this moment. Don't discard or discount them. Don't try to explain them. Just feel all of it. Feel every bit of what you notice.

Please know that the more you stop to sense and feel, the more you will ultimately feel. However, the mind and the body will be checking to see if you're safe and secure. The mind and body will be checking to see just how far you're willing to go while maintaining the normal balance you are accustomed to in your life.

The more challenges you've faced, the more difficult this can be at the start. Most likely, it has taken years and layers of gunk buildup to disrupt the normal feeling and sensing process in your body. Please, don't think one little five-minute exercise will undo years of maladaptation to stressors and challenges of life.

The more you can go in and focus here connecting with the body, the more you will work towards awareness. The more awareness you have, the more you will see that you cannot see at this moment.

Our bodies are meant to have health, but when we've been overwhelmed by our experiences, health is in a far off distant land. When we've not been taught how to adapt and handle stressors in life, it is then that we are like a wanderer lost out in the desert with no supplies to make it through our journey. When you've been abused and traumatized by events in life, any bets are off on having the slightest clue of what will get you through life's journey.

Without feeling and sensing, your journey will be much more difficult. The more numb and disconnected you are, the more you will struggle, and peace, rest, and joy will be the furthest things from your grasp. It is vital that to sense and feel, one must go in and confront their own experiences.

It is not only a mental confrontation because this will only get you so far. It is when you go in and sense and feel and notice that you will gather up the disconnected parts of yourself, leading you to strength and power and awareness unlike you've known so far. The reward is there, but as I found, it isn't easy to get there when your life has faced insurmountable odds.

Many people will pay lip service to being able to sense and feel, but far too many are so disconnected that it does not become a true body experience. I cannot stress enough how this is a body-based practice of healing, not one where we use only the mind and thoughts. It is not something that often comes easy or is a default way of looking at our lives. However, the more we can get out of the mind and into the body, the more we will see our lives in a different way that we cannot imagine at this moment.

Almost every time I go in for a therapy session with Dr. Paul Canali, I may have some physical situation that is causing me a lot of suffering, but at that moment, I don't feel all of what is going on in my body. It is like the brain shuts that off while increasing the physical discomfort I feel. The real reason behind the pain or suffering that I experience is elusive because until I go in and feel the inner workings of my body, I'm only in touch with what is on the surface.

Please do not be too hard on yourself for not feeling in the body. It is part of the human experience. Chastising one's self is only going to push the pain deeper into the body. Instead, work to bring about awareness and consciousness to what lies beneath the pain, and you will find your life transcended far beyond what you currently experience.

When I was working a nonstop schedule of weekly travel and handling 600 emails a day plus being the lead tech support person for a project, I found myself feeling almost no pain. However, even though I didn't feel it, the pain was taking its toll on me through exhaustion.

It was when I finally stopped for a moment that the pain caught up with me, and it was not pretty. I had suppressed it so much that I didn't feel it.

I hear people talk about stress being all in our heads, but that could not be farther from the truth. Stress is everywhere. Yes, some don't feel it consciously, but it is there. Stress impacts us every day, and if we hide from it and ignore it, then it will build up. As stress continues to build, it will get our attention at some point.

If you're going through chronic pain and other conditions, you may be feeling pain, but there is so much other stuff that has been blocked. It pushes the limits of pain to levels that are extremely difficult to endure. It is as if one side of life has been pushed to the max while another side of life has been forgotten and numbed. The more this happens, the more the fear increases and when it gets to be too much, we are shutting down the connection to what is going on in our bodies.

Feeling your body can be scary and frightening. We have plenty of medications and drugs out there to prove this. There are so many pain relievers to help us disconnect and numb from what is happening, including wine, alcohol, and OTC drugs.

It is natural for humans to do this. It is part of our survival mode, but unfortunately, the survival mode doesn't get turned off after stress or experiences or past abuse and trauma. The brain then gets hijacked by all that happened to us or all that we experience, leaving us as puppets, rather than in control of our lives.

The more we can stop and recognize all of this, the greater the chance we have to overcome so much. Toxic stress, painful events, and trauma that we have endured suppress the healing power we have within us.

Just recognizing this in the mind is not enough. It is only part of the equation. We need to go in and feel our bodies. We need to go in and feel every fiber of every muscle and each cell of every tissue. It is through that connection to the body that we give ourselves the greatest hope of being more than we are.

The more we feel in the body, the more we can enact change and make better choices. If we don't do this, the stress and trauma will take over and leave us as bystanders in life. We have the option to connect more than we do and if we do this, the payoff is far beyond anything you most likely can comprehend at this moment.

Try This Exercise

One of the things I do is while I'm in the shower, I'll sense and feel the water on my skin. I may play with the temperature of it, but most importantly, I am just trying to feel and sense. Try allowing the water to hit an area of your skin and then pull it away, so no water is landing on it. What does it feel like before and after? As you do this, you're attempting to rewire the brain so that you strengthen what the body feels as you intentionally connect with it in your mind.

Another thing you can try is lying down in a comfortable, quiet, and safe place. As you do this, begin to allow yourself to sense and feel whatever is going on in your body. In numbing, we shut that down, but when we give ourselves permission to go in and feel, we begin feeling more. If you come up on a tense or painful moment, be there with it, observing and noticing it. Use your breathwork to connect with it and allow your mind to focus on it. This connection might lead you to more than you're not currently feeling. Allow yourself to go there and feel and sense.

Check out the companion CD to this book,

Mind Body Meditation Exercises.
The exercise on "Notice, Sense, Feel" corresponds to this chapter.
https://MindBodyMeditationExercises.com

7. Survival Mode

*"Survival mode shuts down self-awareness. It causes loss of body communication and feedback. This loss opens the door for all kinds of disease and suffering to creep up on us while we are numb and unaware of what is going on." - **Dr. Paul Canali, D.C.**

The more you can sense and feel, the more you can heal. Healing is feeling, and feeling is healing. It is the basic language communicated between the mind and body. Most people have shut this off and become disconnected. It isn't that they have done this purposely but more because they disconnect unconsciously. Unconsciousness is the part of the human experience that keeps us in survival mode.

The trick though is to get out of survival mode, and to do that, we need to feel and sense to stop disconnecting. Survival mode takes us out of feeling and sensing and into pain, despair, depression, and anxiety. It takes us into horrors such as what I went through during the conversion disorder.

Before I was paralyzed and my whole world almost came to an end, I thought I was doing what I needed to do to be a human. I thought I was doing my job well, going to church every Sunday and finding a moment here and there to watch some TV, proving to myself that I was relaxing. Little did I realize, I was living in survival mode. Slowly but surely, all the stresses of the day were connecting with my past experiences. I was oblivious to the stress building up in my life. It was not apparent to me that I was numb and disconnected. I was not sensing and feeling and noticing all parts of my life because I was living in survival mode.

Survival mode is an important concept to understand. If you grow up in a completely safe environment, there is no reason to feel threatened. I'm not sure if this utopia exists anywhere in the world, but for the sake of discussion, we will assume it does. Without threats, the body and mind would more closely function as intended. There would be no outside influences to alter the progression of how our cells function. I may be simplifying life a little too much, but I'm trying to lay the groundwork for what survival mode is.

A life of threats or influences coming from various sources can disrupt the normal cellular functioning in the body. It includes how we view and practice what we've been taught or shown from birth. Threats can be anything from something that jumps out at us to an all-out blown up attack by family members and other humans, to events beyond our control. They can include verbal assaults, perceived threats, and situations where we were knocked off our game. It can include bullying, self-inflicted harm, or other things that take us out of our normal biological functioning.

Threats that bring on survival mode include times that we witness or know of an individual being hurt, wounded, or suffering that we are unable to stop. These threats may be from abusive members of our society. Threats can also be passed down from generation to generation. A war-torn area or someplace hit by a natural disaster can also end up being a threat, taking us into survival mode. It may include some human tragedy or even a tragic event being played out on the TV constantly. We might minimize some moments as if they are not significant, but in reality, they connect us with something that doesn't feel safe.

There are many things that can harm us or leave us feeling threatened, and I have only listed a small subset. Most of us have lived through some experience in life that was damaging, and many have lived through horrible abuse, torture, and trauma. Each one of us knows deep inside what the experiences we have endured have caused for us in our current life. We may not be consciously aware of it, but in the inner depths of the body and mind, it exists.

Stress and the daily buildup of toxic stress act in the same way that a threat does. It knocks us off our game and disconnects us from being one with our everyday human experience. Stress shuts feeling and senses down because it is all-hands-on-deck to confront the intruder. We minimize stress and its impact so much that we don't see how much of a trauma it can become. Because stress is so subtle and sometimes barely recognizable, we don't see it building up into a threat that disconnects us from peace and joy.

We all have our threats in life and the moments where we don't feel safe. We all have our moments where we have been hurt or stressed to the limit and wonder if we can even get up the next morning. There have been moments where we felt pushed aside, abandoned, or not wanted or not listened to as if we didn't matter. Each moment builds upon the previous.

Threats could even be loud sounds that happen at moments of emotional connection to something else that is unrelated. A smell that occurs at times when some other event was going on that was not pleasant can have a devastating impact on our current moments. The look of another person that happened along with some emotion-filled moment can feel like a threat whether or not it is related and connected to the current moment.

Whenever there is a difficult moment or stress or some emotion-filled event taking place, there is potential for it to be recorded by the mind as a threat. These threats can almost seem innocent, but they can pack one heck of a punch to the mind body connection. They can disrupt our normal cellular mechanisms without us even being aware of it.

An example from my own life was when I would do something that upset my father, and his anger would come down as if I was being bombed to shreds. In those moments, I knew that anger came from somewhere inside of him and it was a raging monster that I could not outrun. My only thought was survival at that moment. It was a matter of how I could minimize the impact until the moment was over.

I remember we moved many times when I was a small child. For whatever reason, my father seemed to have many jobs, which left us moving to a new house every six months. I was in so many different schools that I never got to know anyone fully, and I can't recall all the schools I attended.

In one instance, though, we were once again moving in the dead of winter. It was right after Christmas which was always a special time to me, as it was one of the few days where peace prevailed in the house and the abuse stopped. At this moment, the new house we were moving into was not warmed up. The heat had been turned off because no one was living there.

Read along from my journal entry about this moment of survival mode in my life.

As we were unloading all our belongings from the truck, my hands got cold. My hands were always cold. The colder they got on this day, the more they hurt. When my mom told me to go inside and warm up for a few minutes because the heat had been turned on, my father was furious.

He barked at me to get outside and help unload the truck. I tried to tell him that my hands were cold and they hurt. He didn't care as he just gave me a good belt with his hand, hurling me across the room. It didn't matter that my hands were cold and painful. All that mattered is what this monster wanted. I had to live in survival mode because there was no way out. Those moments forced me to suppress and live with a normal biological reaction to the outside temperature. It reinforced once again to me that to sense and feel was not a good thing. In fact, it meant further pain.

When these things happen, we retreat and we seek cover. We look to defend ourselves against the perceived threat, or we run to get away from it. Threats come in different shapes and sizes. Sometimes as in the previous example, there is no place to run, and you cannot seek cover. I could only hide within and turn off any feeling and sensing there was in my body.

Examples Of Survival Mode

Some other examples of survival mode come in everyday moments we deal with in life. Sometimes at work, we have the boss that yells at us, giving us few options. If the boss is yelling at you, you can either stand up to him or cower within, hoping he soon stops. Even if you attempt to stand up to him, it may cost you your job, which only adds to the stress of the situation.

If your car is involved in an accident, you brace yourself for impact, holding all that energy of fear within you with the moment being stuck in time and at a standstill. Maybe the car crash was minor, but the moment of survival caused you to stop feeling and sensing. To survive, those moments could not be in full force.

If you are working day and night, not ever getting a moment to stop and rest, your body is in high endurance mode, wishing and hoping there was an end in sight, but not finding one. You remain in survival because it isn't about consciousness and awareness at that point. You are only trying to get through this and deal with it until it is over.

These examples keep you in survival mode because you must disconnect from the body to survive. Feeling and sensing are not your friends at this moment because the situation would become too difficult. The brain and body attempt to protect us by taking us into survival mode.

If you have been through child abuse or trauma, you know firsthand that there were things you had to do to survive. It might have been contemplating the next move or word spoken by the abuser. Maybe it was identifying what was going to happen next or how you could evade and flee the situation before it got to the point of no return. It might have been that the only way to survive was to disconnect and hope that the moment would be over sooner than later.

There are all kinds of ways that we acknowledge and react to threats. Threats can be very simple, or they can be more complex. Threats can connect to each other and grow into bigger ones which are much harder to navigate as you try to deal with them. It is almost like one threat we're impacted by becomes stronger as it links to previous ones.

Survival mode is how we deal with these threats. It is surviving at the moment in whatever form or way or shape that it takes to accomplish it.

I like to think of it as walking through the jungle and being hunted by a tiger. As you try to quietly evade the tiger, your heart and lungs are ready for action, should you need to run at all out speed.

Body digestion, creativity, passion, and love are not necessary, as the only concern now is trying to outrun or outmaneuver the tiger. Your body is already in a heightened state, ready for whatever action is needed at a moment's notice. You are on high alert. The lungs, hormones, cells, and muscles have readied themselves to do what they need to do to survive and evade the tiger.

Evading the tiger is survival mode. We often live in survival mode because we do not know anything different. We have not been taught that you can come out of survival mode through feeling and sensing. Many times, we were introduced to this way of living early in life as being all that we know about life. If only we would be given an owner's manual to the body and mind at birth, survival mode would be so much easier.

Even if the threat of the tiger passes, we remain in a heightened frame of mind trying to watch out for and evade this tiger and all other potential threats. We are still walking in the jungle as if the threats continue. There is no way the mind or body feels that it is time to stop and rest. We must keep on high alert for the tiger. Nothing that anyone would tell us could make us think differently.

It is the same way the body reacts to toxic stress, painful events, and trauma. What we experience may seem benign, but it is anything but insignificant. It is not helpful to view our experiences as something we cannot control. Attempting to evade them, forget about them or avoid them or act as if they don't exist will only do the opposite of what we need or desire. It will make it more difficult to come out of survival mode when we act as if these threats do not impact us. Yes, we might not have been able to do anything when they happened, but that does not have to be true to this day. We can deal with these threats from past experiences in a different way, even though we may not fully understand how to do this at this moment.

Events will happen every day. It is a given in life. Just like walking through the jungle, the events, everyday stress, and trauma are the tigers. Even the buildup of little events become almost the same as major moments. They seem insignificant at the moment, but often they are not. Survival mode is about being taken over by these moments and experiences, rather than finding healthy ways to release and deal with them.

All of us have a nervous system that is designed to help us function with our response to life and all that we experience every day. When the challenges and moments build up and become too frequent or too difficult, we hunker down and withdraw. The nervous system gets overwhelmed to the point of not functioning as it was intended. We go into our bunkers, and we start closing our hearts and lives off from others. We stop feeling and sensing. Instead of seeing joy and love, we experience more depression, despair, and anxiety. This is survival mode.

Instead of feeling the pains and physical discomfort in our bodies, we turn off all feeling. We end up in survival mode where we feel little or no joy and peace in life. At this moment of survival mode, we are still trying to evade the tiger, even if it no longer exists. Since we cannot outmaneuver the tiger, we make believe that we are handling life. However, if you look at your life closely, you will see that you are coping rather than living.

Coping with things may be necessary at that moment you are experiencing the situation, but they are part of survival mode. Coping can be a stopgap measure in that moment of experience whether it is abuse, trauma, stress, or something else. Coping is meant to be temporary, but we tend to get stuck in it because survival mode does not offer us a way out of the situation.

Often coping is our drug of choice because it makes us feel better. It helps us find some sense of stability in our days when the world seems to be falling apart. It is a strong and powerful mechanism that we use to deal with the things that are hard to deal with or overcome. Coping is survival mode. Even if it has a shaky foundation, often coping gives us a false sense that it is structurally sound and stable.

I remember when it took me a lot of effort, years later, to realize just how I had coped with some traumatic situations. I did not even realize I was doing it until I got to that point in my healing. The practices I was doing every day were normal things for life I thought, but in all reality, they were a continuation of coping mechanisms that were no longer needed. The only thing is that my mind and body did not understand that they were no longer needed.

My therapist, Emma Wallace, was helping me understand that when I went through the experiences I did, I learned to survive. It was the only way I could make it through those difficult moments. However, instead of moving on, I kept the same coping mechanisms going throughout my life. I applied them when they didn't fit the situation. They were what I knew worked and so whether they still worked or not, I continued using them as if they did. It created an imbalance. It caused despair, anxiety, depression, and hopelessness because nothing matched. The coping mechanisms no longer served a valid purpose, but it was as if I was trying to shove a square peg into a round hole.

One such way that I did this was by showing the world everything was fine with me. I smiled all the time, and no one knew how much pain I was living with in my life. However, deep inside I was a mess, and it was eating at me every day. I was coping with the pain by trying to keep it down and ignoring it. It might have been how I survived most of my life, but now that which had helped me in those difficult experiences was killing me. I had to give up the coping mechanism to discover that getting help would be the best course of action. It would help me find hope, rather than continuing to live with the pain.

When I was going through all the sexual abuse and torture, I could not stop to think about what I needed. At the time, my needs did not matter. The only thing that was important in those moments was how bad it would get and how quickly the moment would end. To cope, I put everyone else above me and neglected my life. As the years went by, I continued to neglect my life which almost brought me to the end of my existence. I still struggle with this coping mechanism as I attempt to learn that my life does matter. It is far too easy for me to neglect myself in helping someone else, even at the expense of my own life.

One of the coping mechanisms I still use which often exhausts me is trying to stay one step ahead of everyone I meet. I'm not referring to one-on-one interactions, but everyone I meet on the street. Navigating my house while growing up was like walking in a field of landmines. If I could try to determine what was going to happen, there was a chance that I could minimize what would happen to me. While I was not successful most of the time, my mind constantly calculated and analyzed everything around me that was happening. To this day, I still do that, and sometimes it keeps me in survival mode thinking that everyone is a threat when they are not. Long-held coping mechanisms are not always easy to release.

Most of us are coping with life, whether it is keeping ourselves busy and distracted or consuming substances that keep us numb. We all do it at some point or in some way. It is part of being human. It is part of living in a human body, but the trick is learning how to turn off the coping mechanisms when they are no longer needed and to stop numbing.

Survival mode only brings up the systems in the body that are essential for evading the tiger. After all, why would one want to worry about how to create the future and organize events coming up in the day, if the tiger was hunting you? Creativity or being open to new concepts and thoughts are not required in these moments. They are contrary to what we need to do in order to evade the tiger or the threats in life.

In survival mode, we aren't necessarily concerned with the well-being of other people. Yes, we may have a coping mechanism where we put their needs above ours, but the source and root of this is not pure. We may not necessarily care if we knock others down because we're trying to outrun the tiger or in many cases, the stress, experiences, and situations that have caused us difficulty. If something is standing in your way of evading the tiger, it must be neutralized for your survival. It is the reason why we often do not see fellow humans as they are, but instead, we see them as threats or enemies. Even if we don't think we see them as threats or enemies, we view others with disdain or a lack of respect. We lash out at them as if they are someone that fails to understand what we know to be true in our minds.

We often talk one way when we are going through our day as if we are fooling ourselves into believing all is okay. Unfortunately, we keep avoiding just how much the platform below us is crumbling while we exclaim to the world that we have our life together. That is survival mode.

We may go for years in this capacity of survival mode, and nothing will happen to awaken us. Unfortunately, the more you run from everything, the more it builds up inside you. The more toxic stress, painful events, and trauma continue to go unresolved, the more they begin impacting the body and mind in ways that modern science can barely understand and comprehend. You might escape the tiger for the moment, but as long as you're walking through the jungle, it is still there.

Survival Mode Can Teach Us

Survival mode can teach us if we allow it to be a guide in life. It can help us find our way if we allow ourselves to go in and find the courage to confront the buried threats that we have endured. Courage helps us to get out of survival mode and deal with the fears we face. Sometimes we think courage is a hidden shadow, but it is there as a friend to help us on our journey.

Avoiding, running, and hiding will not bring you to this point and unfortunately, most of our society and world act and believe as if it will. Human civilization is living in survival mode for the most part, whether anyone wants to believe this is true or not.

We find so many ways in our days to avoid and run. We create organized practices and belief systems and protests to do this. Keeping ourselves busy becomes the norm as we hunker down with fear. We buy and buy as if there is no tomorrow and we self-medicate. We consume all kinds of sugary and unhealthy foods. All these ways that we avoid and run away do not bring us anywhere close to coming out of survival mode.

These days, many people are becoming afraid of everyone they meet. If someone is different than them, they perceive them as a threat. Our media and leaders of this country are adding to this, but the participants that consume this stream of information are as much a part of the problem.

I see people walking in my neighborhood carrying sticks and golf clubs out of fear. Someone in the local media told them that they needed to do this to protect themselves. We live in a pretty safe area, and I walk around here without any issue. It is easier when you're living in survival mode to embrace the threats rather than the reality.

When you come out of survival mode, there is a great side of life that most likely you have not seen, or if you have, you have forgotten exists. It is easy to get sucked into the world of survival mode because it looks glitzy and beautiful as it mesmerizes you into thinking that everything is okay when it is not. It is good at seducing you into believing that nothing is bad when you've just covered up those horrors of life as if they barely exist.

Until I was paralyzed, everyone thought I was the happiest person in the world. They thought I had everything together and nothing got to me. I rarely showed my upset or anger towards people or events. I was patient and calm on the outside, but on the inside, I was a wreck. No one got to see it. I learned how to hide it because many years earlier, I had learned how to suppress my feelings and what I sensed. I'll never forget one of my best friends from college exclaiming to me on the phone something he said after I got out of the hospital. "You were the one out of our group of friends that seemed like you had it all together." Yes, to the outside world, that is how I appeared. Deep inside, it was a different story. It was one of survival. Even long after the trauma and torture were over, I was still living in survival as if it was happening at that moment.

While we may like to think that we see the threats in life, often we do not. They are silent and hidden, lurking in the shadows. Many times, they are so subtle that we hardly know they exist until they build up and show us that they are there.

Many times throughout life we are recording what is going on as a threat, but the mind may not fully comprehend it. It becomes just another event that feels unsafe. We may not verbalize that or piece it together, but the brain and the body does this unconsciously.

Survival mode is learning how to live with the threats and the places that don't feel safe. It happens when we do what we need to do to survive and make it through life, rather than being fully connected to the mind and body. When these things are happening, they seem normal to us. If they didn't, we would stop and connect with the body.

The human brain tries to protect us and keep us safe. When these events happen that are threatening or knock us off our game, we disconnect from them. If there is something we can do to alter the course of what is happening, then that empowers us. If we are helpless or unable to alter what is happening, then the mind disconnects and puts us on autopilot.

Survival mode is critical to understand how to heal and how trauma or life's experiences impact us. If we attempt to only focus the brain on positive and happy thoughts without confronting the danger in the room, we're only going so far in overcoming challenges. It is like putting a fresh coat of paint on the walls of our home but failing to see the holes in the wall that need to be patched.

Survival mode, though, is not just in the mind as many believe these days. It is only part of the equation because if you do not involve the body, you'll still have the threats lurking in the shadows. The more you can identify and learn how to come out of survival in your body, the more possibility you will see in your life. When we learn to turn off survival mode, peace and joy and love abound.

When we are in survival mode, it becomes the point where we feel threatened by others, loathed by others, and not wanted by people who truly care. It is the point where we feel we are separated and disconnected from all other people that are reaching out to us with a hand of support.

It keeps us from going deep within and finding our true essence and meaning of life. It holds us back from connecting with others in a way that brings about pure joy and love and life to our hearts. Survival mode keeps us from being in that moment where we are content with all that we have and need.

It holds us back from sensing and feeling and being part of all that the body and the mind and life have to offer. In these moments, we are dimmed and diminished in our senses and feelings. We are oblivious to all that there is because the power of survival mode is stronger than the power of walking out of the jail we have built in our lives.

For me, I learned the hard way that none of this is easy. If you've been through horrible experiences, I don't need to tell you how difficult it is to heal. There have been many times I didn't think I could make it, but now that I've come so far in my journey, I can honestly say, "You can make it too." It may not be easy. It may feel overwhelming, but there is hope beyond your experiences.

Survival mode gives us life, but we also give it life. We give it credibility, but it fakes us into believing that it gives us credibility. We ask it to give up and let us have our lives back, but it is the existence of our lives we are asking to give up and to let go. It is no easy feat for any human, even the most enlightened.

Survival mode is often more real in life than we give it credit. To hide from it and ignore it does nothing that is positive for one's life. It only adds to numbing and disconnect, and the more we do this, the more we cause dis-ease on the body and mind.

When we learn to start confronting survival mode from the felt sense of the body, it may not feel good in the beginning. However, the more we feel and sense, the more we will become aware and conscious. As we become conscious, we have the ability to make different choices for our lives. To me, this is what healing is all about because as we learn these concepts, we discover that overcoming challenges brings us hope and possibility.

<u>Try This Exercise</u>

What are your survival mode coping mechanisms, and how do they show up in your physical body?

8. Coming Out Of Survival Mode

*"Survival mode is when our nervous systems are essentially arrested in a physiological state of fear. This frozen state of trapped energy in the body can wreak havoc on our bodies and minds, without us being aware of what is happening to us." - **Dr. Paul Canali, D.C.**

Coming out of survival mode is a moment when we find meaning in life through deep joy and pure love. It is not just a statement of love or joy, but something that is felt deep within the body and mind at the cellular level.

Coming out of survival mode is finding and discovering the essence of who we are as humans and all that we are meant to be. It is a greater connection to the world where we see the higher good in all things. It is where we see the bigger picture of humanity rather than the shortcomings of the day holding hands with judgment and ego.

I know that coming out of survival mode is not necessarily easy. We have practiced being numb and disconnected for so long that it has now become our life's existence. It becomes the way we know life to be, and so any deviation from what we know is viewed as a danger and threat. The danger we perceive is actually something good, but we have been taught to fear what we do not know. It is what we do not know that becomes our greatest teacher in life or our greatest enemy.

Survival mode is like a mirror fun house at the fair which distorts the image seen. We see what we know to be familiar, not necessarily what really is there. It is part of being human in a human body. There is no need to chastise ourselves for what we see or don't see. Instead, we need to embrace survival mode and walk into the flames of the fire to burn off that which keeps us from seeing more than we do at this moment.

Survival mode can be challenging because it keeps and holds you in the past while presenting to you what appears to be a current moment. The past becomes the future unless we can find a way to recognize and let go of it. The past distorts our vision and our view of all that we know. It keeps us from seeing all that is true and possible and available in our lives.

Until it is turned off, we will keep repeating everything over and over as if it is necessary for sustaining life. We can practice mantras and perform life-saving miracles, but until the switch is recognized and turned off, it will continue as if we are still back at that moment where a horrible and traumatic experience happened.

Moments of survival challenge us through pain and struggle in life. It can feel like the long slow days of the summer heat where you just hope for them to be over and done. During these times, it can be extremely challenging to continue through the day. It feels like life is out of control and never-ending. It feels like we have no say in what goes on. We are giving it life and breath and then hoping it will hide from our consciousness.

Unfortunately, when you are in survival mode, it is often hard to tell that you are in this space. Others can most likely see it, but since it feels like it is the essence of your life, we often fail to see that it is present. It becomes nothing more than an anchor pulling us back into despair and into a moment of a time gone by that we can barely see or remember. We see ourselves as one with survival mode, so to let go of it is to ask ourselves to let go of our lives. There is no separation at that moment.

Survival mode creates tension and pain within our bodies because it is stuck energy that cannot escape. It is the connection to the thoughts we create as a way to disconnect to our potential, while it robs us each day of full physical health and mobility. I have seen and felt it in my own body where experiences of the past have impacted the physical manifestation of pain and other health conditions. Time and time again, I have seen many people exhibit physical signs of trauma and experiences in their bodies while having no clue that these exist. It is evident if you know what you are looking for in the body, but is often hidden because we have no desire to see it.

It Takes Over The Body

Survival mode takes over the body. It is not meant for a higher life existence because that goes against its purpose and vibration. It is meant to help us endure an overwhelming moment that our minds can barely comprehend. It protected us when needed at the origin of the experience we endured, but we are not meant to remain in this mode.

When I was in the hospital going through conversion disorder, my brain was shutting down. I had spent my life hiding from all that had happened to me. Even though the events of my past were over, I was still living in survival mode. Life tried to get my attention in many ways, bringing intense pain on my body before the paralysis hit. However, I ignored it because I felt safe in survival mode. It was what was familiar to me, and so I chose to live my life with my eyes closed. In what almost became my final days, my brain was shutting down everything in my life but what I needed to keep myself alive. If I had not awakened and begun dealing with my life, survival mode would have taken away completely all that I knew of my existence.

You cannot wish survival mode away, and you can't make statements to rid it from your life. It holds power and energy within the cells that you feed daily. It is fed both in the mind and in the body. Often we think that if we can change our minds, we take care of it. While this can be a powerful part, there is still what is housed within our cells. If the experience where it came into existence is not dealt with and released from the core of the body, it will continue to grow and strengthen. It will consume more and more of your life until you can barely tell the difference between your life and survival mode.

Survival mode is crafty and smart and sneaky. It knows how to disguise itself by becoming who you are. You, of course, know how to become what you are by becoming one with survival mode. To let it go, you must let yourself go.

By going into survival mode, we will begin to find ourselves. It is by going in and harnessing all that has been stored for eons that we will reclaim our power. By going in and touching the center of all that is locked in the jail cell of your life, you will find the strength to begin opening the jail cell door.

It is done gradually by waking up and becoming conscious and aware. No, it is not an overnight process, but it is a process that can move us forward towards freedom and awareness. It is about beginning to open your eyes and allow for the thought that you are in survival mode. It is about beginning to make choices that allow you to go within and discover all that you are.

You can always choose not to go in, but at some point, it will deal with you. It will consume you and your life, your mind, and body. Taking every possible ounce of energy and strength from you, it will leave you lying beside the road of life. Survival mode will take away your joy of life and your love for others while replacing it with pain and heartbreak.

Notice today throughout the world how we seem to hate one another. We seem disconnected and separated from others that don't match up to what we see as our existence. As proof, look at the lack of respect, care, and concern for others that don't look like us or talk like us or think like us. Survival mode individually and collectively takes us into separation from one another. It removes joy, love, feeling, and healthy sensation. It is replaced with judgment and hate.

Coming out of survival mode can employ different tools and procedures. Using mantras can help sometimes. Breathwork can be transformative. Bodywork is powerful if it is grounded and engages the individual in feeling and sensing.

Overcoming survival mode is about going in and becoming aware of it by recognizing that it exists. Feeling and sensing it in its entirety is where you come face to face with how much impact it has on your life. Only by stopping and resting and taking yourself out of the busyness of life will we notice it. It is about coming to terms with how you distract yourself from thinking and believing that it does not exist, while realizing that it does. We all distract ourselves from the truth we are in at this moment because as humans, we are masters of distracting ourselves.

Just as survival mode kept us protected from feeling the moment of the experience when it was created, so it also goes with distraction. It is our protection mechanism that went awry. It becomes our escape from moments we don't want to face.

We even convince ourselves years later that we have somehow magically put the moments of survival mode behind us. We convince ourselves that we have moved on and healed and it has no impact on our lives - that we have it all together and these things no longer have any influence on our day. Boy, how wrong we are!

Unfortunately, most of the time these things still have a trickle charge on our lives. If they are not a direct impact to our current day, they often work in the background orchestrating other series of events that come together to pack a punch. Healing and learning to overcome survival mode is a daily process of discovering further awareness.

I'm not saying that there is a never-ending moment for these things, but that they are there helping to push us and move us and change us into all that we can become. We tend to hide our potential when there is more to our day to discover and find further awareness. These minor moments of survival mode and connected pathways can bring us front and center to all that we are meant to be. It is up to us to choose how far we go, not exclaim we are past every experience we've encountered.

Instead of looking at them as something you need to get over, look at embracing them in a way that they continue to teach you about your own life. By doing this, you shift out of fear mode and into a moment of awakening and learning where you reclaim more of the power you hold. If you stand in opposition, there is no way to know what is waiting for you.

When someone says that they have healed completely from a very horrible experience, I know without a doubt that they are distracting themselves from reality. Maybe there is a small percentage that can say this with all honesty. However, I know from experience in my own life that we may move on to higher plateaus from these experiences, but they stay with us. They have worked their way into every pathway of our being and to rid them is a lifetime of work, not a momentary result.

Please don't get me wrong in thinking that I am saying you cannot heal from these moments. It is completely against what I am saying, and I want to make this point very clear. We can move on from those moments, and with each healing experience, we move on a little further.

It is like a train leaving the train station. The further it gets and the more it picks up speed, the harder the station is to see. It still exists because it is the place where it began. However, as the train moves further away, the origin no longer matters as much. Looking ahead towards what is possible matters more.

It is a progression of growth in our lives that is the real life builder. It is in learning how to incorporate those horrible experiences that can become less fragmented, that we can enhance the world for all others who suffer through similar things.

At one time, I thought my life was cursed, but now I see that from what I went through, there are ways that I can impact the world. I can help the world as others travel through those dark and horrendous moments as I have. Without those moments, how could I be there for others and know what they were facing? Sometimes to shine the flashlight for other people, we must first understand how to turn the flashlight on in our own lives. Without these experiences, we don't know where to find the switch on the flashlight.

It Is A Process

Look at coming out of survival mode as a process that helps us move forward, not just one that is horrible and horrifying, which it often feels like it is. Try to look at it as holding the key to the jail cell of your life, rather than holding nightmares in for the rest of your life. See it as a way of connecting with the universe in a way you may not even be able to imagine at this moment.

Survival mode is hell when you go through it, but the people who have been through the worst have been given the keys to unlock so much that most of the world does not understand. If you want to help change the world and make it a better place, the ones that have toiled in the trenches of horror, pain, and despair are the best ones to lead the way. The evidence seen in our world today proves this more than ever, I believe.

Remember the story of the man who was walking down the street and fell in a hole? Different people came along and offered him platitudes, prayers, and advice. The one that could help jumped into the hole with the man. He was the one that knew the way out. I'm not saying platitudes and prayers and advice are not helpful. They have their place. However, when someone knows the way out, that's the person you want standing beside you.

Survival mode is not just your thoughts and how you think. To come out of survival mode, it requires that we find the courage and strength to go deep within and get acquainted with every part of ourselves and every part of the experience we've faced. I cannot say it enough because the cells of the body hold the energy of those moments. To ignore the body component is the same as holding yourself back from all you can be. Survival mode comes from a time when we faced more than we should have had to deal with, but in the healing, we find the true essence of life. We find the true essence of ourselves.

I cannot tell you how many times I have questioned my journey, where it seemed like I would never find some comfort and peace of mind as well as rest. It felt like it would never end. Many others who saw me toiling on this path thought that the steps I was taking were unnecessary and unbearable. However, I learned to recognize that they were viewing my journey through their eyes. I knew deep down from the time I became paralyzed that to heal, I had to find healing within my body. Yes, I had to change the thoughts and programming in my mind, but without the body component, I was shortchanging how far I could go.

Just like when the tiger is chasing us in the jungle, we are often in survival mode. It isn't about reciting a mantra during that time. It is not about pondering the meaning of life. To evade the tiger in the jungle, one must either outsmart or outmaneuver the tiger. If you don't, it will most likely consume you.

Survival is hopefully a momentary thing in that life can get back to normal when we have successfully evaded the tiger. Our breathing can return to a normal resting rate and so can our pulse. Our blood flow and heart can find a normal routine. Breathing and respirations can resume a balanced state. The mind can slow down and begin to see life. Our thoughts can align with a greater purpose.

Digestion can re-regulate itself along with skin tone and complexion, and all matters related to the health of the physical body. Since we no longer are running from the tiger, there is no need to be in an alert frame of mind with heightened sensitivity. We can return to a resting state.

When you have been through trauma or the daily buildup of stress or even witnessed something horrific, it is hard to convince the mind and body to return to normal. It is hard to convince the individual to say "it is over, and now I can rest." To get the mind and body to realize the threat has passed, we must recognize that we are in survival mode. What we learned as survival, has become the crutches that prop us up in life. Often, we do not see how we can walk without them and if we try, our legs wobble, and we go back to the crutches.

The mind believes more of what happened in the past than we sometimes try to convince it in the present. It isn't just the mind that does this either like some may suggest. There is a strong connection located in the body that fuels our thoughts. If you don't deal with the trauma or events, the body issues relating to these things will continue to fuel the endless loop of survival mode.

Many humans forget this part of the healing equation. Part of survival mode is that you are operating in your head rather than your body. Think about being chased by the tiger. You are most likely not thinking about how much love you have for humanity at that moment. You're probably more in your head trying to determine every advantage you can get to outrun the tiger. That is survival mode, and this is where traumatized victims end up.

Thoughts indeed are important in healing and recovery but realize and know that they come from within the body. The body is directly tied to what we experience in the mind. What your body is experiencing, so will your mind experience. What your mind thinks, so does your body experience. It is opposite ends of the same spectrum. That is why we must focus not only on the mind or the body but the mind and body together as one. You cannot separate them and have true and deep meaningful healing. Yes, you will find healing and awareness, but if you want to go to the outermost depths, the body will be just as important as the mind.

As I continue in my own life, I keep working on going from survival mode to deeper healing. It can be a challenge based upon all that we have experienced in life, but it is possible to heal very deeply and without re-traumatizing yourself.

As humans, we often trick ourselves to follow the easy road of healing. At the least, we follow a road that we believe is healing, yet in all reality, we are just waving to different windmills. I do not say this is an absolute, but healing will be further enhanced when we go deep into the body, rather than stay on the surface of thought-only focus.

Getting to know ourselves is a lifelong pursuit. It is not for the faint of heart. It is something that we as humans should aspire towards because the more we know ourselves, the more whole and authentic and real we become. The more we run from ourselves, the more we live in despair, anxiety, stress, depression, and a never-ending nightmare.

Getting to know ourselves takes us out of survival mode and into a realm of getting to understand our purpose on this earth plane in a much greater way. It is our ticket out of the challenges we have been through in life. It is the ticket to greater peace and joy and love than we have ever known.

If you think you know what deep peace, joy, and love are all about, wait until you experience a true awakening from the deep inner core of your being. When you discover how much you are in survival mode and then come out of that, the world is different on the other side. It is beautiful and precious and so much more than most humans fully understand. When you see this, you will desire to go further, not worry about how far you have to go to heal.

Survival mode is not something we wish to stay in, but we struggle to move beyond it. We choose to do this, even if it is unconscious - and most of the time it is. We do not always understand or know any different until circumstances and issues in life get our attention.

Life gets our attention through physical pain and emotional pain and moments that bring us to our knees. It is trying to say, "Wake up and deal with these experiences." It is trying to urge you to awaken to something much greater than yourself. We all have terminology for this in our respective groups and belief systems, but the underlying concept is the same.

We can use the difficulties we experience to help us become more aware of our lives and the world around us, or we can hunker down in a cave and hide. The choice is up to us. I know it is not easy. I've been through some of the worst moments in life that would pull many completely under, but I've found the way out. I'm the man that jumps down in the hole because I know the way out.

We must elevate our world to a much higher plane, and we do that by elevating our lives. Realizing we are living in survival mode is when it is time to wake up, find the door, and take a step. We elevate our lives by going deep within to those moments of great significance and reclaiming the parts we left behind.

Yes, we leave parts of us behind in those moments we try to forget. Every time we have an overwhelming experience, we leave just a little bit of our essence attached to that moment. We begin to become fragmented every time this happens. If we don't go deep within to reclaim those parts, we continue in life as a fragmented human. We live in survival mode hoping and wishing there was something better, when we have it all the time within our grasp.

Survival mode is not meant to be a life sentence. It is not meant to be the essence of who we are. It is meant to be temporary. This place we are in is meant to help us through these moments of great significance when things were beyond our control.

We have all had these moments where something happened to take us away from who we are. It doesn't have to be great trauma to create the survival mode. There can be a minor experience that has an emotional connection to it. It can be a moment where we are a witness to events beyond our control. It can be from experiences where we were in the care of those that did not know any better and consciously were not living as all they were meant to be.

When we become acquainted with how we are living in survival mode, we may see some ugly truths and parts that we may not wish to see. That is normal. They may make us angry, anxious, suicidal, full of despair and living in a world of depression. Our days may be agonizing and filled with so much difficulty that we wonder if we can go on in our awakening.

We may have so much anger within us while living in survival mode that we barely recognize it. We may recognize it but not be able to get in touch with it, for it is locked within the never-ending cycle of that moment that happened to us.

We may have so much despair that we cannot even see any way out of the situation. Life may feel hopeless like there is nothing to live for tomorrow. It may make us think, what is the point? We may not even care if there is a point or if there is hope or if there is a tomorrow.

These are all moments that are part of life, but our lives are so much more. Life is more than survival mode of just getting by and taking what happened to us lying down. Our lives are pushing us to become much more so that we can be there to help shine the flashlight to the rest of the world as they walk their path.

I see humanity as a chain of people holding a flashlight. We are all connected to one another, so if we don't discover how to turn our flashlight on, the person behind us may struggle more. If we learn how to turn our flashlight on, we help complete the illumination for humanity on that path. Each one of us plays a vital role to the next, for waking up in our own lives impacts all of civilization.

Survival mode can be hell, and I know that all too well, but I also know that there is a bridge to the other side, out of the torment, pain, and despair.

Chasing Rainbows

Sometimes we try to chase rainbows when we want to come out of survival mode. Rainbows can be pretty and colorful and perfect at the right time, but if we're not careful, we will be doing nothing more than a dog who's chasing its tail.

We can subscribe to the beliefs and opinions of others that are vocal and seem to have their verbiage together, but at the end of the day, many healing methods may not add up to a hill of beans. It may be nothing more than an illusion of water in the desert mirage.

Many times, we follow these things in the hope that we have latched on to something great and life-changing, but all too often we will find ourselves let down. Then, we move on to the next and greatest light bulb in the package, only to find out that it burns out just as the other things did. Sometimes these things are necessary for our growth to lead us to where we need to be, but often they become distractions on our road to healing and living a healthy, grounded, and balanced life.

Pretty healing rainbows come in all forms and shapes and sizes. Survival mode can include the latest and greatest fad of a product or the latest new age philosophy that is being promoted and liked and shared across the land of the internet. There can be data that backs whatever it is, but without the careful vetting of the data, inaccurate or inconsistent conclusions are drawn that don't truly exist.

I cannot recall all the rainbows that people presented to me as the way through my own healing. Sure, they might have offered something valuable, but if I had gotten caught up in them as others had, I would not have made it this far in my life. There are far too many things out there being christened as the ultimate way to heal, but many are standing on shaky ground. If we could only learn to take the essence of what works in them and apply that specific part, we would make much greater progress in the health of this world.

The number of products that have been pushed on me as a massage therapist make my stomach churn. Some of them are billed as MLM's, attempting to get the masses to see them as a powerful healing product using this sales technique. There are some that are so expensive that I question what their motive is. I have even seen many base the sole existence of the product on a summarization of limited research, not realizing they have distorted the true healing potential.

Over the years I've had numerous products, ideas, and beliefs thrust at me. When I was working in a research department of an agriculture company, my eyes were opened to something most do not see. Approximately 85% of all the products that came across my desk did not work. All of these had the stats and research to back them up, but when we put them to the test in our production system, only about 15% of the products gave us a return on the money. I can tell you that the companies fought tooth and nail to invalidate our research data because it did not prove their product would help us. We were a large enough company that if they could have said our company uses this product, it would have immediately helped their sales. Sometimes, it became vicious in meetings because the truth was not on the side of the companies promoting the products. I remember one product rep threatening me over one of the research trials.

It is the same way in the healthcare and new age industries. There is a great deal of money made upon the hype of some new gadget or product or procedure. There is some truth in each one, so it makes it sound plausible, and often proof is presented in a way that leads you to believe what you are hearing. As consumers of medical treatments, we allow our fears to demand that the medical community come up with treatments that work. Unfortunately, it is sometimes nothing more than a placebo. Survival mode does not allow us to see this because we are focused on the symptoms, not the root cause.

I cannot count the many times I have been lobbied hard to accept and buy into the claims made for all kinds of healing attitudes, beliefs, gadgets, and products. It almost feels like when you meet these folks, they only want to push their "healing item or healing cure" upon you without really getting to know you. It feels as though they don't even question what they are saying. They state it as if it is a fact. There are far too many products to list, and I would only invite nightmares if I started to list them.

However, the best way to spot them is to ask this question: "Does the product or cure take you deep into your body and your mind or do they purport to do the heavy work for you?" Everyone can make claims but if the product, cure, or person is not taking you into a place where you discover a greater awareness of something deep within you, then question the need for these things.

To just take you out of pain may seem significant, but it may limit your long-term healing potential. It may help in a current moment, but don't get caught up in the craze of someone else or some product removing your pain. Healing needs to be about going into the pain deep within, instead of a quick fix from some outside force or product.

It feels like many use the high price of a product, seminar, or thought and belief system to show how effective and valuable it is. I'm always saddened by this and hope never to repeat the same thing in my own life. When money making opportunities overshadow true healing, question the daylights out of it. More than likely, it is then that the products and cures are just a hyped sales pitch, rather than something that will truly help you. Again, look for things that take you deep within yourself into awareness, not that will make you feel good on the surface for a few moments.

I think many of these things hurt our society and those trying to heal. Many of these things prey upon the weak and sick at a time where they are looking for anything to help them. We will always have snake oil salesmen no matter what, but somehow we need to reverse the course and quit selling cures created by the ego. We need to see these cures and beliefs stand up to testing and repeatability.

I see very little hard scientific evidence of what people claim to be a cure. While they want you to spend hundreds or thousands of dollars on these things, the data claims and results can barely be backed up in most instances. If you find some data, it is usually insufficient to draw solid conclusions, or it is questionable information. Just because you see data, do not for an instant think that the data is correct or telling the entire story. In these days, we spout statistics, but there is far too much extrapolation in the data to claim authenticity. Often, the data tells part of the story but leaves out critical pieces that would show the whole story.

I am not saying everything out there is wrong and should be avoided, but unless you can prove it with results, or I can experience it firsthand, I'm not too interested anymore. I want to see without a doubt that it is true, and it can be backed up and repeated from person to person. It needs to be more than just a "feel good" item or a belief. The proof is in the pudding, and these days, the pudding is missing.

In all things, there is an element of truth. Look for that and then see if you can do this in any other way. If the product or belief requires you to do nothing, question it. If it requires you to believe it works without questioning, then question it hard. When it does not take you in and connect the mind and body together, question it. If you try it and don't get it the first time or even the second, third, and fourth times, question it. Don't stop questioning it until you prove to yourself that it is helpful or it does not work. Just because someone says it is true, does not mean that it is.

I have seen people feel relaxation for the first time in a long time and believe that was energy. When they start to feel something, especially when coached, they start to confuse the two. When you truly feel energy moving through your hands or in your body, you will know without a doubt that it is much different than the relaxation response. Unfortunately, we live in a stressed-out world of survival, and we've become confused as to what the difference is between the relaxation response and energy.

I still remember one client taking some different drops of stuff from various bottles. They did not even know what was in the bottles and for all they knew, it could have been water. However, they had been convinced to believe what they were doing at different times of the day was a healing cure. It may have been something that would help, but without proper knowledge of what you are doing, you're asking to be taken advantage of and hoodwinked.

You are far better off to question things that people promote to you as true healing than to buy into all that is presented to you. We've got some great salespeople in this world that could sell water as the most magical creation of all time. We've got people who will sell icebergs as if they just invented them. Question everything and if you're not satisfied, go online and search for reviews. Learn to question it from deep within your core body and gut because if you listen to those things, you will find the truth. If you notice any doubt within yourself, honor that and see if it is fear coming up, or it is a clue helping you discover the validity.

A note about searching for reviews online: Don't believe everything you read. Often these places selling cures, ideas, beliefs, and products have sanitized the internet, so only positive reviews show up. They do not let affiliate marketers say negative things that would harm the sales of their products. I know because I had an affiliate marketing company force me to take down a very honest write-up on their product by threatening legal action against me.

Affiliate marketing is one of the ways that most of these products and belief systems are sold these days. It is a great marketing concept because it expands your sales force without having to pay anyone to be your salesperson. However, the pitfall is these affiliate marketers (much like the companies they represent) have one goal in mind. It is to sell the product. Do you think they are going to show the downside of what they are selling to everyone? No, they try to make sure it is all glowing and positive reviews, or the negative stuff is so benign that it no longer matters.

Again, question everything and when finished, see if what you feel deep inside of you adds up or not. Don't just follow the blinking lights because they look pretty and are fascinating. You may just be following in footsteps that lead you over the cliff, rather than bring you to the brink of enlightenment and truth.

I wish that we could have more honest and truly ethical people and companies in the world. However, this is a utopia that seems like the magical land of tomorrow. I believe that many don't even realize how they are playing into all of this, but they sure know how to push their product and beliefs. Some people get hoodwinked by too many and fail to see past the lights and glamour. These companies know how to hook others in and get them to push their products. They aren't stupid! These actions appear to be their only purpose because their desire is to make money. Yes, they may say they desire to help others, but let's be honest and call it out for what it truly is.

Much of what I write about is my own experience. It is the only truth I know that I can prove without a doubt. However, my truth may not be your truth, and so you should measure how my experience lines up with what works in your life. Take from my experience and life what works and hold the other stuff back for another look. I'm not trying to say that I have all the answers, but I have learned a great deal because of my own life's experiences. I've been to hell and back and have seen far too many things that most have never seen.

If we want to accelerate our healing, we should look for the nugget of truth in all things and learn how to apply that to life. Not everything that is preached out there to the masses is the truth. Not everything people dismiss as voodoo and woo-woo is an untruth. You must be careful and learn how to discern between all things. It is lacking in a major way in our world.

I'm not going to name all the things that I find to be extremely questionable as I don't believe that would be proper of me. I am just going to urge you once again to question everything. Search for the truth and listen to your innermost being to see if it is true.

It may sound like I am negative about all things and that is not my intent. My intent is to say "wake up" because not everything that is purported to be the answer to all of life's problems is exactly that. We've been led to believe so much and follow so many rainbows, that we no longer identify or connect with survival mode or past experiences.

You owe it to your life to give yourself every possible chance to become all you can be, but if you chase rainbows, you're most likely not going to find the pot of gold at the end of them. Continuing to chase rainbows in such a manner is the definition of futility.

It does sadden me when I see how people chase the rainbows, thinking it is where they will find the pot of gold or a healing cure. I've seen people do this repeatedly. Every month or two, they are on to a different healing cure that they hope now gives promise. We give up far too much power to things that are not working 100% for us in our favor. Again, there are truths within each of the products, but they do not always rise to the point of bringing about true change.

One of the things that we do as humans is not evaluating things properly, especially when it comes to our health and healing. We don't do our homework. Instead, we follow far too easily what some expert says without question as if it is the only truth. We blindly accept that something is the cure while missing the most important part of the healing equation. Our peers convince us far too easily that they hold all the answers.

Healing is not about chasing cures and subscribing to the latest field of thought or beliefs and opinions that are shared by other people. Healing is not about learning a jargon that makes you sound as if you know more than you do. It is not about accepting the premise of a product and regurgitating the facts to other people.

It is not about moving in one direction or following a recipe that someone created for a modality. Healing is not about feeling relaxed for a moment and thinking you have found nirvana. It is not a moment in time where you think that you have found all you need to do and that you have healed. Healing is not about telling others how much you have healed, but showing them by using that healing to advance your life.

Healing is about taking that moment you've found and learning to apply and replicate it in all areas and aspects of your life. It is about feeling and sensing and seeing the connection you have with your mind and body. Even that statement is far too shallow because it goes much deeper than this. It is a body-based experience, not only a mind revelation.

The more we learn and grow and the more we heal, the more we will see. What we knew today or yesterday will no longer be valid. It hopefully becomes the stepping stone for tomorrow's discovery and journey along our path. If we stop and see it as an end all or the greatest thing since the creation of oxygen, we've lost the point of our own life's journey.

It is human nature not to allow ourselves to go into deeper levels of awareness and consciousness. The ego holds us back and does it with such cunning secrecy that we don't see the evidence of it. To discover more truth about how we operate and function is to begin discovering who we truly are. However, far too many people stop at this point and fail to continue the journey.

Our lives and our healing journeys are progressions. We have all been given so much, and while some have been dealt difficult hands in life, it is about where we go with it. It is how we learn to hold the flashlight for others walking on the path behind us. It is how we impact the world and universe that brings much more to our journey than just the mere difficult moment we are in at this time.

There is so much more out there for us when we come out of survival mode.

<u>Try This Exercise</u>

What things have you embraced on your healing journey?

What worked, and what did not work?

How can you tell in your body what works in your healing?

9. Stress Impacts The Body

*"Sustained or repeated stress can disrupt our bodies in seemingly endless ways." – **Dr. Robert M. Sapolsky. Ph.D.***

I'm not a medical doctor, but I've dealt with a lot of stress and its impact on my body. I think there are far too many times we don't truly understand as much as we think we do about how stress impacts us.

Sure, we know it, and we think we see it, but then there is a disconnect. Alleviating stress takes more than just using our thoughts. What I share here is an attempt to discuss more of what happens in the body from my personal experience and point of view.

Let's start out with an example to help explain this. Say you are outside, building some wood project. You're hammering a nail that you're holding between your fingers and all the sudden, the hammer slips and hits your hand.

"OUCH," you scream!

And rightly so!

It hurts.

Now, let's say, we're back to hammering and we hit our hand again. OUCH is probably the appropriate response. We continue hammering and go through this scenario of OUCH several times. After a while, it is almost like we become so numb that we barely even feel the hammer hitting our hand.

In many ways, stress is like a hammer continually hitting our hand. Even though we would think that we would move our hand away, when we're in the middle of stress, that's the last thing we think to do. We become numb to it to the point we don't even notice it.

Stress is one of those things that the more our body or our mind endures, the way we feel the "ouch" changes significantly. We don't necessarily notice every moment of stress because we don't always stay connected to the body and mind enough to realize when the OUCH happens. We disconnect and numb.

We get busy taking the kids to every event and activity in which they are involved. Our boss comes in demanding we have this project completed, or there is some fire to put out that requires our immediate attention. Emails require urgent responses and come in at record-setting paces in a day. Text messages and social media prompts demand we stop and check them. Your husband wakes up cranky, or the cereal bowl spilled on the floor at breakfast. The car won't start. The child forgets something they were supposed to have ready for the day and so on and so forth. We watch the news, and it is filled with hate and discord, disrespect and insults. I'm sure we all have our list of stresses in the day.

But here's the kicker: we go through all those things just trying to stay up with the day. We don't stop and say, "Give me a minute to focus on my breath." We don't stop for even 30 seconds to catch up with ourselves. There isn't enough time for that. We're already late for work and late to get the kids to school, so we rush out the door, put the pedal to the metal and try to sneak into our desk before the boss notices.

Then, we're overrun with even more stress, and the husband is calling, or the kids are calling demanding this and that. Our friends are trying to text us. Email is pouring in. The phone is ringing. Get this done, get that done. "I need this now," says the boss. Before you know it, you realize that you forgot to eat lunch, but you don't feel like eating lunch. You continue to go through the day, knowing that there aren't too many hours left to get everything done before you must race to pick up the kids, go to their activities, get dinner for the family, and try to catch up.

The thing is you don't catch up. You drop out in front of the TV and fall asleep. No amount of coffee is going to revive you. You've given out and the next thing you know, you're out like a light.

Now you've gotten to the point where it is time to make sure the kids are in bed, and their homework is complete. It is all you can do to keep going. You're beaten and exhausted, but you can't stop. When you finally reach the bed and fall onto your pillow, your mind is racing a million miles per second thinking of all that you need to do in the morning. Your eyes and brain and body are so tired that you can't sleep. You toss and turn all night, only to barely drift off again before the alarm startles you out of bed.

When you get up, you reach for the coffee and start the process all over again. Only a few more days to the weekend, you tell yourself. Only a few more days, you tell yourself with convincing gusto. The phone startles you and emails pop into your inbox. The kids are texting you, wondering where you are. They've been waiting for 20 minutes. You rush from the office, and the traffic is so bad it frustrates you because these idiot drivers are in your way. Don't they know you have places to be?

By the time the weekend gets here, your body is running on fumes. You barely can keep going, and it is hard to focus. You keep pushing because that's what strong people do. It is hard to keep in mind what you need to do, and you daydream of an escape from it all to a place of peace and quietness and tranquility.

The weekend comes, and you figure you'll get a jump on next week and get things caught up. Soon, your to-do list becomes a mile long. About the time you begin to focus and organize your tasks, the kids come in and need your help. They are arguing and fighting. Your husband comes in and wants to know what is for dinner and if you feel like doing something fun, oblivious to the fact that you're in the middle of a meltdown.

The weekend goes by quickly and the next thing you know, it is Sunday night. You're trying to get the kids ready for school, and the restful weekend you were looking forward to did not happen. The mile-long to-do list you wanted to get done didn't even get a good dent in it. You feel frustrated, but there's no time for that. There are too many things to do, and you are lucky to get everyone fed including yourself, and to sit down for five minutes before going to bed.

You hit the pillow, hoping to get a good night's sleep but your mind wanders and runs. You make it a point to drink some wine before going to bed, but it makes your mind fuzzy. It is how people relax, you have been told. You say there's got to be more, but at this moment, there is absolutely no time in the day for these thoughts. If you could only catch a break or a few free moments in your day. If only you could run off to a tropical paradise and relax for a moment. All you need to do is catch one break in life.

The thought of stopping and breathing or noticing your breath is a foreign concept that takes more time than you have. There are too many pressing things to do. "I can't be bothered with that," you say to yourself.

The thought of taking a moment and walking outside in the sunshine and listening to the birds is good for others, but you wonder exactly when you will have the time to do that. After all, that's just for those new age folks that want to meditate all day long. Okay, you don't say this out loud, but you think about it silently to yourself.

Reorganizing your life so that you have more downtime makes you feel like you're neglecting all those that depend on you. It includes your kids, your spouse, and all your friends and coworkers or boss. You know that everything you do is critical to your life and trying to pick and choose is just impossible.

You know that it is just the way things happen in life. You must suck it up and go on. After all, this is life and the way it is meant to be. You can't help but think this way. If you let others down, how would you ever live with yourself among the guilt, shame, and embarrassment?

All these events and more are like the hammer hitting our hand. Every time it hits, we go OUCH. Then we start doing it all over again. The more and more we hit our hand with the hammer, the more physical changes begin to happen in our body.

Our hand starts to swell and get bruised. We may see a discoloration in the skin. We may get skittish every time the hammer comes down to the nail, afraid of hitting our hand. The anxiety increases. The sense of hopelessness fills that action.

If someone picks up the hammer to pound a nail, you cringe knowing how it feels when it hits your hand, and so you surmise that it will happen to them. You project your fears of the stress upon your own body. It triggers those same responses within you.

Little do you realize that there are other ways of holding the nail so that the hammer doesn't hit your hand. There are gloves you could put on or tools such as pliers that you could use to help mitigate the stress. There are things you can do. You could put ice on your hand to help the swelling and bruising, but these are things that lie beyond the disconnect with the pain you are experiencing or the stress you are enduring. They never enter your conscious thoughts because you're lost in surviving the pain of another potential hammer hit.

Takes Us Out Of Conscious Thought

Stress takes us out of conscious thought. Stress takes us away from awareness. Consider the hammer example. The pain of the hammer hitting our hand takes us away from what we could change to help mitigate that. We are screaming out in pain "OUCH," rather than thinking consciously about how we can make different choices. If you're in pain, you're probably not out to try and figure out how to launch a rocket to the moon. You're just trying to get through the pain.

Stress on the body is the same way. When we're in the middle of stress, we aren't thinking so much about getting out of it. We're more focused on getting through it. We disconnect and numb from problem-solving and balance because our mind's sole focus is on how difficult it is. Conscious awareness is at the opposite end of the line of thought from just getting through stress.

So, while we may want to be dealing with our stress and are often thinking we are dealing with our stress, most of the time we aren't. I see this all the time in the bodywork field. In fact, I see it in myself. When we get in the hectic parts of life, we don't truly see what we think we see. It becomes an illusion and convinces us that we do, even if it evades us.

We numb and disconnect so easily. I mean, if you're going to hit your hand with a hammer, you probably don't want to feel all of that. It would get overwhelming. So, your brain begins to adjust and say, "Hey, let's dial this down." With time, you keep dialing things down. You keep disconnecting and numbing. The more you disconnect and numb, the more life gets dialed down until you're not feeling that much.

It is human nature. It is not because you're weak or not good enough or because you haven't reached nirvana. You may think you aren't spiritual enough. Instead, it is just biology. It is just being human in a human body.

All too often we chastise ourselves because we haven't conquered stress. We see this in others and chastise them. We take the view of perfection, and every time something doesn't match up to this, we slap ourselves. It keeps us stuck in the mode of stress and disconnecting and numbing from all that life can be. We don't see ourselves as a work in progress, but as one that is flawed. It does not do anything positive or beneficial to us.

If we see stress and how we react to it as part of our continued growth process, it changes how we can interact with it. Instead of being at war with it, as if it were an enemy, we can begin to see it as something that we can alter and change, to learn to make different choices.

We make choices each day in how we react or don't react to things in life. We choose how much we allow ourselves to interact with stress and events, or if we numb and disconnect. Through the choices we make each day we allow ourselves to become aware and conscious, or we go into fear and survival.

When you are in fear and survival, your choices become discolored by past experiences, triggers, beliefs, and opinions. These past experiences can include trauma and other situations you've encountered or even the daily build-up of stress. All impact us and the more they reside within us, the more they have a controlling influence on the mind and the body.

The past is something we carry with us until we have fully learned what it is trying to teach us. Sometimes the learning process happens quickly, and other times, it is an ongoing teacher. Sometimes it becomes one single moment of learning, and at other times, it becomes the teacher for all the other moments of learning we go through.

To think of your life as just getting over something is limiting all the potential you can harness from it. Life is a process of growth and evolution. It is not so much about finding an endpoint but taking each moment and helping use what you learn to go to the next and discover more. It is about becoming more conscious and aware each day of your life.

It is not just a thought process. It is a biological concept. Stress impacts the body just as the hammer impacts the hand. You can think all day that it isn't going to hurt, but I'm sure if you whack your hand with the hammer, it will.

That is one of the fallacies humans make about stress and situations, or past experiences in our lives. We want to make healing just a mental exercise, not truly and fully connecting to it in the body. Sure, I get it. I know the fear is all too real and it helps us close our eyes to what is truly there. I do it just like the next human does.

The trick is to learn how to go in and feel that gunk in our lives and reclaim its power from the cellular level, rather than living the illusion. The illusion is one of disconnect and numbing. It is all up to how we allow ourselves to consciously connect to the body, rather than hide, run, and flee from it. No, it isn't easy to do this, but if we want to take back our lives, it is something we must learn.

All these stressors and past experiences impact the body. Just like when the hammer hits the hands, the present moment often connects with the past experiences. They build upon one another and influence what we experience at this moment now. If we neglect or ignore this fact, we only will perpetuate the numbing and disconnect within the body.

As the stressors and past experiences impact the body, it is like a chain reaction because other nearby cells talk to one another. While this is more my belief of what happens in the body, I feel it may just not have been studied and realized yet in a scientific view. I watch what has happened to other people's bodies and my own, and this is where I draw this conclusion.

The biological impacts continue because when your hand is swollen from the hammer hitting it, things within your body must mobilize to go to its aid. Whether it is the blood system trying to come to the rescue or your brain trying to release endorphins and painkillers from the enteric brain, the body tries to compensate for what we experience or what we have experienced.

Structurally, and neurochemically, the enteric nervous system is a brain unto itself. Within those yards of tubing lies a complex web of microcircuitry driven by more neurotransmitters and neuromodulators that cannot be found anywhere else in the peripheral nervous system. – Dr. Michael Gershon, M.D.

When one system speeds up and is overwhelmed, other systems suffer and start screaming out for attention. If they don't get what they need like a fully functioning blood circulation system or maybe some chemical substance the brain produces, they start to falter. It is like one system begins to compete with another for what both need. It again continues to take us into numbing and disconnect.

Consider turning the water on in your garden hose. If you crimp the hose, it will fill up with pressure on one side and the other side of it will not get what is coming through from the spout. It will either dribble out in a higher-pressure stream or barely anything at all. It is the same way the body deals with stress and past experiences. We either let the water flow freely, or we disrupt it.

There is no way to tell what long-term effects will come because of restricting one system or part of the body while turning the dial up on the other part of the body. However, there is enough knowledge out there that realizes this turns into "dis-ease" in the body. It is the moment of illness and physical difficulties via pain, allergies, diseases, illnesses, or other physical situations.

The more we hold this stress in, the more it impacts the body. The more it impacts the body, the more it alters not only our consciousness and awareness but also our brain chemistry and physical body biology.

You can't continue to hit your hand with the hammer and act as if nothing is happening. Yes, you might be able to tough it out for a while, and you might talk yourself into ignoring it, but sooner or later, the pain of that moment and experience is going to catch up to you. It is only a matter of time.

You may think you've escaped it for a long time, but sooner or later, enough will build up and push it past the tipping point. We can have a strong impact on our health if we allow ourselves to stop and rest along the way. If we allow ourselves to take a moment to breathe, we can do wonders for our physical health and our mental health.

If we choose to learn more about how to become consciously aware of the body, we can impact it in ways that we are not able to realize at this time. We all seek answers and good health, but we fail to fully understand and recognize just how much influence and impact we have on our own body and mind. We fail to fully understand how the past does impact the current moment.

It is not just a new age thought process. It is real life that we can all observe and look at if we so wish. If you wish to continue ignoring that which is before your eyes, you will never see this. You will keep chasing pretty rainbows, but never find the pot of gold.

Awareness and consciously connecting in the body don't necessarily start with our thoughts and mind. They start with learning how to feel within the body and connect to everything we feel. It requires that we go into the pain that we feel when we stop to notice it so that we can not only learn from it, but also harness the stored energy and power that it holds.

Stopping And Feeling In The Body

Stopping and feeling in the body is the key to begin learning how to handle stress, anxiety, and all that life has thrown us. It often involves the help and assistance of someone that is compassionate, caring and nonjudgmental. It often requires someone who has traveled through the fires of their own life and has done a great amount of healing so that their junk doesn't get in the way of helping someone else or impacting the other person's healing.

We all have our junk. No person is without their junk. It is a continuous process of learning and healing, and the evolving awareness and consciousness of life. What we learn and discover today is the launch pad for what we will become tomorrow. When we've reached that point, it is then that we see the deeper layers that can be peeled away.

Stress and past experiences are not just a momentary struggle in life - they are real, and they are trying to get our attention. If we ignore them, it won't turn out well. If we embrace them and try to understand them, we will be given the gift of knowledge and awareness beyond that which we know. We will find peace that we may not know at this moment.

When we walk into the fires of our own life's experiences and learn to connect with them from deep within the body, it is then that we discharge all that stored up energy which is robbing us of deep and never-ending peace. We cannot be at peace if we're sitting in the boat on the ocean in the middle of a storm. We must move past the stormy waters to find peace.

In my own life, I have done many of the things that I have mentioned here. When I first got out of college, I worked hard to excel and learn all that I could. In one of my first jobs, I started up a research department, not having a clue what I was doing. The general manager believed in me and so off I went to get things going. I worked seven days a week and at least 12 hours a day. I would come home and have a drink to help me fall asleep at night. Little did I realize that this stress was building and trying to catch up with me, so I ignored it. Flu, colds, headaches, and losing my voice were what everyone went through, I told myself. I did not see them as warning signs.

When I thought this job was taking advantage of me, I listened to the wrong people and took a job that did not fit me. I convinced myself it was more glamorous. My dad put pressure on me, making my job out to be something that wasn't good enough. He compared it to jobs he had, not understanding what it was I did. Unfortunately, I listened to him. Six months later, I knew the job was not working out, and so I went on to the next great career choice. In the meantime, I had started a relationship.

Starting the next job was more demanding than the previous ones. I was designated as an excellent self-starter, and so they dumped me into a large territory to manage before I even knew how the company worked internally. I was lost, but there was no way I could let anyone down. Stress was something for the weak, and I had convinced myself that I did not let stress get in the way. In the meantime, I was so busy that my relationship didn't work. When I was told that I was not in touch with my feelings, I dismissed it as hurtful and negative talk, not helpful and constructive.

I poured my life into every moment on the job, not wanting to let anyone down. My days started by leaving the house at 7 AM and did not end until an hour or two before going to bed. On Sundays, I managed to work only a half day, but otherwise, it was nonstop. I'll never forget when one boss told me that I was much harder on myself than they would ever be. Unfortunately, what I was doing to myself didn't sink in then.

Through all this, the stress was building up, and I didn't see it. You could not have convinced me that it was happening. I thought I had life under control and was doing everything that was expected of me in life. There was no way I was letting anyone down.

At the time, I did not realize that I was living the experiences I had grown up with in my past. There was the father that demanded perfection. There were the horrible experiences of child abuse that I wished to forget, and so the busier I could keep myself, the less I had to worry about confronting them. Little did I realize at the moment that the build-up of stress was connecting to my past in such a way that it was overwhelming my body and mind. I was oblivious to it.

I continued to push and push until I went too far. At first, it was not being able to sleep and struggling with headaches. However, I thought everyone gets those, so don't be a weeny and just push through it. "Maybe if I took a few minutes and took a walk, all would be okay" is what I told myself. However, it didn't take long before the things that needed to be done crowded out the walks and moments of fun or relaxation I badly needed.

Next, it was back and neck pain. Once again, I didn't know why I was having so many difficulties. After all, everyone gets these things, so I just needed to suck it up and move on. They made pain relievers for situations like this that would magically cure it, I understood. So, pop a couple more pills. I don't have time for this now, I thought.

Then there was the stomach pain and heartburn. I surmised that I had a nervous stomach/pre-ulcer condition in high school and this was something I would always live with in my life. I figured that I was worrying too much and so I tried to pray harder. I attempted to adjust my diet because I was probably not eating as well as I should have been. None of these things worked, because I didn't realize just how much the stress of the moment was connecting to my past.

As the days wore on, I became more anxious and depressed. It just seemed like life was so difficult, and there was little I could do to help myself. After all, some of us people in life just worked harder than others, and we could not let the world down. In my judgmental view, that is how I saw things. I pushed on at the expense of myself but was oblivious that I was doing it. I was good at making other people laugh and like me, but I could not do the same for myself. While I was happy on the outside, inside I was so miserable I could not see any of this happening.

With each day, things just got worse. I was on autopilot and barely recognized that anything was going on in my life. The minor physical and mental difficulties were just part of life's experiences. I had always demanded so much of my life, and it seemed like everyone around me played into that as I was growing up. I knew no other way. There was no way I could let anyone down because I had to be perfect and the best at what I did. Then and only then would people like me.

A little later a major moment happened in my job that threw my life into a tailspin. One of the farms I was managing had a fire late one Friday night. It was in a remote area, and so by the time anyone noticed and called the fire department, it was too late. As daylight arrived it became obvious just how bad it was. The crying and screaming of the animals was horrifying. I will never forget the smells or the sights that I saw that day. I can still picture it vividly in my mind as if it happened yesterday. We began rescuing all the animals that we could, but many were so badly burned that they had little skin left on them. It was horrifying.

Little did I realize at the moment what this was doing to me. After that weekend, my neck and back pain increased. It got to the point where I could barely move my neck from side to side. My range of motion was extremely limited. My back hurt constantly. There were things to do and so aspirin became my friend. I was seeing a chiropractor three times a week which was helping, but once I left his office, I walked back into the world of stress. The stress would bring the pain back with a vengeance.

All of this led up to the days of the paralysis and complete breakdown I went through in my life. None of it seemed connected at that moment. My family and I demanded that the doctors fix me or give me a pill to cure what I was experiencing. Each one struggled in confusion as to why this was happening. Medical test after test yielded no conclusions that would help me improve and so I went from doctor to doctor with little to show for it. For days, each doctor would send me home to fend for myself.

It would be many years later that I would start to piece the moments together. Yes, the stress was a major factor, but the animals crying and screaming took me back to two different times that my little kittens were being killed or drowned in a gunny sack. As they were slammed shut in a cellar door by my father, they screamed out. I was chastised for attempting to care for them or crying at losing them. I had to hold it all in and be a man, although I was only a few years old at the time. The fire on the farm connected those two unrelated sounds and sent my life into a tailspin. The official diagnosis was a conversion disorder. Events almost 20 years earlier connected the past and the present moment.

You see, it wasn't one stress or action that caused conversion disorder. It was the buildup of everything I had been through in my life. If you had measured how much stress I was enduring in my life, the amount would have been very high.

I often compare the paralysis and seizures of conversion disorder that I went through to appliances connected to an electrical circuit. A circuit can only handle so much, just like the body. As you add appliances on to it, one by one, it will handle them until you push it to the limit. Once you push it to the limit, it will trip the breaker, and everything will shut down just like what happened to me. Is it the last thing you plugged into it or the first that caused it? Maybe instead of trying to pinpoint one thing that led to the breaker being tripped, you are best served to look at the series of events that led up to this moment. Sure, the final snap may be the result of something you can identify, but don't neglect to see all the things that led to this point. They are just as important, as I have learned in my life.

One of the best things we can do when the body or mind breaks down physically is to ask what was happening before it took place. Experiences in life often have a great impact on the physical reality that shows up in the body. If we can spot that and see it, we have a chance to stop the disconnect and numbing and find our way home. If we continue oblivious to it, we will go down a path to the point of no return. When the physical issues show up, ask the question, "What was going on just before it happened?"

The more you can ask this question and see what took place, the more you will help improve the connection between experiences and physical ailments. When you do this, you give yourself the awareness that more is possible in what you can do to heal yourself. This awareness leads to greater consciousness and opens up more possibility to overcome challenges than we realize.

I'm fortunate that I found my way through the conversion disorder, but so many that I know stay locked into the symptoms of what happened while ignoring all the steps that brought them to this point. No, they are not easy to identify when something happens. I understand this completely. However, if we don't begin to try and uncover and discover the stressful impacts on the body we have been through, we're only making it harder for ourselves.

If we don't deal with the stress and experiences of our lives, they will deal with us. There is no escaping it. While it may show up in different ways and different illnesses, we ultimately are in control of what happens. We have the ability to choose differently and either become aware or go down the path like I did when I almost lost my life.

Over 80 percent of doctor visits are stress-related, and while we all may understand that, we are so far removed from the essence of what that means. We keep going just as I did, acting as if you just need to push through stress when your body is telling you to stop and awaken. The body gives us many warning signs, but if we continue to ignore them, we are only sentencing ourselves to a life of hardship, despair, and pain.

Try This Exercise

List your top 10 stressors in life.

Where do you feel the stress in your body?

What can you do to change the stressors you face?

It may be in how you approach them or let them go.

You might need to prioritize and realize you have only so many minutes in a day.

Come up with a plan of attack that puts you in control, not the things that stress you out each day.

Another thing to do is to get frequent bodywork done such as massage. The more you can do things that turn down the allostatic load on your body, the more capacity you will have to see things differently.

They may not end up being as much of a stressor if your nervous system has a greater capacity to deal with challenges in life.

However, you still need frequent bodywork to continue discharging the daily build-up of stress. Schedule a massage today!

10. Fear

> *"When we are able to stand at a distance from fear, observe it, and take it apart as physical sensation along with its related thoughts and images, the fear often dissolves and transforms." – **Dr. Peter A. Levine, Ph.D.**

One of the things that keeps us from going further in healing is fear. Fear is powerful. It is strong. Fear is cunning. It gets us to believe one thing while holding on to a world that is nothing more than make-believe. Fear is alive and well in the hearts, minds, and souls of all human inhabitants of the world.

If you think you have overcome fear, be careful because it is most likely getting ready to pounce. I don't see fear as something I have to overcome so much as something that I need to recognize, embrace, and then reclaim my power over it.

At one time, I had many fears, and those fears had many fears. Fear begat fear. My fears built up on top of one another and soon, many giants were standing on top of many giants. The fears got so great that I could barely make out what life was. I could barely tell that my life existed.

My fears grew to the point where I did not even see them or recognize them. Going through my days, my friends thought I was the most adjusted one and had everything together. I was too good at hiding from my fears and not letting anyone see them. I was a master at disguise, and so were my fears.

Fears come in all shapes and sizes. They often mimic normal events, and so everyone tends to discount that they are even present. Fear gets blamed for many things, even while people blaming others don't see how much the fear is controlling their lives. Fear is alive and well and in control of our days.

In these days and times, fear is leading the way. So many cannot see this, but they tune in to the news shows for another daily dose of fear. They listen to the leaders and the politicians and the prognosticators as if they hold out the answers to their lives. They regurgitate what they hear because it backs up their fearful thoughts coming from the ego. Perpetuating the fear online through social media, they find others that are perpetuating the fears like they are. Together, everyone feels stronger because the fear unites us together as one.

Unfortunately, the fear is not even recognized. It is not even seen or noticed or acknowledged. Everyone notices the fears of others, but not in themselves. Were you to point this out to those engulfed by the fears, they would laugh and scoff and act as if you are the misinformed one. Fear does not like anyone to take away its power. Fear does not like to have anyone in control but itself. It does not like you looking deep within because if you look too closely, you will see its potential.

Fear drives people to the emergency rooms and doctors. It drives people to buy all kinds of health treatments that fail to help cure the conditions they face. While we may mask our physical conditions, these treatments may not necessarily cure us. Fear has caused this country to spend massive dollars on health care, that continue to increase every year. Fear is alive and thriving and prospering.

Fear happens before your own eyes without you seeing it. Fear is not something you find in others while claiming it is not in yourself. It is within you. It is part of you. In many ways, it is you. I realize that you may disagree and think that you don't hold fear within you, but as I stated earlier, fear can make you believe one thing while getting you to see something else.

How do I know any of this? Why do I say what I do about fear? It is because I have lived a life in fear and I have seen others living a similar life. I had so many major anxiety attacks that I could barely function. I suffered from depression to the point of attempting suicide. Fear gave me the fertile ground to become paralyzed from a conversion disorder and have a near-death experience. I was too afraid to face what I had experienced in life because fear kept my eyes closed.

We all have fear within us, and we all live with fear in our lives. The more we try to hide from it, the more we are feeding it. It is when we deny fear that we give it credibility. It is when we shun it, that we are using it to prop up our lives. When we run from fear, it is then that we are keeping ourselves from overpowering it. When we cover up fear, it is then that it has taken away life's joy, peace, and contentment from us.

Fear is hideous. It is a silent killer of the human spirit. Fear is a thief in the night that robs us of our most precious selves. Fear is responsible for so many of our health issues and complaints because it walks hand-in-hand with stress. While we all want to think we are so much more enlightened and intelligent not to hold fear in our lives, we are only fooling ourselves. We can go on fooling ourselves all we want, but at the end of the day, it will not help us. It is our choice whether we want to become more aware and conscious or not.

All too often we run from fear, and while that is a normal biological reaction, we need to stop and see what the fears are that we are running from in our lives. Fear can disguise itself as being so real and so enormous that we think there is no other option but to run.

I've spent my life running from many fears and the fear of those fears. It took its toll on me and little did I realize I was still living in survival mode, all the time afraid to live my life. I didn't realize that the unconscious fears within me were five-alarm fires going off deep inside. I didn't realize that the fears I was holding on to were killing me little by little. They were paralyzing me. They were taking my life from me. Fear was taking a little piece of me every day while I looked in the other direction.

In our day and time, fear is one of the biggest obstacles we face along with not being aware and conscious. Fear is the propellant into behavior in life that we may not normally associate it with and condone. It is the darkness that keeps us from seeing the entire picture even though we think we do.

Fear is one that we give life to, and then we feed each day. It is a motivating force in life, while we cling to a view that does not truly exist. It alters the world around us and makes the physical body work in ways that it would not normally do biologically. Fear physically impacts all the functions of the biological body, including the mind.

Fear increases the tension and stress in the body. It creates a physical imprint that holds us from being 100% healthy. It reorganizes the body's priorities in how it responds and how the mind manages our human experience. Fear keeps us on alert, and if you can imagine all the body systems that are required to stay on alert, you will find the origin of how fear impacts the body.

Imagine the tiger is hunting you down, and you would have a legitimate reason for being afraid. Fear, in this case, would be something helpful to your survival. It would perk up the body systems that you need to evade and outmaneuver the tiger. Fear would get your heart beating and your lungs working overtime to prepare you to try to outrun the threat. It would get your mind focused on what is happening at that moment as the tiger stalks you.

You would become keenly aware of the sounds that could tip you off to the location of the tiger. Your breathing would not be for rest or relaxation. Instead, your breathing would be keeping you pumped and ready to evade the tiger while trying not to allow the tiger to hear you.

Focusing on how much you love the jungle, or the trees or humanity would not be your focus at that moment. Your focus at that moment is not on solving world peace or stopping to take a nap. Because of the threat, your brain would use the fear to help focus on your survival.

At this moment, fear is helping you. It is your life-giving force to keep yourself alive due to threats around you. It would be the extra moment of strength and energy and agility, with your muscles engaged to do whatever you needed to do to keep yourself safe.

In life, we have many experiences that become the tiger chasing us in the jungle. Whether it is child abuse, emotional or physical abuse, emotional pain from loss, or relationship breakups, fear often begins to form in those moments. It could be fear from toxic stress that we don't let go of which builds up, altering our biological response. Fear grows because of these things, and life becomes altered as a result.

Fear can result from many experiences including being bullied or suffering from emotional and psychological abuse and neglect. It can show up from having a work schedule that gives us no downtime in life. You can even see it in moments where life confronts us with overwhelming challenges, when we have no tools to deal with them. It can show up in survival mode from the never-ending moments of stress we fail to discharge. There are many ways that fear can become a part of life through survival mode. It is not only limited to the horrendous trauma that we may have experienced.

These experiences and stresses build up on top of each other. They keep us running from the tiger, even in the years to come. Each layer builds upon another layer, and as they build up together, they become one. The more they become one, the more they blend in together until you can no longer separate them from each other. They become your life, rather than separated from your life.

Fears are crafty because while we give them life and empower them, we feel that we cannot take back their control. We feel powerless to our fears. The fear itself becomes so strong that we begin to lose our lives in them.

I believe the more you live, the more these fears become cemented into life and blend in with our everyday existence. As the years go, it becomes harder and harder to tell the fears apart from who we truly are as human beings. It gets harder with each passing year to let go of the fears and reclaim those parts.

Fear will stop you in your tracks. It will hold you back from all possibility in life. Fear will diminish your learning capacities because it is not interested in learning new concepts. It wants to survive and keep existing. Fear will taint every relationship you have and alter how you see the world. It will show you one thing and get you to believe it to be true while holding all that exists away from your awareness and consciousness.

We are in a time when we don't even see how our fears are piling up each day. We don't see how much our lives and thoughts and practices influence and impact us each day. Our view of the world and humanity is hindered and altered by our fears.

Our Fears Have Become Us

Our fears have become us, and we have become our fears. Life exists in each moment with fears as the template for the next. Fear allows us to choke ourselves from the true essence of life. It knows no limits on how far it will consume us.

Our fears gut our innermost being and rob of us what we truly know about ourselves. They leave us to rot on the vine, while we run from one hope to another. These fears could not care less what we become or what we think as they control our every thought, move, and activity. They require us to disconnect while they continue to grow and feed upon themselves.

When you've gone through an experience in life, fear may have been helpful, but if you don't let go of that fear, you'll continue to live in survival mode. You can think that this is not true, but I have seen it over and over in my life and that of others.

Letting go of fear is one of the hardest things I think I have ever done and that says a lot coming from someone that was paralyzed, lost their memory and had to start over in life once again. It was hard enough to see it and own up to it, but it was much more difficult to reclaim my life.

Do I no longer have fears? No! I still have fears that crop up and connect me to moments from my past. They are everywhere just waiting for the right trigger so they can come out of hiding from their caves. Fears lie in wait and are eager to pounce when the time is right.

Fears seem so much more than they are. They seem like these big gigantic monsters. When I think of fears, I can't help but think of the story from the Bible where David meets Goliath. All the townspeople feared the giant, but little David took his slingshot with one pebble and took the giant down. To me, this represents fear and how we can bring it down.

You see, we are all scared and afraid of what we don't know or what seems bigger than we are. We tend to find a bond together with others, and the fear grows because now we have a collective energy to do this. We sometimes create rules and beliefs and views based on these collective fears. All the while, we don't even see the fears. We don't even recognize them. We are convinced they do not exist. It is everyone else that has fear, not each of us individually.

These fears are alive and growing each day. They are getting reinforced each day as our lives form around them, and for years to come we closely identify with these fears. As we identify with the fears, we begin to lose a little more of ourselves. As we lose ourselves, we get to the point where we now see something that is not who we are. We have morphed into something we don't recognize.

If you try to convince someone they have these fears, they will reject it categorically. There will be no listening to such crazy talk in their view. They will fight you to the end, to prove how wrong you are. The fear has overtaken the individual and has clouded their judgment. The fear has become so much like they are that they can no longer tell the difference between themselves and the fear.

Fear is insidious. Fear appears to be more powerful than we are, but in all honesty, it is weak. It only feeds off the energy and power that we give it. Fear feeds off the brain power that we turn over to it. As we allow fear to consume us, it takes more out of our lives. It finds safety in our cells and tissues as it destroys our physical well-being.

Fear guts our basic wholeness as humans, but we give fear the knife to do this. We can claim we don't, and act like we don't, but either we give fear the power, or we take it back.

We often overlook the fears in our lives because who wants to spend time going into something that frightens us? We become oblivious to it while hiding and disconnecting from it. As we disconnect from it, the health of our mind and body diminishes with each passing day.

Fear can appear in the form of ignorance, hate, belief, one-sided views, and narrow-minded opinions. It can show up in how boisterous we are, or how much we hide through our shyness and quietness. Fear can come in the form of nightmares and sleep difficulties. It can show up in anger outbursts and impatience, condescension, and over-criticizing.

You see, fear will stop at nothing to hide from its host. Fear will stop at nothing to keep us believing that we have it all together or that we are forgiven or healed, or everything is wonderful. Sometimes we have convinced ourselves so much how fear is not part of our lives that we only see happy rainbows, rather than the storm clouds that bring the rainbows.

Fear can show up as muscle tension, pain, illness, headaches, and other physical symptoms. We try to shield ourselves from fear so much that it begins to take over the body. At the same time, we are using our energy to keep ourselves in that fear and away from the reality and grounded experience of the day.

We exhaust the body to the point of pain and illness, pushing the health of the mind and body so far out of balance that other physical issues start to arise. All the time, we don't see the fear and the connection to physical reality until it gets too difficult to overcome. We don't feel how the connections of the past or experiences that have gone by are now impacting our current day.

We don't see how much we have stored in our cellular memories of the body which have direct access to the mind. All we see is the life we are stuck with, but not what we have disconnected from in our lives. It is at that moment that the potential lies. Unfortunately, fear is so strong and powerful and crafty that it keeps us from going there. It keeps us outside of the buffer zone it has built up, so we continue to call fear our master.

Much of this is so unconscious that we don't even realize it is happening. Much of it is so unconscious that we will go through life not allowing it to become part of our consciousness. The horror is too great, and the experiences are too intense to do anything else. It becomes far easier to ignore it and hope that it goes away. We wish it away as if it is anything but reality.

It becomes easier to present to the world that all is fine on the home front. We shout to the world and the full moon how much we believe and how much we know. Unfortunately, we miss the mark of all that is within us. We proclaim how great we are while minimizing the impacts of what we seek to have in our daily lives.

Many times, I have had people tell me that they are fully healed from one experience or another. While it is possible, often so many Band-aids have been put on the wound that it no longer can be seen. It does not mean it is gone, but that the fears have covered it up. It is a way to minimize the pain while trying to survive. Sometimes this is a part of our healing process but make no mistake that even if we think it no longer exists, it does.

Fear keeps us in survival mode so much that we soon lose sight that there is anything but survival mode. We go through our days as if this is normal and it's something everyone does. It's like one TV show where the father came home, and a family member asked him how was work. "Work is work. You go to work and work your hump off, and that's the way it is."

That is how we view fear and survival mode because it seems like this is what happens in life. We go through our days, and we keep ourselves busy so that we don't have to stop and get in touch with the inner workings of life. We do everything we can to hold ourselves back from truly seeing the bigger picture or all that is within us. We do everything to keep us from truly getting to know ourselves at the deepest levels.

It is much easier to hide from ourselves than it is to go in and truly get to know what makes us tick. I'm not talking about a one-time discovery either, but a constant evolution from one moment of awareness to the next. Life is not about a moment in time, but a journey of constantly getting to know who we are and becoming all that we can become.

I know in my own life, the difficult healing sessions were the ones that were a challenge for me to go in and see. My mind did everything it could to keep that from happening, while my awareness and consciousness desired to help me evolve. Sometimes I was in complete denial of what was going on, and at other times, I was too frightened. While I said I wanted to go into the difficult moments and move on, in all reality I did not.

Fear is the sticky trap that holds us in a place apart from becoming all that we are. Fear is the regulator valve saying, no more. It holds us back. It holds us from truly getting to know who we are and discovering all the nooks and crannies of our inner life. The possibility cannot exist when fear keeps us from seeing all that there is to see.

Fear embraces hatred and ignorance. It embraces the view that others have more than we do and that we suck at life. It embraces the need to have medical procedures done without evaluating what we could change in our lives first. Fear embraces the need for medications rather than embracing thoughts outside what we believe to be true.

Fear holds us to the belief that we don't have the power to heal ourselves or fix ourselves. It keeps us believing that others have the answers to help us or fix us or heal us. While others may be a step in helping us discover more wholeness in life, fear keeps us thinking everyone else has the answers. It keeps us blinded from seeing the truth. We succumb to it as if we are under its spell.

Fear becomes a badge of honor in whatever medical condition we live with or what role in society and family we must play. Fear becomes the badge of honor to give credibility to the lot in life we drew that prevents us from becoming much more than we are. It holds us back from our greatest potential.

We are afraid to move into a moment of change because we are leaving the safety of all that we know and diving into the sea of the unknown. We are afraid to challenge our beliefs because our lives are built upon these beliefs. Often, these beliefs are nothing more than sand disguised as concrete foundations. To find all that we are, we must let go of that which we know.

When I was in the hospital suffering from a conversion disorder and my life was quickly slipping away from me, I came to realize that to stay alive and function once again, I had to let go of all that I believed to be true. I had to face those fears by allowing myself to be challenged and embracing those challenges. It wasn't easy, and I was not sure that I could do it. At the time, I wasn't even sure I knew what I needed to know to do this. We all hold things in our views and beliefs and opinions that do not stand up when challenged beyond our capacity to endure.

I have had times when physical things have happened to me, and I struggled to let them go. In the end, it was me who was holding on to them. I was not prepared to let them go. To me, I was afraid of saying goodbye because they had become my existence. I was not sure how I could go on physically without these things I considered to be who I was deep inside. In these moments, no one could have convinced me that it was me who was not letting them go.

Asking yourself if you are ready to let go is a valuable exercise. Fear will do all in its power to distort the answers to that question. It will make you think the question is crazy and ludicrous and from some nutcase that doesn't understand your situation. Yet I found it is an essential question to ask and allow yourself to be asked.

Fear has held me on a path in life where I saw no escape. I thought that I would never make it. From the suicide attempts to the anxiety attacks to the deep depression and despair, fear had me believing this was all my life could be. It took a health crisis so significant in my life for me to start letting this go.

Letting go of fear can take time. It is not as if you say today that fear be gone, and it's gone. It is possible that this can happen, but all too often the fears are much smarter than we are. They don't give up this easily, and they sure don't go away without a fight. Often, we think they do, but they don't.

More likely than not we are just hiding from the fears, or the fears are hiding from us. We think they have left. We think we have somehow tricked the mind into believing they no longer exist. However, remember that fears are tricky little monsters. They know how to disguise themselves and make us believe they no longer exist. All the time, they are sitting in the background laughing because we bought it hook, line, and sinker.

Letting go is a conscious effort, and most of the time we are not conscious human beings. Living in a world of survival, we are more concerned and worried about getting through the next moment of our day, what's for dinner, what the kids are doing or some zillion other tasks. If we are not conscious, fear hardly needs to work at all to hide from us. It is no effort for fear because it can operate normally with no concern for being caught.

Being conscious is not easy for most humans. As we grow up, no one teaches us how to do this, and our society and world do not make it easy to stay conscious. I have a feeling that the most enlightened of all would say that they struggle with true consciousness, and even that is a stepping stone to additional consciousness they have not discovered.

Fear cannot function in someone that is conscious because a conscious person will take the fear and reclaim the power and learn the lesson of why it is there. Rather than being taken under by it, a conscious individual will embrace it, and fear does not like that. Fear works best when a human is anything but conscious. Fear works best when we are not on our game, and we're in survival mode.

Remember, not all fear is bad. If the tiger is chasing you in the jungle, fear is your friend. Fear motivates you and helps keep you safe. Fear increases your survival tools so that you can evade the tiger and not get eaten alive.

If you are walking through a bad part of town, fear can heighten your sensitivities so that you will know if something is lurking in the shadows or you are not safe. Fear can help you make decisions so that you get to see all sides, but at the same time, fear can paralyze you if you welcome it too much and allow it to roam free.

If you are venturing into something new, fear can be there as an alert signal to help guide you through the obstacles you encounter. It is like a walking stick designed to point out what is in your path as you stumble in the dark. However, if you begin to embrace fear as your mode of thinking and decision-making, then fear has become your enemy. It is no longer useful.

We Give Fear The Power And The Leash

We give fear the power, and we give it the leash. We give it the knife that is used to devour us. Once we have given fear these things, then it in no way wants to give them up. It says, "No way! You gave it to me, and now it is mine. It no longer belongs to you."

The only way to get it back is through force. Force comes in the way of courage and strength and determination. Force comes in by taking the little steps and saying, "I'm taking it back, fear. It is no longer yours to keep."

Of course, fear will fight you to the end. It does not want to let go. You have created fear and helped it grow with all the energy you have invested in it, and now it has so much with which to push back. You helped create it but once created, it now has a life of its own, and you must wrestle it down to the ground to reclaim the power.

Too many times, fear looks so overwhelming that we don't feel like we can challenge it. We give up before we even try to take it back. "It is too much," we think. "I'm too tired, or I don't think I can do this," we exclaim. These are the phrases we say because fear is in control. Fear is the one working the ropes, treating us as if we are puppets on a string. It is the one with the power, or so it seems in our eyes.

Fear will push you and pull you. It will not hold back in defending its existence at all costs. Fear will win and keep winning, leaving you to feel like a failure and lost in eternal damnation for all years of your life to come. Fear will mock you, tease you, and taunt you. It will laugh at you. Fear will replay so many things in your mind to prove just how incompetent you are in trying to reclaim all that it has stolen from you.

Fear will not stop for one minute. It is always on duty and looking for every way it can to prevent you from gaining an ounce. It knows that it robs your power, to maintain its existence and supremacy over you. It knows that the more you try, and the more it can get you to appear as if you've failed, it grows in strength and stature.

You can be the most enlightened individual or the strongest person in the world, but fear can still knock your legs out from under you. It is much craftier and sneakier. It does not play by the rules of the game that a conscious individual would follow. Before you can even begin to know what made you fall, it knows how to trip you up and knock you over. Fear will knock you flat on your backside while laughing and making you feel as if you are nothing more than some mess lying on the ground.

Fear knows how to connect events from the past with triggers of the moment. It knows how to use the slightest movement, smell, feeling, and emotion, among other things, to trigger an event that will take you back as if you are right in that previous experience. It doesn't care if you are left lying beside the road for dead. It will win at all costs.

Letting go of fears is not easy. Courage, strength, and determination are the enemies of fear. Fear knows that the more conscious you become, the more it dies a little each time. It knows that if you get control of the knife, you will no longer devour yourself. It knows that if you see through its hollow interior, you will begin to know the truth. The truth will set you free, but you must get past the fear and out of survival mode.

Identifying fears can be very difficult to do because as we discussed earlier, it hides from you in plain sight. It makes it look like life itself and who you are, rather than something that is not truly the essence of your being.

Fear compromises how you see things and the way you see them. It manages to hold the full view back so that you only see part of the picture. Fear knows what it is doing, and most of the time, humans know very little about the inner workings of fear in their lives.

We all want to act as if we have the world by the tail and we know what we are doing. Especially men, who are taught to be fearless. We are taught that if you show fear, you are nothing but a wimp and a baby. These beliefs could not be further from the truth, and yet we continue to teach them to our young.

Unfortunately, to understand fear, you will need to unlearn all that you were taught because most of it is not true. It is each person's choice how far they go into fear and how much they allow themselves to see. It is part of the human experience of learning and discovering who we are that enables our growth.

Learn to recognize and identify survival mode, because as you do this, you will see how fear has taken hold of your life. It will present itself in the body through physical conditions. It will show up in your mental health through anxiety, depression, suicidal thoughts, and despair, among other things, just as it did with me.

If we allow ourselves to travel into the body using the fear of survival mode, we will transform ourselves. Let go of the ideas and beliefs that you are all you can be at this moment. Realize that you have been impacted by the experiences of your life and the belief system you employed to survive. Realize that you are pure at the innermost essence of your being. The possibility of rising beyond the ashes exists in ways you cannot see at this moment.

Try This Exercise

Get as creative as you want but take a sheet of paper or poster board and begin drawing pictures of your fears. You could use images from magazines or anything you want. Make it fun so that you see the fears in a new light. List all that you can think of in that moment. You may want to go further and notate how these fears show up. Are they just thoughts? Is there somewhere in the body that they show up? Do fears impact your breathing when you aren't aware that they are? Are they connected to the pain that you feel in your body? After you attach the images to the poster board, note which body parts connect with these fears you're currently sensing.

In addition, check out the Fear Poem by Joy Harjo. Listen closely to the words because they say so much about fear. Record your observations in your journal. http://JoyHarjo.com/

11. Into The Unconscious Mind

"The best indicator of your level of consciousness is how you deal with life's challenges when they come. Through those challenges, an already unconscious person tends to become more deeply unconscious, and a conscious person more intensely conscious. You can use a challenge to awaken you, or you can allow it to pull you into even deeper sleep." - Eckhart Tolle

We need to talk and understand more about the unconscious mind. We don't pay enough attention to it, and we don't spend much time thinking about it. Yes, we know the right words but mostly we are just speaking them, not practicing them.

My knowledge of the unconscious mind comes from my work in the massage profession, my personal experiences in life, and working with Dr. Paul Canali of Evolutionary Healing. I'm not speaking from a concept based theoretical study. Instead, I am talking about firsthand knowledge that I have discovered in myself that has helped me increase my understanding.

The unconscious mind holds so much within it. It is part of us, no matter how much we want to be involved with it or not. We can ignore it all we want, but it still operates and impacts every moment of our day.

We can think happy thoughts, numbing ourselves in the process while presenting to the world that we have it all under control. Those things do not mean we are in touch with the unconscious mind even if it is what we portray. Unfortunately, in this case, we don't even realize we are saying one thing and doing another.

The unconscious mind is at work with all the input we give it in a day and throughout our lives. It is not necessarily something we think about or interact with consciously. While it impacts our lives constantly, we're usually not aware of those specific ways that it does.

You won't ever connect with the unconscious mind if you're constantly busy and running every moment of your day. If you're concerned about every possible news story and event, your unconscious will be the farthest thing from your conscious realm and mind. If you're stressed, worried, afraid, and dealing with a thousand life-impacting moments, the unconscious is not going to be something you can easily recognize and connect with your mind and body.

However, the more disconnected we are to what the unconscious mind does, the more numb we are in life. It brings difficulty to mental health, brings physical pain, and impacts our role in humanity. Without being fully connected to the mind, body, emotions, and spirit, we are robbing ourselves of the full human experience.

The way to start going in and connecting with it is allowing yourself to stop. When you stop and allow yourself to feel, it is then that you have begun a moment of connection to what goes on in the unconscious mind. We access it through our felt sense and feelings.

The felt sense is where you allow your body to feel, and by allowing your body to feel, you open the gateways into a part of your brain and life that you don't normally connect within a day. It is at that point where you give yourself the permission to cross that threshold and become more aware of who you are and all that you are.

In the beginning, when you stop to feel your body, you're often not aware of anything. It may surprise you at first. You may not believe it and think that you are aware of much more than appears at that moment. When I was traveling in a job where I was gone most of the week, I did not realize just how much I was not aware of and not feeling in my body. I thought I was aware and conscious, but I was not.

It was not until anxiety began to get the best of me that I started to see a glimpse of what I was not aware of at that moment. When I went into a therapy session, I was confronted with what I was trying hard not to see while being numb and disconnected.

In my journal, I talked about how much the stress builds up without us even knowing it.

Journal Entry, July 2, 2015

Over time, the stress builds up, and as the stress builds up, exhaustion begins to increase. We have become so good as humans in hiding and masking the exhaustion and stress that we don't even see it. It continues to build until it takes us down.

I have just gone through this, and I usually am more in touch with what goes on in my mind and body. The days were too hectic and nonstop. The phone calls were relentless. Everyone needed me and wanted me and demanded my time. I tried to push back, but it got to a point where pushing back took more energy than giving in to all the fronts I was fighting. It crept up on me little by little like a thief advancing inch by inch.

While I thought I had things under control in life and I wasn't feeling any pain, I did not realize I had shut down. It got so bad that if I had allowed this to go any further, the struggle to come back would have been much greater.

This is the point that we get to in our lives that most of us are living in each day. We stop connecting because of trauma, experiences, or the daily build-up of stress we don't see. We do not connect internally with the felt sense like we have convinced ourselves that we do.

If we stop and allow ourselves to go deeper and deeper and be there at that moment with nothing else going on, we have the opportunity of once again turning on this connection. Through the felt sense, we flip the connection to a state of awareness. It is then that you enhance and tune into the mind body connection. As the connection is enhanced, you start to feel things in your body that you might not have been feeling.

The felt sense is not something you think about as much as it is a physical connection. When you allow yourself to go into that space of feeling what is happening in your body, you are beginning to connect with the felt sense. It is a point where you begin to notice what is there, instead of disconnecting, and stop being oblivious to what you hide from your awareness. The felt sense is the physical connection with the body that guides you to the unconscious mind.

The unconscious mind communicates through feelings and the felt sense. It is the language vehicle between the mind and the body that shows us much more than we currently know and are aware of in life.

The unconscious is not something mystical that only certain people can connect with in the mind and body. It is something that each one of us has the ability and power to do, but we must quiet the mind and body and permit ourselves to go there. In the Bible, it is referred to as our innermost being.

We hide a great deal of stuff in the unconscious mind that we are not even aware of in our day. When I went through conversion disorder, there was a part of me that knew I was hiding from myself, but there was a part of me that did not want to permit myself to go into that place. Often, we convince ourselves that we are more connected to all parts of the mind body experience than we are. It is how the ego keeps us locked in numbing and disconnect.

As a result, conversion disorder almost ended my life, and I was not sure if I could ever come back fully from it. Many people struggle to come back fully from conversion disorder. For me to go in and reclaim my life, I had to allow myself to connect with the unconscious mind and listen to what it had to say. I had to become aware and conscious of that which I was trying desperately to hide from my life.

The unconscious can be our greatest ally if we allow it, or it can be an overwhelming force that takes us down. It is our choice and our choice alone. No one can do this part for you, but there are those that can assist. No one can decide to allow this to happen for you, but they can help you once again discover it.

Learning from the unconscious mind is part of our journey into being human in a human body. It is where we begin to understand our lives in the context of the entire world and civilization. It is beyond grounding because it is the true essence and nature of our innermost being.

Don't discount the unconscious mind because it can truly help you. Embrace it and learn about it. Allow yourself to connect with it and begin to understand more about yourself than ever before. Use the felt sense of your body to see all of it and discover more of it each day. The answers and life-giving force we need are located within us. It is where the action happens from the spark that gave us life.

We go through our day with our busy moments and list of things to do, but we fail to see the impact of the unconscious mind upon every waking moment we live. It's there, whether you see it or not, feel it or not, or even want to acknowledge it.

The unconscious mind is one that stores data and input from many different experiences and moments of your life. It is the part that automatically knows what to do in any situation that arises. In many ways, it is the rapid response team. It is the way you respond to situations that match up to your conscious mind and awareness. The unconscious mind is responsible for the basic functions of life, including habits and mind-numbed behaviors.

In an unconscious mind, we store many things. These things that we store come from our experiences, good or bad, and they impact our every moment after that in ways we fail to see most of the time. They are so automatic that they happen before our eyes, and we don't even know it. It's part of being human in a human body.

The unconscious mind controls or helps your reactions when it comes to emotions, feelings, actions, thoughts, and words. It knows when you feel comfortable in your responses and works to keep all of that in line.

You can also think of this part of your mind as anything that is not in your conscious thought. In problem solving, the conscious mind would be gathering data to help you solve that problem while the unconscious mind would be working to determine relevance to life events or experiences. The conscious mind would help you in dealing with a client while the unconscious mind would be pulling in many scenarios from your life where you did something similar. It would be doing a compare and contrast to help you in dealing with that client.

Your conscious mind does not think of your body temperature every second, but your unconscious mind knows that it needs to maintain a balance. It will activate other body systems to make sure this happens. If you focus on your breathing, your conscious mind will know that it is breathing, but every minute of the day, your unconscious mind keeps your breathing operating at the rate which is needed to maintain life and functions.

If you can stop and interact with your unconscious mind, there is so much you can glean from it; so much you can use to view your life and the world around you in a different way. There is so much that you don't understand and see because we are all oblivious to the unconscious mind. We are not as aware as we need to be for our lives.

Being conscious in a human body is not easy. There are far too many distractions that take us away from being conscious. We have tasks to do, problems to solve, events to attend, and people to take care of in a day.

If you're driving down the freeway, most likely the best course of action in your mind is to stay focused on the road. Using your conscious brain, you judge the distance between you and the car in front of you or behind you. You scan the road for situations where you may need to react. Having a deep introspective moment with your unconscious mind is not ideal at this moment.

However, if you're sitting in the quietness of your house, the conscious mind may not be needed. It is a moment where you can stop and find stillness to allow your awareness and felt sense to connect with your unconscious mind.

Our conscious mind and unconscious mind play critical roles in not only our survival but how we function each day. It is in understanding more about these parts that we can better live our lives to the fullest.

Failing to learn and comprehend more about the unconscious mind is only going to hold us back.

The More We Begin To Understand

The more we can begin to understand all that is going on behind the scenes, the more power we're given to move through our days. The more we understand and expose what is hidden deep within us, the more we will consciously become aware to make better choices. Without knowing what is impacting us, it is like taking a shot in the dark. You may hit something, but it might not be what you want to hit.

Exposing the unconscious mind allows us to let go of the baggage we have carried from all our experiences. We may not even be aware that we are carrying them, but they become like familiar weights we drag along each day. Only when we expose these things can we decide if they are still needed, or we can choose to let them go.

Consider if you are traveling by airplane. You pack your luggage, and it may be very heavy. You notice the weight as you put it in your car and as you pull it out once you get to the airport. At this point, you may be thinking you packed too much because it is heavy and awkward to handle. At the airport check-in, you begin thinking about other things and the weight of the luggage is no longer as evident.

We store the experiences of our lives in the unconscious and forget that they are even there. We no longer experience the weight of it because our minds have moved on. The weight of the luggage is still there. We continue to drag it with us, and each day we add new experiences to the luggage. All the while, we don't notice that this is happening. It is how the unconscious mind works.

It is all part of our path and journey in life where we learn more about who we are than we knew the day before. It is about getting to know our innermost thoughts so that we become the empowered beings that we are meant to be. Discovering the unconscious is true growth.

We never know enough about who we are or what all we can be. We all have had experiences that have challenged us to the core. Some of us have encountered moments where we have struggled to stand up against the challenges of life.

All these experiences are recorded in different ways in the unconscious mind. It is like information entered into the computer. Even though we may not be aware of it, the unconscious mind is recalling the facts. It plays out more than we realize or even desire to accept.

We go through our days oblivious to the impact of these past experiences on our unconscious. Indirectly they impact the physical body and mind to the point where we experience illness, disease, pain, and mental struggles. While we stay oblivious to the impact, they work hard behind the scenes controlling and manipulating our lives to help us make sense of our days.

As time passes, we learn how to avoid and disconnect from the revelations of the unconscious mind. We disregard the messages our bodies give to us, and we ignore the physical symptoms that arise until it is too late. By the time we notice them, they have already been striving to get our attention.

In all reality, it is not that the unconscious mind is our enemy, but when we fail to listen to it or connect to it, we make it the enemy. We stand opposed to the very nature of what it is hoping to get us to hear and understand. Opposing what is trying to help us is not ideal for the human experience.

We become masters of avoidance and numbing. We get so good at it that we do not have a clue we are doing it. It is as if we are on automatic pilot. If someone points it out, we would think they are speaking a foreign language we don't understand. We look at them as if they have no clue what they are saying and need to be enlightened about our struggles. In many cases, we might not hear what they say to us.

How could we understand or hear? It is the unconscious mind awareness that does not show up unless we allow it to show up. Without connecting to it, the unconscious mind stays hidden. It is not accessible to the logical mind.

To recognize and connect with the unconscious mind, we must first turn off the logical mind and go internally into our senses. It is through the senses that we become connected to something far greater than the logical mind understands. The felt sense is the communication vehicle with which this happens.

Connecting to the unconscious mind is a foundational concept on which it can be used and applied in many ways. Connecting to the unconscious mind is something that the body and the mind can be trained to do. It is possible, but it is a decision we need to make to allow it to happen.

In the early days of healing, when you have a great amount of toxic stress and past experiences or trauma built up, connecting with the unconscious mind is not easy. It is most likely a big challenge to do this.

After being put under great duress for long periods of time, the mind and body don't trust anything you would do to upset the delicate balance these struggles have created.

Even if the balance you have achieved in life is toxic, there is the familiarity that convinces us we don't need to change things. We might know that what we are doing is not working, but the mind is good at tricking us into thinking that change will be worse than familiarity.

I remember one session with Dr. Canali where I was struggling with a rash that would not go away. When he brought me into the room before I went onto the therapy table, he asked me one simple question. "Are you ready to let go of it?" I looked at him and immediately said, "Yes!" After all, this is the reason I came to him.

As I began to think about that question, I grew angrier. How dare he ask that question? I want this gone. Why on earth would I not? Why would he ask a question like that? As I sat there and pondered the question, I realized that maybe I was not ready to let go of it.

Once we started our session, we began to discuss this scenario of thoughts. I was afraid that if I let go of the rash that I might not know what to expect. I would not know what life was. Of course, it was not so much about the rash, but the deep connections to past experiences that had shaped so much of my life. The issue was not the rash, but what it connected to at that moment.

Letting it go felt like I was cutting off an arm or a leg. In my mind, it was not easy to think that I could make it if I no longer had this part of myself. Even if it is a horrible physical condition or mental health issue, we may be getting a negative pleasure from it. Be aware that the mind can and often tricks us into seeing things that keep us in survival mode, not in a conscious thought pattern.

Be patient with yourself if you are attempting to do this for the first time. It may take some time to work with it, and it may take someone that is trained in this area to help. If you've been running from the tiger in the jungle, it isn't going to be easy to convince yourself that you are no longer running. That is at the heart of connecting to the unconscious mind.

Connecting to the unconscious mind is allowing yourself a safe place to stop, without distraction. Stop from the hustle of your day and allow yourself to go in and feel your body. Allow yourself to go in and sense. Be in that moment where nothing else that matters but the physical feelings of the felt sense.

While you may think that this is meditation, it is similar but different. Meditation helps you to turn off your mind and be in the moment. However, what I am suggesting is that when you do this, you do it through your senses. You do it through the felt sense of your physical body. The felt sense of the physical body takes the concept of the mind body connection to a whole new level.

Here is an example exercise to follow to help you see what I mean when I say connect to your felt sense.

As you begin this exercise, stop and be in the moment while pondering or asking yourself,

- *What do I notice in my body?*

- *What do I sense?*

- *What do I feel?*

You are focusing on what you sense and feel, but you're not trying to analyze it. At this moment, you are just observing and noticing it. You are inviting it in and asking what is there.

Senses can be anything from what you feel in your skin, muscles, or tissues to noticing a smell or a feeling of warmth or coldness. It can be noticing how much your breath is holding back or how shallow it may be, or even how deep it is. You might hear a sound that becomes intense or dull. Anything you can sense is valid. There are no right and no wrong observations in connecting with the felt sense.

The more you observe the sensations, the more they may intensify. They may get to the point where you need a safe person trained in these concepts to be there with you, holding the space. A sensitive and trained, conscious individual can help you feel safe to explore these new things.

The more you can stay with these sensations and observe them, the more they have the potential to physically change at that moment. Allowing and surrendering to these things gives you the power to connect and reclaim the parts that have become disconnected. As you do this, you reclaim the energy that is stored up in these areas, which is robbing you of much needed daily strength and a deep sense of peace.

Often, it helps to use your breath to work through these moments, along with sounds and movements. Sounds can be anything from tones and melodies to any simplistic sound that automatically arises. Movements are not wild or exaggerated. They are slow, connected, and observational. Your intent is not to go into the sound or movement but to use it as an observational device to what you are feeling. I always look at it as if I am using a magnifying glass to observe. The way I do this is through connected movement, sounds, and breathing.

All these things keep you in the moment of feeling your body, and when you are in that space, observing and playing, you provide fertile ground for your nervous system to re-balance. It gives you an opportunity to bring in more awareness which leads to greater consciousness. These things allow you to connect and then move the stuck energy out from the body.

The process is more involved than the simplistic way I am describing it. I'm just trying to lay the foundation to more fully understand that there is a way to connect with your unconscious mind. The more you do it, the more you reclaim the disconnected parts of your life.

A Body Oriented Process

This process is not just a mental exercise. It is an exercise that is very body oriented where you connect with the unconscious mind. It is very physical, but not in the sense that we normally understand. It is physical because you are using your senses and observation to connect with something much deeper and greater within your mind and body.

You are not trying to find the reason you think these sensations show up. Don't make the mistake of thinking that if you have pain in one area, it means x,y,z because you will limit this experience. While it is possible that it may mean this, it is far too limiting in the exercise with the mind body connection.

When you start trying to analyze what is happening, you are connected to your thoughts rather than to the felt sense within you. The analysis will not get you to the point where you need to go to connect with the unconscious. There may be a story that evolves from this experience, but it is not the focus of what you are trying to do. You're trying to step out of your logical mind and feel and sense. The felt sense is the connection to the body transformation that is possible.

The power of this concept, once you learn and understand it, is beyond comprehension. I've seen challenging physical issues in my body change and heal right before my eyes. I have seen this happen in other people in some very real ways that would almost be too hard to believe if I had not seen them. In my own experiences, it has not taken days or weeks to change some of these physical symptoms in my body. It can happen quickly! Some may call these experiences a miracle, but the thing is if we understand this deep connection, it is a biological healing mechanism built into our human existence.

The unconscious mind is a powerful force that tries to keep us operating in life even when we throw so much stress, negative experiences, and trauma at it. However, if we avoid and disconnect from it and numb ourselves to it, we make it that much harder to connect to it. By avoidance and disconnection, we sentence our lives to struggles that work hard to take us down rather than to allow us to live. The more you avoid something, the stronger that reaction becomes in your mind and body. Numbing and avoidance are additional layers of concrete added to what you are trying to bury.

I'm not sharing pie-in-the-sky concepts. These are truths that I have discovered through the work of Dr. Paul Canali and Unified Therapy™. I have seen how these things have impacted my life in some very powerful and life-changing ways.

If we all can begin to understand just how much we avoid and numb and disconnect in our day, we can make a different choice of what we do. It is through the felt sense and stopping to notice and observe that we offer ourselves the greatest healing power. That is not new age mumbo-jumbo. It is real healing work that makes a difference. Awareness and the felt sense are the keys, and until we go in and allow ourselves to become one with them, we will live in pain and overwhelm.

Connecting to the unconscious mind through the body is not as difficult as it sounds, but in many ways, it is difficult. Most of us have been living disconnected lives, and the unconscious mind is now a foreigner within us. If it were simple, our entire world would be of conscious and aware individuals. The vast majority of us in this world are not aware or conscious.

This deep work on ourselves requires an effort to allow ourselves to do it. We cannot continue to hide our heads in the sand because we are at a point in humanity that we are not only hurting ourselves, but we are hurting others. It took me a long time to realize just how true this was and how much I was the one inflicting the pain on myself while hiding from awareness.

Yes, certain activities help take us out of being disconnected, but often we have not passed the threshold we need to obtain a greater awareness and consciousness. Even with these mind body-based activities, we stay disconnected. The fullness of our lives is hidden and silent. We get to the point that the unconscious mind is anything but something we desire to be connected to in our lives.

I challenge everyone reading this not to accept where you are. Do not settle that you are mindful, aware, and conscious like you think you may be. That is the ego convincing you of a fake truth. If you see your life in this way, you have farther to travel in the mind body connection.

Try This Exercise

After doing the exercise in this chapter where you sense and feel, record your thoughts on these questions. Leave judgment out of this. You are not trying to analyze them, only observing and noticing all that shows.

What do I notice in my body? What do I sense? What do I feel?

12. Numbing And Avoiding

*"There is such a thing as old emotional pain living inside you. It is an accumulation of painful life experiences that were not fully faced and accepted in the moment they arose. It leaves behind an energy form of emotional pain." - **Eckhart Tolle***

When we numb and avoid, we are not feeling. We are not connected to the body or the mind. Even though we think we are present, often we are not connected in the way we think we are. Most of the time when you are numbing and avoiding, you're not even aware that you are doing it. If someone tried to convince you otherwise, you would have great difficulty comprehending what they were saying and would question how it applies to you and your life.

Numbing and avoidance can appear in many ways. It can be as simple as using food and alcohol or as complex as using drugs and sex. Numbing and avoidance can show up through religious practices, constantly buying stuff you don't need, living in fantasy more than in reality, or just keeping yourself constantly busy.

There are many ways we numb the body, as listed below. It is by no means an exhaustive list. Some of these things by themselves in moderation are not an issue. It is how they overtake our lives that matters, by disconnecting us from the conscious mind and body. The way they are numbing is how they impact, control, or manipulate our lives.

Some Ways We Numb

Food
Alcohol
Drugs
Addictions
Religion
Frequent Unsatisfying Sex
Buying Stuff
Hoarding
Living More In Fantasy Than Reality
Constantly Staying Busy
Living For Medical Procedures And Doctor Visits

High Sugar Intake
Excessive Fitness Junkie
Junk Food
Deep Tissue Massage Is The Only Way To Feel
Turning Life Into A Joke
List Of Medications Becomes Your Identity
Spacing Out
Excessive Web Surfing
Excessive Game Playing
Constantly On Your Smart Phone Device
Adrenaline Junkies
High-Risk Activities Become The Norm In Life
Looking Outside Of Yourself For Answers, Not Inside
Not Drinking Enough Water
Poor Eating Habits
Obsession With Making Money
Obsession With Control and Power
Talking Only About The News Story Of The Day
Getting Lost In Politics
Not Listening To Others
Everything In Life Is About You
Excessive Caffeine
Telephone Junkies
Non-Stop Excessive Talking
Lying To Yourself Or Others
Helping Others At The Expense Of Yourself
Not Being True To Yourself
Excessive Anger
Blaming Others For Everything In Your Life
Looking For Abusive Relationships
Vanity and Narcissism
Divert and Distract From Uncomfortable Questions
Loss Of Taste
Over-Spiced Foods
Avoidance Of People
Over-Emotional Or No Emotions
All Positive All Of The Time
Feeling No Pain
Acting As If The Past Never Existed

Not Sensing Joy
Missing The Beauty Around You Each Day
Having All The Answers
Dissociation
Conversion Disorder
Acting Carefree
Nothing Is Wrong In Spite Of Major Difficulties

When we are numb, we aren't feeling the full breadth of the physical body. Most likely we are not aware that we are not feeling everything. If you are trying to get a hundred tasks completed by the end of the day that the boss is demanding you finish, do you think that you would feel all the pains in your body or how the stress is impacting you? More likely than not, you would not feel these things. They would get in the way of you performing the tasks you need to complete. You would be numb to the unconscious mind.

Pain is not your friend when you need to run the 100-yard dash at the fastest speed possible. To ignore it, numb it, and disconnect from it would seem appropriate to complete the race.

If you're at the scene of an accident and people need help badly, disconnecting and numbing would be helpful. If you are feeling all the events that are unfolding, it may be too overwhelming for you and anxiety would be too great. In this case, it would be helpful because it allows you to render aid.

Sometimes we need to numb the body to handle the current moments, but it is when we don't shut off the numbing that it becomes a problem. Temporary numbing is one thing, but long-term, it causes great damage to the mind and body. The more we numb, the more long-term damage we do and the harder it is to recover. When the experience or situation is over, it is critical to begin feeling in the body once again.

If we can begin to understand how much we numb and avoid the hard parts of life, it will lead us to a much greater awareness filled with peace beyond comprehension. Numbing and avoidance take us away from mindfulness where we are empowered and filled with all that we need to take on the challenges of our lives.

We must first begin to understand that numbness and avoidance are two of our greatest enemies. The more we choose not to see how we numb and avoid, the more we are robbing ourselves of all the potential for our lives. Numbing and avoidance lead to negative pleasures. They help us disconnect, but at the same time, they rob us of our energy and essence of life. Numbing and avoidance keep us from the deep peace within our lives.

Why is it with human beings that things have to get so bad and horrible before we wake up? And then, we forget again. It is like history is repeating itself over and over.

When I think of this, my first thought goes to peeling the layers of an onion. When we look at an onion, we see that it is made up of many layers. If we could gently remove the outer layer, we would see another layer. As we keep pulling layers back one after another, we see more of what lies beneath it. However, until we pull that top layer off, and then the next top layer off, we will never see what lies beneath it.

It takes courage to go in and remove the layers. It takes strength and confidence and a willingness to leave all that we know while venturing into the unknown. The ego is strong which makes this very difficult to do for humans. The ego holds us back from truly seeing all things or allowing ourselves to see all things. Our experiences in life hold us back from seeing what we need to see, but that is part of the journey as we discover ourselves more each day.

Sometimes it is not easy to go in and deal with life and all our baggage and experiences. Sometimes these things are so difficult and intense and horrific that to muster up the courage and strength to go in and see them requires great strength. The ego and mind tell us instead that it is easier to survive and numb out or hide and disconnect from all of this. We convince ourselves that to neglect and avoid this stuff is by far our best option, when in fact that robs us of the strength we need to heal.

Often, we don't know there is an alternative. How life plays out in the present moment seems more normal than going in and uncovering that which appears odd, strange, and anything but what we think it should be. We are often conditioned in our early years of life to accept what we are shown and taught and to disregard anything that falls outside of these parameters. Even the most horrific moments that we endure can become so commonplace that we have no idea that there is anything beyond them. We cannot see that other people don't experience the same thing.

We live in a society where people urge us not to rock the boat and upset the apple cart. Often, if we do challenge the status quo, we encounter others who would rather remain asleep because to wake up is just far too difficult. It is easier for them if we don't travel on our journey because it leaves them feeling like they are out on a limb all by themselves or that they are damaged. They desire not to see it, and by our journey of discovery and healing, it creates a moment where our lives become a mirror reflecting to them what they are trying desperately to avoid.

Sometimes, it is just a moment where we are growing and learning, even if it seems like we are revisiting history and have not made much progress. These horrific moments of pain and suffering we have lived through are not easy. They have often lasted a lifetime and are connected to so many neural pathways with fingers stretching to other moments in life. Even when it seems like we are revisiting those moments, it is then that I believe we are going in and reworking the networks of all the tiny little neural pathways.

It is not easy to do this all at once because it would be far too overwhelming for the mind. The mind wants to protect us and keep us alive, so if we throw everything at our awareness in one moment of time, it will be too much. It takes time to go in and dissect the neural pathways of the brain and consciousness. It requires us to look at the inner layers in a much deeper way.

Healing does not unfold in a linear sequence. There are parts of one pain that are worked on while other parts of a different pain may be unfolding. Those little parts of different pains may be connected in some way that we are not aware of or conscious of, and yet they need to happen before the next step takes place. Without these various parts, we cannot build the foundation we need for longer lasting healing that goes deep into our consciousness.

If you have watched a computer hard drive defragment itself a few years back, you would see that some of the bits of information need to be moved out of the way so you can rewrite that part of the memory. It isn't that all the parts are bad, but they are standing in the way of seeing the complete picture and allowing you to view life in a new way. Once you organize the parts and clear the empty space, the memory begins to function together better. The computer can use its resources more effectively just as we can enjoy a life of greater peace and joy.

If you went to a class to learn some new technique, I'm sure you could repeat the class and learn so much you didn't get the first time. Our minds can only comprehend and understand so much at one time, based on our circumstances and experiences of life. Even though we think we've learned the lesson, there are most likely parts that have yet to be learned. If we learned everything in one single moment, we would diminish the future lessons that life has in store for us.

It may be that the history of our lives is repeating itself, but often this means some parts have not yet healed and are finally able to surface so we can begin to look at them. This part is the unconscious connections to things from the past and how they fit together in the present. As they come up and then come back for us to look at again, we are often stronger and more focused and more able to have those ah-ha moments.

Emotional And Physical Pain

Emotional or physical pain is often at the root of numbing and disconnection in life. It is not easy and often overwhelming when avoiding the pain appears to help us function in life. Even if the issue causing the pain may be toxic to our lives, it results in numbing the physical systems of the body and mind. It is one of the things at the root of so many ailments and conditions we experience.

Pain is rooted in the emotional and energetic parts of the body more than we realize. I don't buy into the statement that the pain of life happens and there's nothing we can do about it. Of course, there is also pain from injuries that may be more difficult to do anything about than the regular emotional pain of life. These days, I'm not convinced that physical or emotional pain is outside of the possibility of what we can do to alleviate it.

Even a current wound or physical injury or some psychological and emotional issue can connect back to past experiences, even though it would appear there is no connection. That neural pathway touches another neural pathway and then it connects to another. It is almost like having a friend on social media where now you touch their friends, and then you touch the friends of their friends. We may not all know each other, but we are all connected.

One example that I went through showed how much I was numbing and avoiding. The memories of my past were flooding my mind so much that the pain got so intense. In fact, I could barely move my right leg or my back and neck as I made the way to the emergency room. It was difficult driving myself there. Doctors gave me muscle relaxers and painkillers which knocked me out for the next day or two, but at least I could once again move and function. For a short time, the painkillers kept me from feeling the pain. However, neither of these things solved the underlying issue that I continued to numb and avoid.

I've seen with pain, that there is much more going on in the mind than in the physical body. It shows up in the physical body. However, to convince us that this is true is like asking someone to climb straight up a mountain with no rope. It is not easy to see, do, or consider. Believing there is a connection when you're in pain is asking a great deal from our human existence. The mind impacts the body and the body impacts the mind with pain and numbing. I think in cases where someone has experienced trauma to varying degrees, pains tend to be more noticeable or there are many more connections left to resolve and reprogram in the mind body connection.

The one thing I've learned not to do is avoid the pain. Yes, sometimes this is the way we deal with it in the immediate moment, but if we fail to go into the root of the pain, it will grow into a bigger monster as the hours and days progress. Ignoring pain is never a good thing in the long-term. It is a messenger of the body and the mind that something is wrong or there is some issue to resolve. Pain is the notification that we need to address something in life. The more we ignore it, the more we are taking away from ourselves.

Shortly before paralysis from a conversion disorder, I was experiencing so much stress. I was seeing a chiropractor because I could barely move my neck from side to side. In the treatments, I was getting relief, but once I stepped back into life, the stress was overwhelming. It brought on numbing and a disconnect to what was going on in my nervous system and neural pathways. I did not want to deal with things I was facing, and so I hid them and buried them so deep that I could not see them.

We often disconnect from pain. I know I've done this many times. It is part of being human. To feel pain isn't a bad thing, although trying to convince ourselves at that moment can be a challenge. Instead, it means you are alive and connected to yourself, feeling what is going on in your body at that moment. Some may see that as a horrible thing they want nothing to do with, but to disconnect from it means you are feeding it massive amounts of energy, shoving it down.

As we numb and disconnect, the energy continues to grow, taking away vital resources for our lives. Pain is a way we interact and learn more about ourselves. It is a way we find our limits and then build up to push past our limits.

When I hear people say "I have no pain," I truly feel sad for them. We cannot go through life without feeling pain. If we are feeling no pain, we are numb and disconnected. I've lived a life that has shown that concept to me a million times. Please don't get me wrong that I am saying we must live with pain, but most of the time we do not notice it. If we notice it, we do not connect it to what is behind it because we numb and disconnect.

Sometimes we have the "pains" that we notice, but often time those are masking much deeper, profound points of awareness. Pain that we notice is only part of the complete story or situation we are dealing with, and when we focus solely on it, we're missing the bigger picture.

For those that are dealing with pain beyond what it seems they can comprehend, the nervous system is distorted. The pain button has been pushed past notification to the point where it demands our attention. It is saying, "You have ignored me for so long that you can no longer ignore me." Unfortunately, in our society, we don't have enough people that understand how to turn the pain dial down without impacting all other body systems. We think the many different kinds of medications and treatments do this for us, but more often than not, they take us further into disconnect.

As I've found in those horrendous moments of pain, sometimes I need to find a way to alleviate the pain for a moment, so I can go in and see what is happening in my life. Intense pain blocks that signal and information flow in our mind body connection. However, I try to be careful that I don't get so lost in the "pain alleviation" that I forget to go inside and look at what is behind it. My goal of helping to reduce the pain is to allow myself to go deeper and find out why it is there and how I can go to the root and let it go. Masking the pain is not a helpful long-term solution or strategy.

If you have been in deep pain for a long time, this process is not easy. It can be a big challenge to find your way through it. Don't be like the guy I once knew that was trying to wake up, but the minute he started feeling the intense pain, he reached for the things that took him back into numbing and disconnect. It is far too easy to do when you're dealing with that much pain, but it will become a never-ending loop that will be harder to free yourself from in life.

At one time, I thought pain was something you lived with in life. However, now I've learned over the years that pain is not something you have to accept. I know that goes against so much of what we believe in this world, but I have seen the evidence of it in myself and others. I know pain is difficult to deal with, but the more you learn how to interact with your biology, the more you will see there is a way past it. Just because we don't understand what to do at this moment and all seems hopeless, it does not mean that it is.

We learn as a child that we have to get over the pain. Pain makes others around us, including our caretakers, uncomfortable. Often it is not easy to see someone in pain, and so we get all wrapped up in their pain as if it were our own. I'm not talking about holding back on compassion and empathy. When we see someone's pain, it causes an interaction with our past experiences. Often there is something that touches and connects within us that we don't even see.

I'll never forget the people I was around, in a therapy session dealing with conversion disorder. Even though I barely knew them, my body and mind felt what they were going through in an instant. I didn't even recognize it at first, but as I observed myself, I realized that the language of conversion disorder was felt deep within my mind and body. Even if I could not articulate it, the connection was there. Other people impact us, especially those that we are close to or have some connection with in life. I know people sometimes put a label on this, but I believe that as humans we are wired to connect that way. It is a natural part of being human in our world.

From birth onward, we are taught that if we fall and scrape our knee, someone such as our mom may kiss it and make it all better. The pain from the moment will disappear. Whether the pain stops at that moment, the message of mommy kissing our injury tells us to move on and not feel it. Instead, the more we could sit with that pain for a moment and not numb or disconnect, the more it would heal. We would see that we have the power within us to heal the body, and not necessarily look to an outside person to do this for us. When we push the pain aside, we only add it to our inventory of neural pathways that are left unprocessed. It does not matter how minuscule they may be. These experiences combine and add up with each additional year of our lives.

Numbing from pain is unconsciousness. Feeling no pain is not a normal thing in my view. It is being disconnected and numb. Feeling the pain is consciousness and awareness because then you can choose how you will interact with it. Often pain is a bigger threat than it appears, like in the Bible story of David and Goliath.

The more we don't learn how to deal with pain, the more intimidating it becomes. Even watching our caregivers deal with pain teaches us so much about numbing and disconnecting. These are the things that we

must often unlearn and re-evaluate in the light of awareness and consciousness. They are part of our biological growth as humans.

The more we go into the pain, the more we not only help alleviate
the pain, but we build ourselves and our resolve up to take back our
power. We empower ourselves with every little pain we can negotiate
through, to be stronger for the next layers and next rounds and next
discoveries into further consciousness and awareness.

The more we ignore pain and numb our lives, the greater it builds
up. The more it builds up, the more difficult it is to deal with because
now it is so overwhelming. The dials are turned to maximum volume,
and we're left in an overwhelming situation. As we ignore and numb,
the situation gets worse and more complex. Even though it can still be
turned around, it becomes more difficult. By the time you're at the overwhelming pain in life like we are now in society, you've added many
layers of concrete over the earlier experiences in life.

Pain is not an easy thing, and when it rears its ugly head, it makes the
mind and body go into fear of the worst that could happen. We see it as
an enemy to avoid, run from, and flee. Sitting with the pain and breathing into it or just allowing it to be there for a moment without going into
a fear response is not easy. However, there is great healing that comes
from learning how to be with our pain.

Recently, I was dealing with a rash. When the itching would kick
up, the pain would become all too real. At first, my fears raised their
ugly head and said, "it could be life-threatening." While I knew this was
a possibility, I also knew that I had been through this before and had
found healing. The previous experience, though, did not stop my mind
from going into the fear response and numbing my mind and body to
keep me from focusing. Once I got myself to stand up to the fear and
put it in its place, I was able to start making good choices that helped me
find relief and healing.

One person I once knew said they felt sorry for me because of the
pain that I dealt with in my life. It was something along the lines of "I'm
so sorry you have to feel pain like that." I thought it was strange that
they thought this was odd, but then I remembered that most humans
live in a constant denial of all that they feel. We are mostly unconscious,
so we don't feel pain and we often don't feel the full range of life's possibilities. You can't have one without the other, in my view. If you have
one without the other, it only means you are most likely numbing and
not conscious of your pain.

Pain can be a good thing if we can get past the fear and if we are not living in an overwhelming state of agitation and excitement. It is just that we are conditioned to look to others to alleviate our pain. That takes away our personal power of learning to work with it, and using the awareness of it to help further our paths. I believe pain is the bumper rails of life. It helps keep us in the center of the path and keeps reminding us of where the edge of our path lies. The thing is, we stay on the sides hitting the bumper rails, rather than using them as guides.

Numbing and disconnect are real parts of the human experience, as we are humans living in a human body. They are often our go-to default mode when in reality they take us away from living our life fully. When we are numbing and we disconnect, we miss the joys of life while our energy is robbed from us.

In this world, we are so numb that we cannot even begin to notice it because it is so commonplace. We focus on what others do and how they don't live up to our expectations, but we fail to see our role at the moment. All you have to do is observe the discourse currently taking place or the high levels of opioid addiction that we are facing in this world.

Numbing has taken us so far off the beaten track, and I hope and wish for the world that we find our way back. However, this means that each one of us individually needs to grasp the concept of numbing and how we do it, even if we don't admit it to ourselves. As long as we don't admit the prevalence in our lives, the world will continue to falter.

The hardest part about waking up from numbing is that when you are numb and disconnected, you cannot see it. It is only through the felt sense of connecting the mind and body together that you start turning numbing down and living the life you were meant to live. Until you are in your body, feeling and sensing fully, the numbness is a thief that robs joy, peace, love, and contentment from you. It consumes your energy and every part of yourself it can take. Again, this is a body-based moment, not just something that you focus on with only your mind.

Try This Exercise

In what ways do you numb and avoid things? Use the list at the beginning of the chapter. While some may be immediately obvious, there are most likely others that are not. Take a moment to stop, sense, and feel, giving yourself time to see where you avoid and numb. How can you notice, in your body, when you're numbing and avoiding feelings or difficult emotions? What can you do in the moment to pull you back to grounding and find a way to dissipate these?

13. The Magic Pill

*"You can give a guy a drug-coated stent, but if you don't fix the stress problem, it won't really matter. For so many conditions, stress is the major long-term risk factor. Everything else is a short-term fix." - **Dr. Robert M. Sapolsky, Ph.D.***

Way back many eons ago, when I was trying to deal with conversion disorder, I figured out something that I didn't completely understand until I wrote this book. Most of the doctors and physical therapists didn't have the answers I needed at that time. In those days, there was no internet to research information and no one I could reach out to for support.

On my own, I started doing the things that made my body feel good. No, I'm not talking about drugs or alcohol or meditation or any of the other things you might be thinking of at this moment.

I'm talking about the felt sense – feeling deep in my body. I did not know what it was called at the time and I could not articulate this. I just knew that deep inside there was something to the feeling part.

When I went through conversion disorder, I was dead at one point, and they brought me back to life. It is interesting to note that the limited hospital records I have in my possession don't depict what truly happened that day in the hospital. I know the truth, but it was not recorded because I think they know they made a medical error.

However, at that moment, I could not feel anything. I was beyond disconnected from my body. My mind didn't even care what happened because there was no connection between it and my body. In many ways, my mind was trying, but my body had given up.

I still remember them putting a needle in the bottom of my foot and asking me if I could feel it. As ticklish as I was, I did not feel a thing. I believe you could have cut my foot off and I would not have felt it. That is how disconnected and numb in my body I was.

We all numb and disconnect with the body. It is part of the survival response because to feel what is being done to you isn't necessarily a good thing at that moment something horrific is happening. No one would be able to endure being raped, molested, or tortured if they felt anything. No one would be able to endure being beaten if they felt everything. You could not withstand the onslaught of stress every day without finding some relief from it. So, the body goes into shutdown mode, and it stays there.

Often, when we stay stressed out every day, or we try to burn the candle at both ends of the stick, the body says, "Ok if you want to do that - go right ahead. I'll numb and disconnect while you destroy yourself." It isn't necessarily something you see happening and unfolding. This scenario goes on within you and without your conscious mind realizing that it is happening.

In conversion disorder, this becomes a normal response in your body. You learn to maladapt to trauma and experiences and stress to the point where feeling in your body is foreign to you. Even if someone points it out, you cannot see it, because you are so numb and disconnected.

You have no way to see it because you never learned the skills to know how to react or deal with it. It becomes the life that you know. To even begin thinking about letting go of what you have used to survive up to this point is like asking someone to jump out of an airplane with no parachute. To the person at this moment, nothing helpful and healthy makes sense.

The thing is we don't recognize what is going on, so we have no way to figure it out and no clue to begin to heal the effects of surviving this way. Yes, it does affect and impact the body. Don't kid yourself that it doesn't! You may not be recognizing all that it is or how it is impacting you.

When we entertain the thought that we have survived this way, the conscious mind says, "Oh no you don't! You're not going down that road. You're being conned because if I allow you to go down that road, you're going to destroy all the secrets I hold inside." That's what goes on in the mind. To wake up is not easy and to find the courage to do it is even more difficult.

So, then, we end up going to different medical procedures or therapies that give us no long-term cure. We take all kinds of medical tests, medications, and alternative products. We look for what will help us temporarily. At the same time, the answer that we most need is in the part we stop ourselves from going into and taking a hard look at in life.

We give up, thinking that our diagnosis is the way things will always be. There is no hope or any way out of what we are going through in life. It is the way things are, and anyone that tries to tell us differently has no clue what they are saying. They are harmful and hurtful to us, we conclude, and so we dismiss them like waste in a trash bin.

Keep in mind that when we injure ourselves, often it connects the current pain to some experience we have lived through. I'll never forget when my dad fell off a truck and broke his hip. Even after his hip had physically healed, he was having constant back pain. The pain did not make sense to the doctors and would not stop.

They sent him to the Mayo Clinic in Rochester, Minnesota for extensive testing. The diagnosis was that it was all in his head. He grew angry that no one could tell him why he hurt. The doctors didn't have much to offer to help him other than pain pills. He did not like the diagnosis in the least bit but did little to find any other way to heal his body from the pain.

If you watch the movie, All The Rage, you'll quickly see that Dr. John Sarno discovered something most other doctors missed about pain. For the most part, his medical colleagues thought he was practicing something that did not fit into their medical knowledge paradigm. He would tell people that the pain they were having was not from physical issues in the body, but their emotions and how they reacted to life. Unfortunately, Dr. John Sarno passed away not long ago, but the movie, All The Rage, is about his life's work. I would urge you to check it out because it has some very good information.

Stanley Coen, a Columbia psychoanalyst and author, suggested that the purpose of the pain was to distract attention from frightening, threatening emotions and to prevent their expression. – **Dr. John Sarno, M.D., The Mind Body Prescription**

Is it easy to go into these difficult places of pain and struggle? Nope... no way... no freaking way! It is hard because you must stand up to all that you have lived through in life that has helped you survive and say, "You know what - you're not serving my best interests." Of course, the moment you try to do that, fear rears up and slaps you so hard that you spin around the floor as if it won't ever stop!

Our society and family structure are built around us not waking up in life. Try sharing a physical ailment online or with people that know you and see what the advice is. They will often tell you to take this product or pill or go through some procedure. No one will be telling you to go within and find that place of healing inside yourself. They often don't know that this exists and many times, energetically, if you go into these places, you threaten their stability structure in life. It most likely will be a 100% unconscious reaction from other people. If you look for it, you will see it.

Then we start looking for the magic pill of healing. Surely some healing modality or some belief system or spiritual person will have the answer. We are bound and determined to get to the point where we feel we should go, but we're still clinging to the 5000-pound weight we're dragging behind us. We convince ourselves that this pretty and shiny new idea will be the magic pill we are looking for in life.

If we're not careful, we will start chasing those that appear to talk the talk, but not walk the walk about healing one's body. People have the jargon of the day down and sound believable, but they miss the body experience of healing. There is no depth and repeatability to what they say. Yes, they'll hit some good points, and they will have some success, but the deep internal self will remain hidden from view.

In one of the episodes of The Andy Griffith Show, Aunt Bee got suckered into buying a healing elixir that was supposed to make their lives better. The traveling medicine show guy was great at telling people what they wanted to hear. He draws a crowd and gets them to buy his elixir. Soon, it becomes clear to Andy Griffith's character that the elixir is nothing more than alcohol. Of course, they are feeling better because they are sloshed. This scenario is what happens time and time again in the world of healing. We drink the elixir of the day, thinking it is healing us.

Emma's Blue Pills

There was another episode where a new pharmacist comes into Mayberry to run the drugstore for her uncle. One of the ladies in the town by the name of Emma comes in for her blue pills but has no prescription. Of course, the pharmacist will not give her anything. Emma convinces everyone in the town that she is going downhill fast because she can't get her blue pills. She develops all kinds of symptoms, and in the end, the pharmacist gives in and gives her the blue pills she wants. However, the twist to the story is that the blue pill was nothing more than a sugar pill or what we would know today as a placebo.

As we look everywhere for the magic pill, we fail to see, listen, hear, or realize that it is within us. If we want to find what we need, we must go deep into the pain and the horror and the stuff we don't want to see.

Many times, we don't even know what exists. We've become so good at hiding ourselves from it, that we can't even remotely begin to see it.

The magic pill is where we go into the stuff that is at the root of difficulty in life. When we push past the fear, it is there that we find all that we need and the answers to what we're missing. The magic pill is the point where we go into life's experiences, not avoiding, disconnecting, or trying to outrun them.

Yes, we can keep trying to disconnect and numb, but trust me - it only takes you further down into despair and hopelessness and death. No, I'm not going to sugarcoat any of this. I have lived through this experience of trying to get back the felt sense of my physical body.

By now you may be saying, "Well that's all fine and good, but it isn't that easy." You might also believe that I don't know anything or understand your situation. In fact, you might see this as something that is contrary to your belief system, and so you dismiss it before you even consider it. You are free to do that, but I can tell you without a shadow of a doubt that the difficulty of the physical reality you experience will continue.

If we look for the magic pill everywhere else but where it is, we're never going to find it. Yes, there might be some things that help give you some temporary relief, but until you go to the source of what has caused the survival mode, you're just like a dog chasing its tail. It gives you something to do and makes you think you're doing something, but in all reality, you are just going around in circles.

The magic pill isn't out there in the wild blue yonder. You're not going to find it in some person, procedure, or substance. It is within you, and until you figure that part out or at least entertain the thought, it's not going to be an easy life. Yes, some things come along and help us temporarily by giving us some relief. However, if you're not looking for the long-term solution or one that takes you into the depths of your mind and body, you're missing out on the healing potential for your life.

My Body Felt Something

So, now, let's go back to my story. Somehow, I figured out that when we did the relaxation exercises in the hospital, my body felt something it had never felt before. My body recognized that this was a good feeling, but it went beyond this feeling. My body knew this was some good stuff that I was discovering! I wanted more of it, and I knew I needed to figure this out. I did not understand it at the time, but I noticed that it existed. It was the first key to my new awareness.

Let me make it very clear that it was not the feeling of relaxation that made me feel wonderful. It was about how it made me feel deep inside my body. It was a visceral connection that went far beyond a moment of relaxation. For me, it was the beginning of understanding the felt sense in the body. The only thing was, I didn't know what to do beyond recognizing the felt sense. There is so much beyond that point that the majority of us in this world do not discover.

So, while I knew very little about relaxation, I started my quest to figure out why a guided relaxation exercise made me feel so good. I wanted to understand it and reproduce it. This experience started me on a path of reclaiming my life.

I remember buying a guided relaxation cassette tape and listening to it as I went to bed at night. It helped greatly, but it still left me searching because it didn't resolve anything. It just started me on the path of awakening to my inner mind and body connection.

Yes, the talk therapy I was doing and the medication I was taking helped. Yes, the physical exercise and stopping to smell the roses helped. There was more, though, and I was intent on finding out what it was. Inherently, I knew there was something more to connecting deep within the body, but there was no way for me to articulate that at the time. It all seemed foreign to me.

The thing that started me on a path to healing was when I made the connection that my mind and my body were out of sync. Little did I realize, I was beginning to see that I was in survival mode, while not even understanding what it meant at that moment. It was with me trying to understand what was happening deep inside, through the relaxation, that I was at the beginning of my healing. The mind and body together are a powerful force to help us, if we allow this to happen.

Deep inside, I had never felt relaxation and peace and calmness like this, and it propelled me to keep searching and asking. Sometimes we want grandiose cures when what we need is that tiny spark of a moment where we begin to see something in a new way. We need to be open to it because otherwise, we will miss it. If I had gotten lost in the relaxation feeling, I would not have traveled as far as I have in my healing and recovery.

I didn't ask anyone I met how to find more of this relaxation because, at the time, I wasn't sure what it was that I found helpful. I had already seen that no one had answers. Others would tell you happy thoughts and slogans, but no one could offer much when I asked about how not to worry or how to relax. Yes, many tried, but it was just words spoken. The things that others said to me were empty because they had not found the way through in their lives. I had to learn this for myself.

In high school, I had a nervous stomach and ulcer which landed me in the hospital. There were many people with so much advice. I was told to recite the Serenity Prayer. Another person told me not to worry and let everything go, like water slides off a duck's back. Some told me to pray. However, none of these things solved the issue I was facing. The things happening in my home were the source of my stress and struggle.

I remember asking these same people, so how do I not worry about it? They struggled to reply as they stammered in giving me an answer that was nothing more than a water bucket with holes in it.

There was one lady that told me after I came out of the hospital for conversion disorder that I didn't need these doctors and psychotherapists. She stated to me that all I needed to do was pray to God and not see a psychiatrist. Unfortunately, I had been praying to God for years, and my prayers went unanswered. It did not deliver me from the hell I was living through in my life. I remember replying to this lady and asking her that if her arm was broken, would she just pray about it or go to a doctor? You can probably guess that she said she would go to a doctor.

Why people give half-hearted advice still baffles me because most of it does not help. It does not hold up when challenged. Unfortunately, it doesn't stop people from spreading these thoughts as if they are the morsel of all truth. I'm not saying God can't help (however you see God), but you have to be careful because so often these statements are anything but conscious. Many do not realize how the mind and body together create the experiences we live through in life. Even in Chapter 139 of Psalms, the Bible recognized the innermost being of the mind and body.

All I know is that most of what people told me to do was not helpful. If I had continued to listen to them, my path would have had a lot more difficulties in it. I knew deep down that I was on a quest and a journey to discover more. Relaxation was the beginning step toward leading me to understand the felt sense in the body.

It took me years and much difficulty. My life would experience situations that would almost take me down. It wasn't a step-by-step process, but more like a tidbit here and a tidbit there of something that helped.

It took me many years to begin piecing those things together, and to this day, I still struggle to tell anyone what I did to heal. The concepts are hard to explain because they are more of a body experience than a thought-based reality. We get so lost in our world, thinking we know the answers rather than experiencing what the body understands and feels.

While there may have been people that could have helped speed this process along, I did not trust everyone. This lack of trust turned out to be a good thing. There was nothing concrete I could state as to why I had little trust, but I knew this was a journey I had to take alone. I'm glad I did because far too often we are taken off our course by those who believe they have the answers. It is nothing more than a mirage in the desert. There is far too much money made off of products and concepts that offer little more than a placebo.

There are elements of truth in much of what people do and believe, but then those elements of truth become the entire paradigm. When that happens, a person is led to the conclusion that the answer is in the practice, product, or therapy, but not within the mind and body of the individual. The elements of truth get in the way of what makes the difference.

I will never forget one experience while learning a type of massage. In a practice exam I was required to do, I started doing the work on the person while trusting and feeling my intuition. They stopped me and asked me why I was going in the direction I was around the body. I explained that I was following my intuition. Of course, the instructor corrected me, saying you had to go a certain direction around the body for the work to be effective. I was dismayed because it went against my intuition that was very strong that day. It was the day that I began to see how the rules of this particular massage modality got in the way of the true mind body connection. The paradigm blocked true healing.

I see many that will evade truth for something shiny. Many will chase the rainbow, instead of feeling the rain. People will go to the ends of the world in search of someone telling them what the answer is when the answer is right there within them.

Yes, we do want a quick and easy fix. Most of the time, we want to take a pill or go through a test and procedure and say, "I'm cured." The thing is, until you fix the source of the situation, you're only going to be a dog chasing its tail. Medications and procedures often mask what is going on, but they make it appear as if they have solved the issue. Be careful not to be fooled into seeing what is, and what isn't helping you to heal. It is far too easy to be fooled.

I understand that when you are suffering or are in pain, the last thing you want to do is be patient with anything that doesn't take the pain away immediately. The discovery into the mind and body connection is not welcomed because you want the pain and suffering to stop. I get this! I've gone through it more than I care to remember. However, the quick fix is not the cure. It only takes you from going into your body where the root of all the suffering is.

We are a civilization that embraces what the majority claims, rather than checking to see how true it is. In the dark ages, people did some horrific things to cure people that of course never worked. These days, we gasp at some of those. The one that completely amazes me is how in ancient times they thought that blood was a bad thing in the body and it needed to come out. We now know this is ridiculous, but at the time, the masses believed it was true. In fact, you dared not say anything contrary to this belief because you might have been put to death.

It wasn't that long ago that medical people fought against the new idea of washing their hands before doing medical procedures. Many thought it was ridiculous and a complete waste of time. Now, we understand that it is needed and cuts down on infection and disease that's passed from one person to another.

We are beginning to understand more and more just how much some of the procedures and "cures" of our day don't stand up to scientific testing. Often some of the research is one-sided, and the side that some don't want you to see is hidden and deleted. Placebos often do as much as many of the current medical treatments and drugs, yet the groupthink of the day ignores this.

My Grandfather And The Placebo

About the time I was in kindergarten, I remember my grandparents coming to stay with us for a weekend. On the way, they were involved in a car accident. While they were not badly injured, they were shaken up and their bodies a little bruised. In those days, seat belts were not the norm, so I think they got beat around a little in the car. My mom tried to make them comfortable on the beds in the room I shared with my brother, but they were in pain. The doctor had prescribed a pain pill for them. However, my grandfather was a cranky person, and so he went through the pain pill prescription quickly.

Since we lived in a rural area and there weren't so many pharmacies like there are today, there was no way to refill the prescription that weekend. My mom was growing weary trying to take care of my grandfather. Nothing she did was enough for him as he just continued to complain. Yes, he was in pain, but he was not attempting to work with her on anything.

Finally, in desperation, she came and got some of our Halloween candy, specifically the sweet tart candy. She took them out of the package and went to convince my grandfather that they were high powered painkillers. They were special ones that the doctor had prescribed in case the other ones did not work. Somehow, she convinced my grandfather that these would work and help him sleep. The next thing we knew, he was sleeping like a baby, without pain.

The placebo effect was working wonders because it was nothing more than a piece of sugar candy. While I understand there is a time and a place for prescription medications, sometimes I think we give up too easily on the power of the mind and body to help us.

I'm amazed when I turn on a TV and see ads about pharmaceuticals, just how many side effects there are. It is almost as if this is a badge of honor. No one pays attention to all the harm that comes from taking these drugs with beautiful names on them. I don't believe that taking the numbers of medications every day that we do is a good thing for the human body. However, if you are not in touch with the felt sense of the body, survival mode leads you to believe this is the cure. I'm not saying every drug or procedure is bad, but if we're not doing the internal body-work we need to do, we're only chasing rainbows.

Discovering this truth about the felt sense of the body is the magic pill. It does require you to go into the pain and horror and experiences you so badly want to forget. If it is done correctly, though, it isn't as difficult as it may sound, but anyone helping you needs to understand this and to have traveled through their own experiences of life. You can seriously harm someone if all you do is bring up someone's trauma without getting them through to the point of resolution.

Too often we think that what comes out of an emotional release is the sign that we are resolving the trauma. While healing can and often does connect with our emotions, without going deep within, we are not touching the source of pain. Let emotion guide you, but don't allow it to dictate the terms of where you need to go. Don't let the release of emotions trick you into believing that you have let go or resolved the deeper issues. Allow the emotions to be there in the way they need to, not becoming the paradigm of truth in your life.

In figuring out what the magic pill is, therein lies the lesson of what you are to learn. It is that lesson that propels you forward. It takes back the energy that was robbed and stolen from you and the innocence that was taken from you. The magic pill helps you gather all the fragmented pieces of your life that have been scattered along the highway of experiences you have faced. It helps to give you the magnifying glass to observe and see all that there is in your life.

The magic pill is not a quick fix. It is designed to take you to the source of your suffering. When you find the source of what is causing you to stay in survival mode, that's when you have begun to find the essence of your life and all that it offers. While it is not a quick fix, physical and mental change can happen fairly quickly. The more I see that in my own life with physical challenges, the more I am amazed at the power within us.

Anything that takes you away from feeling deeply in your body and connecting to it may offer some short-term results, but will miss the bigger picture. As much as we may not want to hear this, suffering and pain are there for a reason. To access healing we must access the innermost self, for that is where the magic pill of healing truly exists.

Try This Exercise

Watch the movie All The Rage and see how it applies to your life. Allow it to help you understand the mind body connection. http://AllTheRageDoc.com/

14. Avoiding Healing

*"We've in fact conditioned ourselves to believe all sorts of things that aren't necessarily true—and many of these things are having a negative impact on our health and happiness." - **Dr. Joe Dispenza, D.C.***

So how did I avoid healing?

First off, I put the happy face on display for all to see. I acted as if everything was okay. Outwardly I could not let anyone know that anything was wrong inside. In many ways, I would not even allow myself to know that anything was wrong. The happy face helped me hide every bit of it.

In addition, I tried to avoid healing by playing the game of healing. Sure, I wanted to get better, but hey, whatever the therapists or psychologists wanted me to do, I was game! I could hang in there with the best and fool the rest. They thought I was engaged in the healing, but I was much too clever to go in and heal.

Sometimes I just thought I knew it all. After all, whatever some therapist was trying to get me to do took me into territory that I didn't want to be anywhere close to seeing. So, in these cases, I would prove that I knew more and could see all.

Every idea some therapists came up with, I tried to play off like nothing interested me. I mean, I would go out of my way to object to every idea that could be helpful. The smart ones figured out what I was doing, and so they had an endless supply of ideas to help move me beyond where I was.

I tried to avoid healing by being afraid of going into those deep dark places of hurt. Yes, the fears were strong, but instead of taking on the fears, I would avoid them at all cost, often putting on the "everything is fine" approach.

Not asking for help was one of the things that I did well to avoid healing. I knew that to survive in this cruel world, I had to go it alone. I had to be in complete control. There was no way I was letting anyone get under that layer and even attempt to help me. There was no one I trusted and even the ones that came close to being trusted, I kept under a close eye. Throughout my life, accepting help meant that I would be used, abused, controlled, or manipulated with strings attached.

After some time in therapy, I tried massage as a healing component of my recovery. Of course, that brought up all kinds of fears and memories and I quickly just laid the blame of an inadequate body worker at the feet of my altar to fear. It was easier to avoid the body component and pay later, rather than go into all the trauma that was locked up in my mind and body.

I will never forget the day I went in for one of my first massages ever. It seemed like a good idea, so I nervously booked the appointment. When I arrived at the place, the massage therapist was very nice. The room seemed safe. Everything looked peaceful.

The massage therapist explained things to me and asked me questions. Everything she was doing felt so good and was very relaxing. I was enjoying the experience. She began to work on my lower back, and that's when it happened. Something frightened me. Where her touch had felt so good, now it felt threatening and scary. I didn't realize it at the time, but something I was unaware of triggered me.

Instead of voicing what was going on and trying to work through this, I did the only thing I knew. I told the therapist some excuse that I can't even recall to this day. I got up and ran out the door, barely having enough time to put on my clothes. Racing to my car, I got out of there as quickly as I could, not understanding what had taken place.

Humans were not safe creatures to me, and my body knew it. It was much easier for me to avoid this level of healing in my life than to go in and connect with it.

I don't believe I was ever able to explain what happened to the massage therapist. Maybe she figured it out, but there was no way I could talk about it. My only reaction was to run.

I'll never forget a client I once worked on that cautioned me not to touch one part of their upper body. While I understood and made every attempt to do that, I made a slight move and temporarily forgot this request. The person allowed me to finish the massage, but after that, I never heard back from this regular client. Yes, I know I triggered them inadvertently, but again, it was a way for them to avoid healing.

In bodywork, if we are not careful, it is easy to trigger clients on the table and be triggered ourselves. If we are not aware and conscious, we may not even notice when it happens. If we have not done the healing work on ourselves, it may appear as a healing experience, even though it is not. In these moments we retraumatize the people we are trying to help.

When I went to massage school, which in itself was an accomplishment for someone like me, it was difficult to deal with my touch and fear issues. I am not sure how I got through those initial moments in massage school because I was afraid to be touched and afraid to touch others. Avoiding healing was my default go-to-moment.

Even when I started to feel safe with someone during a bodywork session, I still hung back. I still would only allow myself to go so far. It wasn't anything I wanted anyone to see, and so I avoided healing. After all, the mind and the body store trauma memories. That meant someone had to go in deeper, but I was not ready to deal with it.

Sometimes I wanted a quick fix because I didn't want to deal with all of it. It was the ultimate form of avoiding healing in my life. If I chased every technique and idea and therapy out there, I could act like I was trying to heal without truly doing much. It helped me to avoid healing and keep everyone some distance from me.

In some of my early experiences with Dr. Canali, it was all he could do to get me to feel and sense anything in my body. I had spent years numbing and staying disconnected from everyone, but this therapy helped take me from avoidance to beginning to feel.

My Senses Had Been Turned Off

My senses and my feelings, as well as my emotions, had been turned off for so long. It was the only way I survived. I still remember one relationship I had where they told me that I was not in touch with my feelings and emotions. I got angry at that statement because I thought I was, and I felt they were wrong. There was no way to convince me that I was not in touch. I have seen this in other people who went through conversion disorder or other somatic situations, where they don't physically, emotionally, or mentally connect with what is happening. It happens to a majority of people in this world.

We as humans have powerful ways of avoiding healing that seem to be built into us and turned on without much thought. When you've been abused, beaten, and molested, your body has no desire to connect with others. The avoidance of asking for help or allowing others to help you heal keeps you in a life that is no fun. It may be easy to explain why you are this way, but connecting in the body is a whole different story.

Even with the daily onslaught of stress, we get where we start avoiding everything that matters. It isn't safe to feel because that takes you away from surviving this moment. The more you feel, the less it feels safe in those moments. Avoidance tricks you into thinking that surviving is far more safe than healing and knocks you off your path.

One of the best ways I ever tried to avoid healing was not feeling and staying disconnected. The less I felt, the easier it was in dealing with things, I thought. To not feel and disconnect helped me avoid that which I needed to go into and explore. It kept me on the surface of healing but allowed all the toxic poison to hide below. Feeling was not my friend. Being connected to the body was not my friend.

I looked at all the healing as just too much and sometimes felt that it was too big of a hassle. It was much easier to walk away from it and act as if I had my healing all finished, and that life was 100% better. In my mind, it was easier to act as if nothing from my past bothered me any longer. Talk about avoiding healing!

Time and time again, those of us who have been through horrible trauma will act as if we are healed. Sometimes things are so overwhelming that it is too much to think about, but we fool ourselves into believing it is true. Avoiding healing is like trying to hold your breath underwater indefinitely. Sooner or later, you will have to come up for air. In healing, sooner or later, all of this will catch up with you.

When all our trauma, negative experiences, and toxic stress catch up in the mind and body, it is not pretty. While we may understand that from an intellectual level, we disconnect from the body-centered experience of it. As these things build up, they cause all kinds of pain, anxiety, depression, and other physical issues. If we don't go in and deal with them, they will deal with us.

No Avoiding Experiences

You cannot avoid your experiences or neglect them. In the short-term, you might think you can, but the more we avoid and push these down, the more the experiences build up. Each experience becomes potential energy just waiting to find an exit. As these moments look for an exit, our body systems are impacted in ways I don't think modern medicine understands. It is far too easy to claim we are under stress while ignoring what lies beneath the surface. It is far too easy to simplify our current experiences into a diagnosis while failing to see the impact on our body systems from previous experiences.

Sometimes to avoid healing, I would get so wrapped up in my own story that the story became my avoidance. Don't get me wrong, the story had to come out and it was my strength along this road, but I used it to the point of reliving it and just not dealing with it.

Now I have come to a place where my story is part of my life, but my life is much more. I remember sitting with other survivors at dinner before the Oprah show we were part of, in one of her last episodes. Everyone wanted to know what my story was, and while I understood the reason for asking the question, I realized I had moved on from my story. It no longer felt like it had the control over me that it did when I first started to come to terms with it.

Sometimes I wanted healing in my life to happen right now. I didn't want to wait. I didn't want to go through the process, so I would look for ways to convince myself that I was done healing. Little did I realize for a long time that healing is a process. As uncomfortable as it gets, you need to go into every part of it to reclaim those pieces of your life. It is part of life's continuing journey, bringing us closer to getting to know our authentic selves.

At times, to avoid healing, I just wanted to be left alone, but I wanted someone to care. While I wanted someone to acknowledge my pain, I also wanted to avoid it. I wanted to be loved but could not accept love. I wanted to be understood but I was lost and confused or I kept people away. There were moments when those things happened simultaneously. I didn't know how to interact with people for fear of being abused, and so the easiest way to deal with it was by avoiding it altogether.

As you can see, there are many ways that we avoid healing. We can chase pretty rainbows all day long, but if it is keeping us from going deep inside, why are we doing it? That's a question we need to ask ourselves constantly. We need to be brutally honest with ourselves.

We can't be complacent in our healing. We can't avoid things and expect to heal. Yes, at times the journey gets long and difficult, but it is then that we must learn how to reach out. Sometimes we need a rest, but in those moments, we have to be honest with ourselves and truly see the big picture. Otherwise, there's a good chance we are avoiding everything we need to be doing.

Avoidance is something that does not allow us to become aware and conscious of what is going on in the body. It keeps us from connecting with the innermost healing parts of life. If you're walking through the jungle, and you know a tiger is hunting you down, but all you want to do is gaze at the beautiful sky, there's a good chance the result will not be what you want. The same goes for avoidance.

Healing is not easy. I won't claim that it is. It is a process that sometimes makes you want to give up in frustration and anger and despair. Sometimes healing is exhausting and difficult work. Avoiding it and acting as if it does not exist is not going to help you heal. It will prolong it. The longer you avoid it, the more it will impact your body in physical ways.

We may think we're getting away with avoidance of our healing, but in the long run, the body will do whatever it needs to so that it gets our attention. If we continue to avoid and ignore, numb, and disconnect, it will bite us harder in the hope of getting us to wake up.

Things To Try To Stop Avoiding

Here are some things you can do to help yourself stop avoiding, and to connect consciously with your body and life around you:

- Spend some time outdoors listening to the birds and feeling the rays of sunshine on your face. Feel the wind or breeze on your skin.
- Spend time playing with animals, where you can see the joy in them and connect deeply with something that is life-giving, not life-draining.
- Focus on your breathing for 30-seconds or a minute, in various times during your day. Observe your breath. How shallow or deep is it? How fast or slow does it go? Can you notice your breath or do you find you are almost holding your breath?
  If you spend 30 seconds observing your breath, you will see quickly how much it can change.
- Take ten deep breaths in through your nose and on the last breath, hold it in your chest for as long as you can. When you can hold it no longer, allow your body to deflate like a balloon. You might even notice a slight vibration in your body when you do this, which is normal. It is stress releasing from your autonomic nervous system.
- Take time to be in the moment with your body and mind, shut off from the outside world. Leave the phone in another room and lie there silently observing what you feel in your body. What do you sense? What do you feel? Be the observer and notice all that is taking place.

The more you can take moments out of your day and stop to connect and feel, the less you will avoid. Yes, you can do mantras and positive affirmations, but connecting deep within the body is the key to long-term peace and joy in your life.

The more we feel and heal, the less we are avoiding and numbing. If we have spent a lifetime avoiding healing, we will not change this overnight. It will take time. Even once you begin to feel and stop avoiding your healing, there will be times that will take you into survival mode. For most of our lives, it has become the default go-to-place for how we react to life.

Avoidance tricks us into thinking we're getting somewhere, but if we're not careful, it will drive us over the edge of the cliff. We need to start noticing how much we are avoiding, because that is the only way we'll understand that we should not rest where we are, but keep walking forward on our path.

Try This Exercise

Choose one of the exercises below and note how it impacts you.

- Spend some time outdoors listening to the birds and feeling the rays of sunshine on your face. Feel the wind or breeze on your skin.
- Spend time playing with animals where you can see the joy in them and connect deeply with something that is life-giving, not life-draining.
- Focus on your breathing for 30-seconds or a minute, in various times during your day. Observe your breath. How shallow or deep is it? How fast or slow does it go? Can you notice your breath, or do you find you are almost holding your breath?
  If you spend 30 seconds observing your breath, you will see quickly how much it can change.

15. Loving That Negative Pleasure

*"Be miserable. Or motivate yourself. Whatever has to be done, it's always your choice." - **Dr. Wayne Dyer***

We all do things that are good for us and some that are not so good for us. I'm no different. Yeah, I may not have all the bad vices others do, but I've got my negative pleasures. They aren't helpful in healing, but often they are part of our healing.

So, let's get into some of the ones I have struggled with, and you can see how this applies to your own life. We may not see them or currently recognize them, but if you look hard enough, they are there. If you've been through serious trauma or stress, more than likely you are experiencing these things.

One of the things that I get negative pleasure from is thinking that everyone is avoiding me and not wanting to be around me. In my mind, I become this person that no one wants, and no one loves. It becomes who I am to the world and how I interact in a day.

I can back it up, proving with observation through my own set of facts, that what I think is true is true. It doesn't matter if my viewpoints are not calibrated with what reality is. I see everyone as avoiding me and having nothing to do with me. I become the unwanted child like I was so many years ago.

It is my negative pleasure because I begin to lose myself in how I find my identity in this image of what my life has become. Even if the image is different from reality. At this point, I see nothing that I need to change in my life because it is just the way things work, I tell myself. There is no convincing me because my mind is trying to protect me with a view that is far from real and conscious. It is how negative pleasure works. I succumb to its every wish and demand.

The more I do this, the more I feel like no one wants me and I feel alone. It feels like the loneliest moment and place on this earth. It feels like no one loves me or has ever wanted me even though I have people in my life that care for and love me deeply. The more I allow myself to go there, the more I push them away and the lonelier I feel. It becomes a self-fulfilling prophecy.

It is my negative pleasure because what makes me feel safe and secure is pushing everyone away and withdrawing back into my cave. So, while that feels positive in a twisted sort of way, the negative comes in how I'm doing much harm to myself while allowing my mind to see safety in a distorted manner.

Sugar is another negative pleasure of mine because when I am in its presence, I cannot resist it. It calls for me, and the moment I get near, it tantalizes my taste buds with joy and excitement, wonderment and awe. If I try to resist it, sugar grows furious with me that I am ditching it and avoiding it and abandoning it. It demands my loyalty and my return to the ecstasy that it provides me.

Sugar is an addictive drug that creates a high. It is pushed on us by those who are not concerned with our health. The more you consume it, the more you want, and the more you want, the harder it is to walk away from this addictive pleasure.

I try to summon the willpower to say no to the temptations of sugar, but it comes at me with full force, attacking me on all sides. It sends the message to me that I am not strong enough to let go. I end up being loyal to sugar at all cost to my health and well-being. I will not and cannot let it go, sugar whispers in my ear. Sugar is tricky that way.

It tastes so good, and it makes me feel comforted when life gets stressful. Sugar makes my taste buds dance in ecstasy and joy as if it is the greatest thing. It does not let me rationalize that it is anything but joy and happiness. It is my comfort food of choice. Sugar has me hoodwinked.

I believe what sugar tells me is true because of how it makes me feel. I give in to its desires and wishes almost as if I no longer exist. It has become my negative pleasure because of the enjoyment I get from it, but I am no longer in control. The negative pleasure of the sugar is now in control.

Self-pity is another negative pleasure I have wallowed in throughout my life. When the healing moments were difficult beyond belief, I wanted to step into my cave and push everyone away. I wanted everyone to feel sorry for me and to feel the pain I was feeling. It was my existence and my life. It was who I had become at that moment.

Sure, the horrors were many, and the memories were like flooding water suddenly coming over me. At one time, I struggled to walk and talk. I struggled to function normally in life. Walking into a store produced so much anxiety that others had to do my grocery shopping for me. It was who I was. It was all that I was.

My Misery

My misery became the misery of the world. I saw nothing but misery. There was no hope or possibility, and there was no way out. I was sure everyone saw it too, and if they didn't, I had nothing in common with them. They just didn't understand, I concluded. I saw others as being lucky, and I was unlucky. I saw them as having this wonderful life, but my misery proved to me that I would never have that life.

The misery tricked my mind into self-pity, thinking that this was just the way things were. I was doomed in life, and no golden ticket would lift me out of it. It fed off me and I used it to prop myself up because self-pity had become who I was.

The self-pity I had was on full display, but I could not see it. I'm sure others around me could, but I was oblivious to how it took control of me. It was all I knew. No one could tell me any different, for the negative pleasure of self-pity through misery was the movie of my life.

Suicide Attempts

Suicide attempts are another negative pleasure I deal with in life. It has become a life companion that I dread and hate and despise, but it has given me purpose and strength. The purpose and strength, in this case, are not necessarily good things because they have altered how I view my escape. Losing my strength and purpose happens because it whispers loudly in my ear that it has my back. It tells me that everything will be okay if I listen to it. At times I believe it because it convinces me it is my escape in life. During these moments, the pain and difficulty are so great that I want to be anywhere but going through what I am facing.

The things done to me were beyond most people's comprehension. Escaping from them for just a moment was more than I could hope for in life. Suicide attempts provided that awesome moment of relief and hope and possibility. It enticed me by saying, this is the way out. It tricked me into believing that this is how you get beyond these horrors you are facing.

Sure, we all know suicide is the last stop on the train of hope, but when it becomes your negative pleasure, it looks like the answer to all of life's problems. It looks like the moment that takes care of all that you need to handle. It appears as the savior of your life because it tells you that it will make things all better. There will be nothing more to worry about in your life.

Suicide is a negative pleasure because it tricks you into believing that which is not true. It covers your eyes from the entire truth and alters your brain into what does not exist. That's how negative pleasures are able to bring us down. Their existence and energy are derived from your adoration and acceptance of them. The more you give in to them, the more power and control they have over you.

It is not easy to stand up to negative pleasures just like it is not easy to stand up to your fears. However, you must learn to stand up to these things if you want to overcome them. You may not be able to do this overnight, but with time and work, you can begin to see what truly exists. We don't have to follow the trickery of negative pleasure.

Thinking I Can't Do Something

Thinking I can't do something is one of my top negative pleasures. It is like the banner and billboard of my life saying, "This is what is. It is who you are. Here is the motto of your life. Go ahead, believe it, dude, because it is true."

It doesn't matter how much I have accomplished or how far I've come. It doesn't matter how much someone tells me that I can do something. No matter if all evidence pointed out to me is true that I can do something, it does not matter. The negative pleasure has convinced me in my mind that I cannot do it.

I hear that little voice become powerful in my head. It tells me that "If you think you can do something, who are you kidding? What makes you think you can accomplish anything? You are worthless and if you need evidence, look at all your failures."

It convinces me that there is no need to try because I am just going to fail. It leads me to believe that I should save myself the time and effort of looking for the ways that I might succeed. The negative pleasure leads me to believe those ways are never going to work.

Negative pleasures know how to twist and distort what you see. They know how to convince you that you can't do something even if the evidence points to the contrary. Trying to deceive them and prove that you can succeed is an exercise in extreme courage and determination.

Negative pleasures don't want you to see the logical facts that everyone else sees. Negative pleasures want you to see things in the distorted way it has managed to get you to see. After all, they are the supreme rulers of your life. Yes, it will allow you to observe other things that can control your life, but it knows that this is just an illusion since it has ultimate control.

It will let you walk like you're enlightened and all-knowing, powerful and conscious, but in the background, it is pulling the strings. It is like the man behind the curtain that plays with your emotions while toiling with your fears and convincing you that he is in control.

Sometimes I can get so engrossed in whatever I'm doing and although I'm accomplishing things, avoiding what I need to do becomes my negative pleasure. I can get stuck in the daily details and miss the big picture because it feels safe and normal. It looks like I am doing the responsible thing. It looks like I am doing something good when I'm just doing busy work.

Accomplishing things is good, but when I do one task to avoid another, then I have turned it into a negative pleasure. It keeps me busy. It keeps me focused on something, but at the same time, it takes me off the goal I am working towards achieving. It shows me that this is what I need to do, but at the same time, it hides the true intent from me.

If I own up to the true intent of where my life is going, then it may mean that I need to make changes that I do not want to make. It may mean that I want to sit in the security and safety of my current moment, rather than risk looking like a fool for what matters. While it is far too easy to be seduced by negative pleasure, I allow it to happen even when I know it is not in my best interest.

Thinking I am not good enough is another of my negative pleasures because it becomes the point where I stop myself from doing all that I can. It is the point where I convince myself that there is no sense in trying because I'm just not going to be good enough to make it happen, so what is the use?

Thinking I am not good enough goes hand in hand with some of my other negative pleasures. It becomes the fixer in my life, helping give credibility to the other things. When I know that I'm not good enough, it does not matter if I think I can do something. The decision about the outcome has already been made.

It holds me back from all that I can become while it convinces me that I can never become all that in life. It gives me a sense of purpose knowing that I never have to risk myself beyond the lines of all that I know.

If I argue with it and tell it that it does not dictate my life to me, it laughs and scoffs in my face. It tells me what an idiot I am. The negative pleasure tells me how stupid I am. It tells me how ordinary I am and I should never expect any more from life. I listen to it, yet am disgusted by it, but it has its control over me. It knows how to manipulate me and shame me. Negative pleasures know which buttons to push at the right moment.

Negative pleasures give rise to not being vulnerable but being filled with shame. They show me that without them, I have no existence and I am nothing. The thing about negative pleasures is that they don't want you to be conscious and aware because when you are, they no longer can live in you. They deceive you, and convince you, that you are aware.

Enemies Of Negative Pleasures

Awareness and consciousness are the enemies of negative pleasures. Without them, we don't see all that we are and all that we think or understand. Awareness is at the birth of something different in life. Awareness is the moment where the healing process launches into new dimensions. It gives rise to consciousness.

Often I thought that I was aware and conscious, but the more I went into these moments of insight, the more I realized I knew less than I thought I did. Awareness and consciousness operate outside the vacuum of what we cannot see. They are beyond our reality in this moment and beyond our grasp. If we ignore them, we will never embrace them as fully as we often think we do.

To become aware, we must give up all that we know and think we know. Giving it up and letting it go, is when we begin to see the outer edges that we did not realize existed. It is in seeing that bigger picture or even realizing that the bigger picture exists, that we get a glimpse into a consciousness we have yet to discover fully.

Becoming aware and conscious by coming face to face with negative pleasure is the way we push ourselves to greater heights. It is not easy to do this, and sometimes it takes all the willpower and courage and determination just to move our foot a fraction of an inch forward. We must go into the felt sense of the body to find awareness that leads ultimately to consciousness.

That is okay because in awareness, it is not a race to the finish line. It is a process of unfolding and letting go. It is a process of understanding that negative pleasure exists and then allowing the edges of awareness and consciousness to appear.

The more we become aware of the negative pleasures in life, the more we can influence and impact what is taking place. It is a never-ending unfolding of a process that takes us deeper and deeper into our consciousness. The more we explore the edges of all that exists, the more we will find what exists beyond what we know.

It is like traveling into outer space. We can only go so far before we are at the edge of our own galaxy. We can only see so far before we can see nothing more. The more we travel to those edges, the further we see. It is in this process of seeing and moving forward that we become more than we are at this moment.

All too often, we ignore the impact of what is happening in life or what has taken place and how it impacts us physically. We know how to speak the jargon of the mind body connection, but we have not gone in and touched our innermost being where the felt sense connects the mind and body together as one.

When I was paralyzed and unable to walk, and barely able to speak or take care of myself, I struggled to believe that I would ever do these things again. The negative pleasure in my mind was that this was all my life had become. It was my awareness at that moment.

I had to fight to shift my awareness and begin believing that there was more. The paralysis in my case was not as much physical as it was mental. I didn't believe I could walk. I didn't believe I could function and it took me reversing those thoughts like nothing else I had ever faced in life to begin walking and talking as I had once done. However, along with the mental part, I had to go in and connect physically in the body with the experiences holding me back.

It was a process that unfolded for me. At first, I wasn't sure where to go or what to do. I held on to the hope of finding and discovering the way forward into healing for my life. I embraced and sought out things that helped me discover myself. I didn't stop at these moments, though, for they would have become my own negative pleasure, even if they were part of the healing process.

We often create a world of torment that we force on our lives. I've had plenty of experiences that helped create the suffering I lived in, but I learned that I had to step beyond it if I wanted to heal. I had to go in and ask the hard questions of myself, discover the negative pleasures, and then work towards greater awareness and consciousness. None of this was easy, but it was necessary.

We can't change the past. It was there for whatever reason we could not understand while in the midst of dealing with it. I had to struggle hard with not being able to change the past, and dealing with all the negative pleasures that had become a part of my life. I knew if I wanted to heal and get beyond this, I would allow the struggle to take me forward, rather than hold me back.

I remember cursing all that happened to me and some days I still do. When you've faced the horror of being raped and molested, beaten and ridiculed, there is hardly any other emotion but anger that seems appropriate. I knew that if I stayed in these moments that I would not heal.

I'm not suggesting that we avoid anything or any experience. I'm not suggesting that we avoid the negative pleasures or emotions we face. Instead, I'm suggesting that just like I have learned, we must go in and embrace all parts of ourselves. We must hug it with love until it transforms into a deeper awareness and consciousness. If we don't, then we will risk becoming one with our negative pleasures and past, instead of using them to become more than we know or we are at this moment.

Sometimes it can be good to wallow, and I often see people talking against this. Yes, I have wallowed, and sometimes I needed to do that while I was trying to figure out what was ahead.

What is one person's wallowing may just be where they are discovering the road ahead. To some, it may not seem that way. However, the caution here is to not get stuck in this muck. If you're not finding the answers you need, try something different. Look for the things that take you into your inner discovery, and not just from a mental perspective, but from a body based approach. The more you can find the help that takes you into your body to find the answer, the more you will propel toward overcoming the challenges you face.

I don't see negative pleasures as reasons to beat myself up. As I write that, I realize that I do chastise myself for being the way that I am. It is part of human nature. Maybe while I'm writing this, I realize that another one of my negative pleasures is being self-critical. I can criticize myself with the best of them. So, see, even this is my process as I write about what I face.

Growth, though, is not about counting how many things wrong we can see within ourselves, even if that is our current practice. Instead, growth and healing are about becoming aware of these things and then working to let go and heal them, one piece at a time. It is about embracing the negative pleasures so that we take back the energy and power they hold over us.

Negative pleasures are good at robbing us of not only our thoughts and views but keeping us stuck in such a critical mode that we never see them. It is often easier to numb and disconnect and ignore these things than it is to go in and find the key to removing their power from them. We can tell others what they need to do, but we often fail at telling ourselves what we need to do.

It is a continual process of moving forward and identifying our negative pleasures. It is not a one-stop healing moment where we know everything there is to know about our lives. Being human and living in a human body is a continual growth process, bringing us into consciousness and through awareness. To think that this is an endpoint in a process is limiting us from all that we can become.

The negative pleasures I have included here in this chapter are some of the ones that I readily recognize in myself. It is by no means an exhaustive list for myself either. They are the ones I'm choosing to highlight. For you, the negative pleasures may be something different. You may find them showing up in different ways than I do. It is perfectly okay because to get caught up in the process, comparing my experiences to yours, will not move you forward.

Each of us has our uniqueness that we must discover and embrace while moving forward. Letting my process become your process will not ultimately help you. However, learning from where I have traveled will help give you a greater ability to see road signs along the way that might point out things you may have missed otherwise. I share what I've been through so everyone reading this may understand their own process a little more.

Keep in mind that fear has a major role in how negative pleasures come through. Fear is the vehicle of distortion, and together with our life's experiences it often holds us back. We give fear the leash, but then we are surprised when it tries to choke us.

Recognize fear for what it is. It is there to protect us, but it can also keep us from discovering and moving forward from our negative pleasures. When you recognize it and then realize that it has only the hold over you that you allow, you will be able to embrace it, taking power away from it to create gigantic steps of healing and change for your life.

Negative pleasures in life do exist, but the goal should be to learn to identify them and work to resolve the underlying issues they raise. We do this through the felt sense of the body because even while we try to believe they are in the mind, the source is in our neural pathways and cells. The mind will only help us so far if we do not go in and discover the connection to the body.

Try This Exercise

What are your negative pleasures? List what you do and see if you can recognize the origins of them. Now, as you look over your list, what do you feel and notice in your body?

16. Dealing With Our Insecurities

"It takes tremendous energy to keep functioning while carrying the memory of terror, and the shame of utter weakness and vulnerability."
- *Dr. Bessel van der Kolk, M.D.*

Many of us, if not most of us humans deal with insecurity. If you don't, then we might consider you a superhuman. I think part of being human is to deal with our insecurities. To be human is to have parts of us that don't feel secure.

To me, it is biological. It is just part of the human makeup in the mind. It is how we roll. After all, there are many parts of us. Some we choose to confront and others we choose to hide from in life. It helps us grow if we choose to allow it.

Some may have insecurity when it comes to saying anything because they don't feel like they will be believed. Others might feel they will be ridiculed. Many times, this comes from the messages we grew up with from the time we were born. Whether our parents, teachers, or other adult leaders unconsciously taught this, most likely it was there. Some of us had better caregivers than others, and some of us did not.

Others may struggle thinking what they say is not enough, that no one will understand, or that maybe they are saying too much. Insecurity comes in many forms, and sometimes we were shot down as a kid so much if we said anything, speaking the slightest thing might bring great anxiety.

I remember growing up in a house where every idea you had and everything you said was ridiculed. Nothing was ever good enough, and you were the dumb one in the family when you opened your mouth. It didn't matter if you were right and backed up by fact. If the other person didn't buy into it, you were the wrong one.

At the church we went to while I was in high school, everyone was wrong except for what the king of the family or the minister in the church proclaimed. Your insecurity and self-esteem were mocked at every turn. These people in my life interpreted the Bible to fit their views, and so you had nothing to back you up against what they said. It was what I lived through, and I knew no different.

When I was a kid, I recall being at my aunt's house and needing a glass of water. We were so controlled in those days that you didn't dare interrupt the adults. Under no circumstances did you ask for anything. Even asking for a glass of water that I badly needed was beyond question. I might not have been punished there in front of them other than a look that said I was in major trouble, but I knew what was coming later. Silence in front of others was my safest bet. After all, my dad constantly repeated, "Children are to be seen and not heard." He meant every word of this statement.

Insecurity can also come in the form of how we look or act or behave. If we are dealt with a great deal of shame, we might never feel secure in any aspect of life. We may overcompensate by becoming boisterous and mean-spirited to others. We may undercompensate by becoming so withdrawn that no one ever hears from us or we don't feel strong enough to let anyone hear from us.

Growing up, we had very few clothes. While I know that we had little money and needed to make do with what we had, this went beyond something normal. We lived on a farm and worked with animals, yet we were supposed to wear our clothes multiple days in a row. We were also discouraged from taking more than one shower or bath a week, and that was before we went to church on Sunday. You could wash up in a sink a little, but that was it because I remember being ridiculed if I tried to take an extra shower. There were the showers that you could take with the monster, but I declined those as much as I could. Some days I lost those battles.

I always felt dirty and unclean. It did horrendous damage to how I saw myself in life. I didn't realize for a long time that body odor was not normal, but I had no understanding of it. Supposedly we needed to save water, and yet we lived on a farm with a well that provided all the water. I never understood it then, and I don't understand it now.

The shame I felt was enormous, especially as a teenager. Of course, I had come to know this as the way things were. Baths and showers were for Saturday night, so you were clean before going to church. It was their only purpose. Clean clothes smelled so fresh when the laundry was done, but the fresh smell didn't last long. It all added up to insecurity.

Thinking I'm Not Good Enough

I constantly struggle with thinking that I'm not good enough. Worst of all, I often think everyone does not like me or hates me or is angry at me. I go through many days not always being able to see that they do not. When this happens, the anxiety and depression build, and I feel completely isolated. It is an area that I still struggle with in my life as I continue to heal those old traumatic wounds.

Another related insecurity is when someone doesn't respond quickly or goes too long without speaking or writing. I think I did something wrong, or I upset another person. I fear I wasn't good enough for this person or some friend. It is insecurity about feeling abandoned and unloved among other things.

Sometimes we have faced insurmountable odds, and we've dealt with situations that leave us feeling so wounded and beaten down. We become insecure about getting anywhere in life. We often believe that we are too wounded to change our lives or progress forward or truly find and discover all that we are. Overcoming those challenges can be monumental no matter how hard you try to employ positive thoughts or affirmations.

Insecurities like feeling like we are too skinny or too fat can lead us to spending many dollars on clothing and treatment that we would otherwise not spend. It can lead us to eat too little or not care what we put inside us. It becomes a disconnect from the mind to the body because while the body tries to say one thing, the mind is having no part of listening to it.

All you need to do to see evidence of this is to look at the advertising that is pushed out every day. Everyone desires to be the perfect person so that someone else will desire them. We all have the things within us that we hate about ourselves. Overweight people want to be thin and thin people want to be not so thin. Short people are envious of tall people, and the reverse applies. Being able to talk in front of others is envied by the introverts while extroverts sometimes miss the deeper connections of highly sensitive people.

There are other struggles people face, such as thinking we aren't a good enough lover or provider, or making people angry at us. While anyone could sit there and try to reason with us that this is not the case, all the past neural pathways of the mind are telling us something different. It affects and impacts everything we do and say and our interactions with one another.

Everyone has something that they hate about themselves even if they only voice that to themselves in private. It is hard for us as humans to accept ourselves unconditionally. Many may claim that they do this, but the evidence is so clear that we all struggle with this.

Not feeling smart enough can be a big insecurity for many because they have led themselves to believe it is true. Even some of the most intelligent people I have ever met feel like they are not smart enough. They compensate by trying to prove that they know something. Even when the world is listening to them and regards them as an expert on the subject, it is never enough to convince their mind that what it is hearing is true.

When I was growing up, I never was smart enough or good enough for my dad. He would constantly berate me and tell me how little common sense I had. My dad would make fun of the things I did, the decisions I made, and the things I said.

I still remember when I needed to build a hay bunk for my sheep because they were eating off the ground. Anyone who's worked with animals knows that having them eat off the ground is not good. It can cause many kinds of health issues. So, after begging my dad to help me build a hay bunk for them, I finally gave up and decided to build it myself. Now, I'll be honest and tell you that it wasn't the prettiest thing. It probably wasn't the sturdiest thing, but it was functional and solved the issue. When my dad found out that I had done this on my own, he wasn't happy I did. No, he was furious that I didn't have him help me and so he criticized every square inch of it. He left me feeling deflated and horrible and that I could do nothing right.

I'll never forget learning to drive. Not only did I have my dad screaming at me about what I should do in the car while driving, but I also had my mom offering advice and my older brother thinking he knew it all. It would get so bad that when I pulled into a store parking lot, I had to wait for them to battle over which parking place I should pick.

One of the things I started to do on the piano as a kid was learn how to create songs from a place within me that was so deep. Sometimes the music would flow, and sometimes the notes would clank a little together. One day my dad, disgusted about having to listen to me, said "There was a lot of mistakes in that song. What is the name of that song?" This critique came from a person that had no musical ability. I replied, "It wasn't a song because I was just playing around trying to create something." I wanted to tell him that if he could do better, the piano was all his, but there was no way I was going to say it to his face. There was no doubt in my mind of the action that would follow.

In college, my father made sure I knew that anyone attending college was an overeducated college idiot. While he didn't name me specifically, it was inferred in what he said. Time and time again, I would hear this phrase. In my first job after college, he would tell me how I was nothing more than he was, working on some menial job. Except, I was managing a multi-million dollar system and once again, just as in the college situation, he was jealous. It all made for that insecurity reinforcement that I had heard almost every day of my life.

We have insecurities about money and taking steps to move towards where we need to be. Often, we convince ourselves that because of past situations, what lies ahead will be a failure. We won't go there because we can prove to ourselves, some other similar situation has not worked out. It is easier to have the idea and give up than push through with courage into the unknown.

How many of us have lived through moments where food was scarce, or a house was not adequately heated? Those things that we experience can have a direct impact on how we see money and abundance in our lives. These are silent stalkers, but they are very powerful in proving to us that since we did not have our basic needs met, we will never have enough.

At the heart of our insecurities is fear, along with our past experiences. Our past gives us the foundation we stand upon for what lies ahead. The things we have been taught and shown give us the view of how we see life. Even as a small child, we learn to mirror that which we see. Whatever adults show us through the example of their lives, gives us the framework for how we see life. No parent or caregiver is perfect because they are often learning as they go. It is our responsibility to unlearn the bad and relearn what we need for our lives.

What we know gives birth to how we approach life. It gives the framework and boundaries of how far we go or what we decide to do. The more adverse experiences we have in life, the more potential there is to succumb to these things as if they control us. To break free from this is not impossible, but neither is it easy.

Seeing life in an insecure way begins to take away from the possibility of all that exists. It keeps us from knowing the full framework of what is out there. It keeps us from believing in all that there is and all that there can be. We become people who know no different. That is part of the human experience. It is part of who we are and what makes us into the people that we see before us today.

The sad part is we buy into the reality of those who cared for us. Sometimes our caregivers were horrible to us, and sometimes these people were not aware of what they were doing. They passed it on unknowingly and unconsciously. We had no way to know they were doing this and how to make different choices. We were following those that were there to help care for us.

Sometimes the caregivers around us did not comprehend or were not aware that they were causing us great difficulty ahead in life. More than likely, they were doing what they had been taught and shown. If they had not healed their difficult experiences and overcome these challenges, they would be repeating them unconsciously.

What we mirror to others, especially young children, through our own lives is extremely powerful. Kids are a sponge that soaks up everything in the environment around them. It is how they learn, but unfortunately, it is also how they learn unhealthy behavior. When a child is born, the parents become the infant's sole source of food, sustenance, warmth, and training about how to respond to life. What the parents mirror to the child is what they form the basis of in all that they learn and how they experience life in the years to come.

When we got to the point where we needed to begin taking care of ourselves on our own, the information we had to draw on was from those that taught us through their words and actions. It became the basis for all our decisions, thought processes, and views upon how we saw life.

If you add into it the experiences that we now face, we add more layers upon what we learned in life. The fears wrap it up with a beautiful bow and delude us into thinking that we didn't know best, but fear did. The fear kept us from fully seeing what we thought we saw and kept us apart from all that we would ever come to know.

The fear showed us a distorted image in the mirror, even though our eyes and minds and emotions thought we saw something normal and true. It gave us the grounds to have altered realities of what was truly there versus what we saw. The mind, our thoughts, our emotions, feelings, and views were all in this together.

Now that we've reached a point in life where we hopefully begin to see differently, we must give these things up. However, that is easier said than done. To give these things up is essentially to let go of the life that we know.

One of the things I had to do in my healing was to walk away from my parents. They had become so toxic that to stay in communication with them at all, meant I was still attaching myself to their toxicity. They were desperately trying to reign me in and tow the family dynamic, but I knew that if we stayed connected, I would lose myself. It was one of the most difficult things I've ever done.

When I let go of them, or at least when I thought I did, I found out that so much of what I had been taught growing up didn't serve my life in the way that I thought it did. I was so locked into their beliefs, views, and opinions but did not realize this until years later, after stepping away from them. All of what I had been taught was so ingrained in me that it just seemed normal. Far too often in this world, we as humans are locked into what we are taught, not what we have come to know or understand.

I found out that many of my insecurities came because of trying to live their truths and beliefs and opinions about life and me. I had to fight through each one of those - including religious dogma - to begin finding out what I truly thought and felt and found to be true.

I Had To Question Everything

One thing I found while searching for how to deal with insecurity was that I had to question everything. I had to so I could find out what things fit and what things did not. We often give lip service that we do this, but most of the time we are fooling ourselves. It was no easy process, and it was a continual process of waking up and becoming aware that a greater consciousness is alive within us.

The more I questioned things and asked, "Is that true or helpful to my life," the more I found out that many things were not. The more I did this, the more I chipped away at the foundation I had been standing on, only to find air pockets below. Once exposed, they allowed me to see further into what existed.

It reminds me of when I was learning to weld in high school shop class. For a test, we had to weld the end of a pipe together without adding extra metal to it. It was not easy, and even though it looked like we had been successful, often it took several attempts to accomplish it. As you welded, you had to chip away at the slag that formed. Air pockets would form in it which added no strength and would allow water or air to flow through them. Passing this test in shop class meant that we were successful in getting the pipe to hold water.

Just like in the welding experience, if we didn't chip away the slag, our pipe would not pass the test. It was only through pounding away at it with a hammer that we found the pieces that were not as strong. It is the part that we tend to avoid in life because it is not an easy process. However, to become a conscious human, we have to chip away the slag.

It is easy to get ourselves to believe that what we think is true, really is true. Unfortunately, those are often illusions. We succumb to our own worst nightmare of living a lie while believing it is the truth.

When we live a lie, we don't want things to change around us. We want others and the world to be the same as we have known because if they change, our foundation gets threatened. Most of the time, this is an unconscious reaction and moment in life, but if you look closely at it, you'll see that the slag needs to be chipped away.

Yes, this is a process that unfolds and happens over the course of a lifetime. I don't believe there is an endpoint, but a continual process of becoming more and more aware and conscious. It is how we wake up and become more than we were yesterday. It is how we evolve to a higher point in our lives and become more than we are at this moment.

Far too often we think we've done a few things to grow in our lives, and so we close the books thinking we have moved past everything. We say, "I'm past it" or "I've moved on" or "I'm healed" when in reality, we're just numbing to what is hidden. It is too easy to fall into this trap. These old tricks need to be exposed for the lies they hold so that you can become conscious and aware and overcome challenges.

Insecurities are there for a reason. We may have good reasons to hide from them, but ultimately these things will rob you of so much energy, strength, and forward movement. They are thieves in your life. Their purpose is their existence, not yours.

We live as they dictate to us who we are, all the while covering up the true person inside of us. These insecurities hold us back from becoming all that we are and can be in life. If we let them go too long, they bring physical and mental pain and stress, altering how we see the world and how we live.

Granted, some of us have endured far too much. We've had to face the odds of life that most would have given up on much sooner. Sometimes these remnants become who we show to the real world. We are so much more than we realize.

It takes time to go through this process, and it requires that we build upon what we've already discovered. We should be careful not to let our insecurities in life rule us. Let us dig deep into them and see where the air pockets have formed. The more we dig deep inside, the more we can fill those air pockets up with material that helps us stand taller and more solid.

It is not just a thought process either. It is important to understand that, because so often we look at all these things as only being mental issues. The experiences we have lived through are stored in the cells and tissues of the body. They are imprinted on our neural pathways. If you do not go in and make these body-based connections, then the mental process of healing will be limited.

I know it can be scary letting go of these things and daring to stand apart from the biological family unit or society in which you live. You're venturing into the unknown, apart from all those that have been standing close to you. Just don't let that get in your way because it will hold you back. It will prevent you from walking your path into self-discovery and awareness and consciousness.

When I walked away from my parents, it tore me apart inside. Even with their toxic nature, I still longed for that family unit. The letters from my parents got so horrendous and hurtful that I had to have a friend read them for me. They stopped at nothing to keep me in line with the family unit and their consciousness.

This part of my process was so painful. If I could have avoided it, I would have at all cost. However, I knew I had to let go to heal because my family was sucking the life out of me. I would not have made it if I had held on to what I knew. It was not easy convincing myself to do this, but the cost of not doing it would have meant my life would have ended.

Daring to step out and not stay connected with them was extremely hard. I'm not going to sugarcoat it because it just about did me in. It takes great courage and strength to do this, but I knew deep down that if I was going to live another day, I had to walk away. I had to find myself, and nothing could stand in the way of that.

Do I have insecurities to this day? Yes, I most definitely do. They still exist, but on a different level where I actively work with them. They are no longer hiding in the shadows. Some may still not be in full view, but I am now more open to going in and rooting these out of my life. If they come up, I try to observe and learn from them. I try to focus on letting them go and reclaiming another piece of my life rather than just holding on as if they were my life's sustenance.

Sometimes these things kick my butt hard, and other times I win major battles over them. I do not wish to let them take refuge within me like hidden poison because they will do long-term damage to me physically and mentally. The conversion disorder showed me just how far these things would go, and end up bringing significant harm.

When you work to let go of insecurity and face the fear and truths you have based your life on, there may be many things that will attempt to hold you back. From people, beliefs, religious dogma or other opinions, you may experience a very strong force that will do everything in its power not to let you discover your true self. You must be strong in these times and keep walking no matter what. When you start to confront the things that hold you back, there are powerful forces that will stop at nothing to prevent those changes from taking place.

Family and religious dogma want you to stay locked into their sets of beliefs because if you don't, it shakes their foundation. In no way do others want you to shake their foundation because by doing that, they may be forced to confront their truths and who they are in life. However, that is their path and their set of issues they must work through. It is not yours.

Even if you're not sure how to walk into the discovery of all that you are, start heading in that direction with that thought. If you keep questioning it, you will discover more about who you are. Have courage and don't let anyone stop you or delude you or trick you into thinking that you're on the wrong path.

When we do step out in the discovery of truth, we will find that others are walking with us. We may not see them initially, but they are there. It takes us choosing to begin the journey to discover a life that is beyond what we know at this moment.

The more we discover about who we are, the more empowered we are to become more of who we are. Life is not about following what everyone else thinks we should follow. It is about discovering our true essence and awareness of what is our existence. It is being human and learning to live in a human body, full of possibility for greater consciousness.

Others may claim they have your best interests at heart, but if it does not match up with every cellular component of your body, set it aside and find your path. Look for those things that help you progress forward, heal your life, and put into full view all that you think you know.

It is not an easy path to walk, but it is a necessary one. It does have rewards for you, but until you step out on the journey, they will not be shown. I believe we are meant as humans to become all that we are and to grow in awareness and consciousness. In my own life, something propels me forward from all that I thought I knew into a moment of discovering what is possible.

As I continue to walk, I am discovering truths and possibilities that I did not realize existed. The more I walk on this journey, the more I discover. I hope that you will confront your insecurities and use the fear of them as a motivating power to help you walk forward in your life.

Try This Exercise

See if you can think of one or two insecurities you have and make a note of them. Now, as you say those or think about them, see if you can notice anything in your body that happens. Does a pain show up? Do your muscles tighten or tense up? How easy or difficult, light or deep is your breathing? What do you notice physically when you think about these words? Don't judge the sensations, just allow them to show up.

Another exercise to do is listen to the song, "How Could Anyone" by Shaina Noll. Try singing along with the words every morning and evening for a month and let the words help re-center your mind on who you are as a person. https://www.ShainaNoll.com/

17. My Experience With Anger

*"Deposits of anger are made not only during childhood but throughout a person's life. Because there are no withdrawals from this account, the anger accumulates. Thus anger becomes rage; when it reaches a critical level and threatens to erupt into consciousness, the brain creates pain or some other physical symptom as a distraction, to prevent a violent emotional explosion." – **Dr. John Sarno, M.D.**

People struggling with anger is a growing epidemic in our world. Yes, anger has been around since the beginning of time. However, there are far too many people smiling to the outside world while silently struggling with anger in their lives.

The evidence is in what we see posted and shared and liked on social media or in the news. It is almost as if we as humans need to vent and rant and scream constantly. It is almost as if we as humans need to let the world know what our opinions and beliefs are, even at the expense of other people. Our anger comes forth like a bomb going off on the planet. We live in a world where stress is so prevalent that there is no outlet and no way for people to deal with the anger they experience.

Some people will say, "you should not get angry." Some will exclaim, "anger is a bad emotion." Other people will treat anger as a very bad thing, forcing those with anger issues to burrow deep underground. In many ways, they are only inflicting more harm on others and themselves.

Anger is a normal emotion. However, it makes most of us uncomfortable when we see it. In the Bible, even God and Jesus got angry. The harm of anger comes in what you do with it. It is where you direct the anger that matters, especially when innocent people bear the brunt of it. Turning the anger inward on yourself is just as harmful.

People are not being helpful when they tell others all anger is wrong. Anger is there for a reason, and it is not helpful to judge others for it. We should be helping people discover how to let it out in a safe way and get to the source of it. Being human isn't about judging others and informing them of how you see what they do as wrong. It only forces people to suffer in silence.

Anger is a valid emotion. My personal belief from what I've experienced is that you can't have happiness without anger. You need both ends of the emotional spectrum. Anger in itself is not bad. Sometimes we need it to protect us or push us forward in a direction that may be difficult. It can be a very beneficial emotion.

Anger used in inappropriate ways becomes harmful, for anger can be used to hide what someone feels deep inside their mind and body. It causes them to react in ways that hurt others, disrespect others, or do things in life that aren't for the best of humanity and civilization. The more we hide anger, the more it festers and grows.

When anger is used to control and manipulate others, it is used in the wrong way. We can see evidence of this at every turn in life. The evidence is in what you read online, in a social media news feed, or hear in people's conversations. Many times, it shows up in how people respond to you and what they say to you. It might even be in how you respond to others or what you share, because often anger blinds us to the deeper truths in life.

Often, we use anger to deflect our insecurities and insufficiency in life. Rather than us healing deeply, we turn that anger from the pains that have been inflicted on us onto innocent and unsuspecting folks. They bear the brunt of our own unwillingness to go in and heal.

Anger is something that festers within most people. I know, no one wants to admit that, and everyone wants to think they are beyond anger. Unfortunately, if you see what is before you, the proof is clearly visible. It is evident if we open our eyes. From bombs and mass shootings to leaders controlling and manipulating the masses, anger is there. From people who lash out and call each other names or use and manipulate others for their own good, anger is there. When people fail to listen to one another but push their ideas and agendas on others, often anger is unresolved in their lives.

I once had a boss who would scream and yell at me constantly. To this day, I think the guy suffered greatly from so much anger that he had no idea how to deal with it. In the office, he'd slam his fists on his desk and bellow at people at the top of his lungs. Everyone was afraid of him. He did get results, but his toxic anger he displayed harmed many in his path.

For those that struggle with all kinds of mental health issues, anger is often just under the surface but almost too difficult to reach. It may come out far too easily because the lid of the steam kettle can no longer be contained. It often hinders people and inflicts more pain, holding them back from discovering their true self. I know - I've been there! It isn't any fun! Anger can also cause people to hold everything in and not deal with all that they have experienced. They are too afraid to let anger show up, and so it is silently inflicted upon their body.

Anger is also one of those emotions that is hard to deal with in life. It is too easy to attempt to hide it because there is no safe place, time, or way to bring it out. If your anger shows up, most people are not comfortable with how it comes out or when it comes out and will quickly tell you to put it away.

Often anger is a danger to those around people who struggle with it, and it hurts others. I remember growing up in a house where it was common to see it on display. My dad would get so angry at the drop of a pin, that you never knew when or where or how it would show up. The one constant in our house was that my dad's anger would be present, most of the time surprising and shocking us.

I remember being punished for not putting silverware away correctly in a drawer, even though I was only a few years old. To this day, I'm still not sure what I did wrong, but it didn't matter. My dad's anger was raging in full force. My dad was good at screaming and ranting and raving. He was good at hitting whoever was close to him.

As a kid, I remember learning to wash the dishes. I would have to stand up on a kitchen chair next to the sink because I had not grown enough to reach the sink. When it came time to wash the greasy frying pans, I would struggle to get them clean. As a result, my dad would sometimes take his foot and kick me in my rear out of anger that I could not get them clean. I still remember my little body being slammed into the kitchen sink counter and so badly wanting to cry out in pain.

There was one time that he got so angry at my dog because she had chewed on our shoes and boots. Most puppies go through this stage, and especially when they are left alone, they want attention. My dad made us keep her outside as she was not allowed inside most of the time. Well, that day, she got attention from my dad. My dad picked up the shoes and hurled them at her. Unfortunately, what his anger prevented him from seeing was that she was sitting next to the window. The shoe missed her and hurled right through the window, shattering it into a million pieces. By the time everyone realized what happened, it was too late. I think my dad wanted to crawl behind a rock and hide. At least he didn't pick up the shotgun and fire it at my dog that day, which was his other go-to-device for when he got angry at our pets.

Other times when he was angry included one time when I was out working in the garden. He was not able to walk because of an accident, and so he was sitting in a lawn chair near the garden barking out orders. Of course, there was nothing that I could do right, and so he would be screaming and yelling, demanding that we do what he was not able to communicate clearly. He was always criticizing me for everything I did. Without paying attention, I got a little too close to him, so he picked up the garden hoe next to me and whacked me a good one in the head. He wanted me to do what he wanted, and his anger got the best of him. To this day, I never remember my father having much remorse for his anger filled actions.

My older brother was always showing his worst side to me. He had to one-up me constantly, pick at me, and generally was just a bully. I remember one time when he had picked on me and went a little too far, forcing me to stand up to him. I chased him out of the house with a kitchen chair in my hand, ready to wrap it around his head. He outran me of course, but I was so angry at his taunts that I was ready to do serious harm to him.

When I was getting ready to go away to college, I was trying to pack my stuff so that I would know what I had and where it was. My dad did not like how I was doing this and proceeded to tell me how stupid I was and how poor of a job I was doing. "Use your common sense that God gave you," he would say. I had learned not to say anything to him in these situations because you would find yourself slammed into a wall. I knew my days of living in this house with him were limited, and my only desire was to escape and leave. Unfortunately, at that moment he saw me roll my eyes. The next thing I knew the verbal assault started.

When we would go on vacation or camping, there were always anger filled moments that we had to endure. I loved to travel and go camping, but the torment we went through in the process was almost too much to bear. Nothing was good enough, and you never did anything quick enough for the man to be happy. He would kick you, hit you, assault you. He would verbally tear you to shreds as if you were a complete idiot. Packing the car was a nightmare of verbal assaults.

There was a moment, when I was in kindergarten, that my dad got so angry at my older brother. I have no idea to this day what had gone wrong, but my dad dragged my brother to the barn. To this day, I can still hear the screams of my brother as my dad wailed on him so hard he could be heard inside the house.

These were some of the tamer moments I endured as a kid. Throughout my life, I was so afraid of anger that I stuffed it down. I wanted nothing to do with it, and I did not show it. The anger felt like a complete danger to me as in losing control and hurting those around me.

I remember arguing with Dr. Paul Canali in an early therapy session. I believed anger was a very bad thing. He struggled to get me to hear that anger has a purpose. Sometimes it motivates us to act, and sometimes it helps us clear out things we no longer need. If we bottle it up inside though, it causes great harm physically. If we continue to bottle it up, we end up lashing out at those that care about us while often not realizing how much harm we are inflicting upon them. Anger dealt with appropriately can be a good thing but left to fester and grow into unconsciousness is a recipe for disaster.

The trouble is, we often end up mirroring how our parents and others around us display anger. The way they show how they deal with anger is how we learn to deal with it. In our current day, we're modeling the unhealthy behavior of anger to kids and others everywhere in this world. It is sad watching this unfold with adults that seem completely oblivious to the harm they are inflicting. It is far too prevalent because we are not learning how to deal with it in healthy ways.

How many times do we hear reports of someone snapping and doing something horrible to other people? The news reporters interview people close to that individual and everyone acts as if this was beyond comprehension. However, no one sees what is going on right before their eyes. We are often too unconscious to see it in ourselves. We wish not to see it building up in others, and even if we did, most have no idea how to help someone walk through the fire. They are far too busy sending memes online that do little to help humanity.

If you have been through this in your life, you may realize that you must teach yourself how to deal with anger. If you are like me, you may come to understand that what you were taught and shown about anger while growing up has no healthy basis for what you do in life.

It is not an easy road because if you employ a numbing consciousness of only being positive or having happy thoughts, you're causing your body internal harm by ignoring anger. Yes, many convince themselves that this is the way out, but I know from firsthand experience that it is not. What we don't deal with in the body, the body stores and turns on itself. This energy looks for an exit but often hides within the cells and tissues. Anger that is unreleased is very harmful to the cells and tissues of the body. If we don't deal with anger, it will cause many mental and physical and emotional issues.

Often right below the anger, there is deep sadness, hurt, and pain. Sometimes we're taught that the only way to deal with it is by suppressing it. Rather than allowing ourselves to go in and touch the innermost corners of anger, we act as if it does not exist. We exclaim that we are happy, and that anger is wrong. Unfortunately, as much as we think we are right, we are only fooling ourselves.

Most of us have few people who understand and can help them walk through the healing journey from anger that's consuming their lives. It is easier to think happy thoughts or act as if anger does not exist than it is to confront it, deal with it, and find healing. Our go-to-choice of dealing with anger is avoiding it.

All too often, we don't have healthy skills for releasing anger. We were not taught appropriate anger releasing techniques. We often saw our caregivers show anger in ways that weren't healthy, or downright inappropriate. When we grow up in a world where anger is an unhealthy norm, we become so afraid of it and so unsure of what to do with it. It becomes what we know to do, not what we have discovered is a healthy way to release it.

At times, people explode and then we're shocked and surprised. At times, people fly off the handle and they feel horrible afterward. More commonly, you can see anger in everyday behavior.

While anger is a valid emotion, it can often be misused and mishandled. It is in that essence that we need to begin to learn how to handle the explosive side of anger.

Here are some tips on handling anger that I have learned. For me, it is still a work in progress. By no means am I an authority on it because I struggle like all the other human inhabitants of the world. Please don't kid yourself to think that you've got anger under control, like you may have managed to get yourself to believe. Use these tips to help yourself release anger in a healthy way.

First, recognize that the anger is there. See all of its edges and corners and moments. When anger is consuming us, we often don't fully see it. We are blind to it in these moments, and I am not kidding. This is part of the problem because if you can't see anger taking place and your role in it, your reaction to dealing with it becomes harder. Anger is often an unconscious moment for us.

Others around us see the anger in us more plainly and clearly. Enlist their help to begin recognizing it. Discuss it with those close to you who bear the brunt of anger outbursts. It impacts them more than you may realize and if you look and listen closely, you will see and hear that from those who care about you. The angrier you get, the quieter those around you get. It stifles them and forces them into a world of dealing with your anger as if mortar shells were raining down on you.

Come up with a safe word for when you get in those moments. This way, those around you can help by just saying the safe word. It gives you a moment to consciously connect with the state you are in and helps them lovingly assist you. This action empowers them. Safe words help you feel less threatened because they help you be more conscious and aware. Often anger drives others to feel insecure and quiet and may often trigger them back to experiences they have had. A safe word helps you honor them while trying to move towards a more conscious life where you truly and fully see your behavior for what it is. People who are extremely angry or get angry often do not fully see how frequent and intense their anger outbursts are. They may think they do, but often they do not.

Work on deep release from emotional pain and conflicts in your life. If there is toxic stress that is overwhelming to you, find ways to begin dealing with it. What can you change in your life to lessen or alleviate it? How can you alter how you look at it? If you've been through difficult experiences or toxic stress, what steps can you begin to take today to heal from them? Remember, it is a process, but if we continue to hold in emotional pain and experiences from life's past, it will catch up with us sooner or later in some form or fashion or way. Rather than suppressing these things, learn how to resolve them.

Anger is high energy and often not conscious. Anger is overwhelming and powerful like a bomb. It needs to be frequently diffused because if you don't, it builds up quickly. Find a way to diffuse it daily. Even if you have a day that doesn't feel too full of anger, you still need to do activities that help let it go. It could be going to the gym and connecting with your mind and body, to help give your body a way to let go of the anger that is building. Yoga, Qigong, meditation, and other mind body practices can help you let the anger go and diffuse things. Deep breathing and enteric brain work can help you move the energy out of your body and release it while becoming more conscious and aware. (Also see https://MindBodyMeditationExercises.com)

Since anger is a physical reality in the body, mind-based practices will only help so much. Working to connect the mental anger that you express with what is in the body will help you move through it in a healthy and safe way. Bodywork helps you work through things because if not, you're only playing with half a deck.

We are too quick to think that anger is something that happens in the mind. It is a thought process reaction, we conclude. However, by the time you connect with the mind on anger, the source of it has already been pumping in the body. From my own life and experiences, I believe anger is generated within the body before the mind reacts. While this difference may not seem significant, I believe it is.

All too often, I have heard people say that there is a split moment between something that happens and a point where you get angry. It is in that split moment that you can find a different reaction. However, as much as I'm sure this might be possible for some, it often leads other people to feel like they have once again failed. Deep anger originates in the body first, then shows up through the mind and our reactions.

One of the things about anger is the more it happens, the less you feel in control of it or how it's expressed. When anger leaves you feeling helpless to control or work through, it feels like there is no way you'll ever get to the point where you can conquer it. Each time it shows up, it feels like the mountain gets a little harder to climb.

Anger shows up in the body, whether we want to realize it or not. It is a physical reaction that may not necessarily make sense to our limited consciousness and awareness. However, I have seen in my own life that I can be on the table in a therapy session, and we can easily recreate it. Sometimes it is recreated through tense spots, or places of pain, or with a movement that connects to the felt sense.

*"Anger is simply a natural instinctive response to obstacles in our path and to many different circumstances where we feel powerless or victimized." – **Dr. Peter A. Levine, Ph.D.***

Memories or even general conversation can bring it up. The more you have endured in life, and the more that an unhealthy life has been mirrored to you, the more anger will be there. There is no getting around it, other than learning to work through it. We work through it by first acknowledging its presence and then working to find ways to release it from our lives.

I'm not a big lover of using anger management techniques to deal with it. Yes, they may help in the short-term, but if we are not careful, they will become an addictive medication. These techniques will become something that keeps us from going to the root of the issue, rather than living with it and altering it at its core. We want to focus on finding the source and releasing the source of our anger, not just masking it or trying to hide and cover it up.

Realize that anger is a process of learning how to let go. Recognize that most likely your caregivers did not know how to deal with anger appropriately, so these things were passed on to you unconsciously without you or them realizing it. Know that the more conscious you become of your own mind body connection, the more control you will have as you learn to let go of these painful experiences.

Yes, it can be a difficult process to learn to deal with anger in our lives. Find those little steps that offer a simple moment of accomplishment and build on them. The simple moments help you know you have some impact on it, and you need those to make you stronger so that you can discover the sources of it within your body.

I cannot emphasize how much the anger comes from within us and in the body. The mind is secondary, in my view, of where anger originates. I believe this is why we struggle with anger, because we chastise the mind for becoming angry when it is just feeding off of what is happening deep within the body. It is deep within our awareness and consciousness, but until we allow ourselves to go there, it will remain hidden.

When there is so much anger generated in the body, it becomes as explosive as a bomb detonating. By the time the anger ripples through the body to the mind, there is very little that can be done. I am referring to a split millisecond between that point of anger generation and it reaching the mind. It is so quick to happen that when we notice it, much time has passed. When it reaches the traffic cop of the brain, the power of that anger destroys the traffic cop to bits. There is no way to react because the thing that should be regulating the anger in a healthier and more normal pattern is now destroyed. That is the point where we see the anger displayed to the outside world, and it happens so quickly that we don't get a chance to see the reaction until after it is too late.

You can compare anger to a tsunami. I almost hate to use this example because of how destructive a tsunami is, and I don't want to make light of the devastation that has happened around the world, yet it is a good example to use. When the earthquake in the ocean occurs, that is the moment of anger. No one knows it is coming or that it is happening until it occurs. The earthquake in the ocean is what happens in the body. As the power of the earthquake begins to build the water into a tsunami, it travels towards the shore. In our case, the shore is the mind. Even though we see it coming, we may try to hold out our hands and say stop. Maybe it is possible to stop a tsunami with your hand, but so far no one has been able to do that. The only thing left to do is run for the hills as it devastates all that it touches.

If we can go in and stop the tsunami from even happening in the first place, which is the source or root of anger in the body, then we can impact what happens after that. I'm not saying we can stop a tsunami, but am using it just as an example of what happens with anger in the body. If we can go into the body and connect with the anger and release it, we've got a chance to alter how we react to these situations.

Again, this is not only a mental exercise. It is an exercise that originates in the connection between the source in the body and the mind. It takes time to heal the origins within us, but to fully deal with anger, that is where we must go.

We can suppress anger by not showing it to others, and that is something we do all the time. If you stop and observe people and watch them at all points of their day, you'll notice it. Suppressing anger, though, is not helpful, and it does not mean that it has gone away. It just means you have become good at keeping it hidden from the world. I believe we are masters of suppressing anger shown to the world, and it is becoming much clearer that how we are acting to one another is giving it an outlet. We can no longer suppress it.

The more we suppress anger, the more harm we inflict upon the body. I believe it can lead to heart attacks, stomach ulcers, chronic pain, and muscle tension. Suppressing is not the way to go. Maybe in the short-term you need to do this, but be careful because you can only keep it bottled up inside of you for so long.

There is a difference between getting upset and angry. Being upset, I think, allows you that split second to determine how you will react. Being in a full-on moment of anger that is coming from deep within some unconscious part of your body does not allow the same determination of reaction. There are different levels of anger. Much of what I am talking about in this chapter are the full-on moments of anger.

I know anger impacts many in this world. Because of my issues, I recognize it and spot it in others. I see in them what they may not see in themselves. It is so prevalent in the world, and the reactions we see on social media give evidence to back up what I am saying. People do not realize how they play into the anger and how it is controlling them, but if you read their social media feeds, it is easy to spot. It isn't just the other people displaying it either as the more we interact with it on social media, the more we become part of it.

I see people blame it on having "Irish or Italian or German" in their blood and I find that disturbing. To me, it is not only racist and bigoted but flat out wrong. It is an unconscious statement if I have ever seen one. Making a statement that you have Irish or Italian or German heritage in your blood, or whatever it is that you say, makes it sound like you cannot change things in your life. While it may feel helpless and hopeless at the moment, numbing and avoiding it does not mean it is true and does not help.

Regardless of how you choose to constructively let go of it, getting to the source of it is the key. Without going to the source and diffusing the bomb, your anger will build until you explode or it causes major physical pain. It may take extensive work for a significant time to get to the source of anger within your body. Ways to help release anger are many, and the following discussion is by no means a complete work of reference material. However, these are some things that I have done which have greatly helped me.

Using The Swimming Pool

Using the pool, you can dissipate a lot of anger. Fortunately, I have the option at home, but even if you don't, try a local fitness center or a friend who maybe has a pool. When you're in the pool, there are a couple of things you can do.

First, start off by trying to build up the intensity of motion in your body. You can swirl your arms around in the water by standing in a spot that isn't too deep. In this scenario, you are trying to push the water around from one side of yourself to the other in a pinwheel motion. The aim and goal are to build up the activation in the body. At the same time, you're allowing yourself to connect with whatever it is that is bringing the anger up.

Sometimes, just the act of doing this can help you push the anger out through your arms. Picture all the frustration you have in life as you let it fly out through your hands. You can punch the water, slap it, push it, or even kick it. You're not going to hurt the water, and it should be gentle enough to do these things without injury to yourself. Be careful and conscious to not injure yourself, but take your frustrations out on the water.

In the swimming pool, you can allow the anger to build up and keep forcing that anger into the water. Think about the things that are currently pushing anger up in your life. Allow things to build up and allow your breath to increase to match the anger and resistance. You are trying to put everything into the water that you can.

Now, take a deep breath and go underwater and push a scream out into the water. You're trying to scream as loud as you possibly can underwater where no one can hear you. Of course, when you've pushed the air out, you need to surface so you can catch your breath. Be careful in all of this and make sure you take care of any safety precautions that you need to, so you keep yourself safe. Don't risk your life to do an exercise if you do not feel comfortable doing it.

When you get to this point of exhaling the scream into the water, you might find your body will want to lie down and rest. You might notice that you take some deep breaths and then your body goes into a recovery mode. Find a comfortable place around the pool where you can lie down and allow all of this to happen. You're in recovery mode now from the exercise and if your body shakes a little or trembles or gets lethargic, give yourself some time to rest. The rebalancing of your mind and body is taking place. The autonomic nervous system is doing what it needs to do to heal you.

Most likely, you will feel different when all this is over. There is a good chance that you will feel lighter, calmer, and more peaceful. You may experience other things, but allow yourself to connect with all that is going on in your body. Be the observer, trying not to explain what is happening, but experiencing everything as it occurs. Feeling as much as you can in the body is critical. Repeat this often for best results.

Hot And Cold Baths

Another exercise you can do involves hot and cold water. I used it more for a rash that I was struggling with, but it came out of emotional stress and anger that I was dealing with in my life. This method helps move that overabundant fire energy out of the body and is something you can do in your own home.

While there are many practices out there that deal with removing fire energy from your body, this one is something you can physically feel. When you put your body in ice water or hot water, there is a physical sensation that can directly connect the mind or the anger with what is going on in the body. It is not something you will need to spend time thinking about, because it is such a strong visceral and emotional connection. It takes you deep into the areas where anger is residing in your body.

I realize that even to think about doing anything with ice cold water baths for some people is very difficult and I fully understand this. Make sure you are physically and medically able to do this before starting and if it is too much for you, keep reading for additional ways to deal with anger.

This method focuses on the rash I had that was a result of anger and other issues in my life. You do not need a rash to benefit from this because this method helps push the anger out through the body. Anger is fire energy and water is the opposite of fire. In fact, an ice cold bath is a strong opposing force to fire and anger. Take note that as I describe it, I will be including the information about the rash because I believe that is helpful in addition to the exercise to release anger.

Step 1

I filled my bathtub up with cold water and added approximately 20 pounds of ice to it. You may need to adjust it for the size of your bathtub but use your judgment on this. I wanted to get the water very cold to maximize the effectiveness.

Because the fears were coming up, I began to prepare myself for the process mentally. I told myself that I would not be a long time in the ice. Also, I knew that I could stop it at any time and I wasn't going to die from the cold water. It might make me feel uncomfortable, but since I could crawl out of the bathtub, I could control the effect of it on myself.

I also knew that I was going to refill the bathtub with warm water after this, so I had something to look forward to after the ice. It was the reward or the comfort after subjecting myself to the harshness of the ice water. The key in all of this is to plan and prepare so that you can do everything without too much thought.

Step 2

During the healing ice bath, I had some Holosync music playing in the bathroom. Holosync is a great CD program to listen to and helps the mind find balance. You could use any music that helps you relax and balance your mind. Maybe you want to use some more up-tempo music in the beginning and then gradually slow down the tempo. Possibly you need the calming music to help with the fear. Use whatever music that helps you achieve maximum results.

I planned not to stay in the ice cold bath for too long. If my body started to feel numb from the cold, I was prepared to exit the water. In this case, though, I employed another technique that helped me go further with this. If you have never heard of Wim Hof or the Iceman, check out his videos on YouTube where he explains what he does with a breathing technique. He has been on TV in a tub of ice water, and with his breathing method, he can melt the ice while staying warm. I'm not saying you can easily melt the ice without a great deal of practice, but the breathing technique helps keep your focus, and it helps you stand up against the fear. Also, it helps move energy through your body, and that is the whole point of this exercise.

In my version, I used the breathing that Jeff Primack had taught at a Qigong conference in Orlando. This breathing technique helped me stay focused. Also, it helped me keep from feeling overwhelmed by the fear of the healing ice bath. The breathing is a strong focal point of strength and to do this exercise, I needed every bit of strength I could get. It was difficult climbing into the healing ice bath, but the breathing helped me move past the fear. I was surprised at how long I could stay in the cold water with the help of the breathing. The first time, I didn't stay in the ice water bath as long as I did the next time.

Step 3

Allow your body time to experience this healing ice bath process. You may find that your body starts to shake. There may be emotions and crying that appears. I ended up screaming into my hands, which at the time just seemed to be a reasonable reaction. Be very in tune with what seems and feels right to you at that moment. Your purpose should be to connect deeply with your mind and body in a very physical manner.

My reaction may be different from yours, but what matters is what happens to you. As I went through the process, I noticed my legs and the pelvic area started to shake. No, it wasn't from the cold water as much as it was my autonomic nervous system re-balancing. There is a difference because the autonomic re-balancing is generated from deep within your core, not just your skin or muscles shaking and shivering.

Connecting the breathwork with the screaming is a very powerful moving force for energy stuck in your body. You may want to connect after the screaming with some calming sounds you can make. The Holosync CD playing in the room helps me release and let go of some deeply held stuff in my mind body. It is a physical release, not just a mental release, and that is extremely important to recognize.

It is a physical body connection with the mind that, when you get to this point, moves tremendous energy through the body. When it gets to the point of autonomic re-balancing, that is when the possibility of healing begins. It does not need to be a mystical or spiritual thing as this is a normal built-in process within the biological body that we have long ignored on this planet.

As I felt my feet start to get a little numb and tingly, I began to drain the water and step out of it. Quickly grabbing a towel to keep myself from getting too cold, I started to fill the bathtub back up with hot water. I wanted to give my body something rewarding after pushing through the fears of the ice water.

Step 4

Once I had the bathtub filled up with warm water, I added about 1/3 cup of oatmeal powder. I ground oatmeal up in my NutriBullet to a fine powder for this purpose.

There is something about oatmeal that is so soothing to a rash and helps calm anger. Most over the counter products do not work, I have found, and that includes essential oils and other alternative remedies. In this case, it was a soothing thing to do after the harsh ice water.

Next, I just allowed myself to soak in the warm water. It is important to note that when you have a rash, try not to get the water too hot. Hot may feel soothing, but I've found that it can irritate the rash, so go easy on the water temperature. Make it warm enough to be comfortable, but not too hot. Combining the ice water and the hot will help the fire energy of the anger to continue to dissipate.

In this case, I just allowed myself to relax in the warm bath, and I think I zoned out for some time. I'm not sure for how long because I did not time it. It seemed as if time passed quickly, which usually happens when you're deep into that relaxation moment after pushing your body into the moment that is not comfortable.

Once completed, you'll want to make sure you rinse your tub and yourself, so the oatmeal doesn't dry and stick. Following it up with a warm shower feels good.

Results

When I got done, I felt so relaxed from this and could feel a significant shift in my energy and my body. I noticed both the rash and anger had calmed down. Overall my body felt much more at ease. I did not notice the physical difference in the rash until the next morning. At that point, I realized the irritation, itching, and pain from the rash had subsided so much. I noticed that it looked much better than it had for days.

More importantly, though, I know I was able to push a lot of anger and fire energy out of my body. I could physically feel the calmness and peacefulness in my body. Tension had drastically reduced, and my energy had shifted. This simple technique with ice water followed by warm water can help make major changes. Yes, you still need to go to the root of what has happened in your life that kicks the anger up, but body-based methods like this will greatly enhance any other work you do.

The healing ice bath worked well and helped give me some serious relief from what I was experiencing. It greatly helped reduce the anger level in my body, and I began to find some joy and peace in my day. My body and my mind were much more relaxed and at ease. Without a doubt, I could tell just how much this shifted my physical body. Since doing this, I have repeated this process to help me deal with the stress of the day that sometimes builds up.

Even though I knew about alternative healing and hydrotherapy, this experience opened my eyes. The breathing method I used in this was a significant part of the success.

No, it isn't easy getting in a healing ice bath, but the rewards outweigh the fears. This process helps connect the mind and body back together while relieving stress. It helps get rid of the fire energy that is in excess. Also, it helps balance the autonomic nervous system for optimal health.

Primal Screams

Primal screams can be excellent, and even more powerful if you can connect together the mind and body. Sometimes we all need to let out a scream, but I'm talking about something more powerful than that. If we focus on the scream, we're not fully engaging the mind and body together. However, if we can connect the physical body with the mind and then let the scream come forth, it will transform us.

Depending on the state or condition you are in, focusing on breathwork can be helpful. Using breathwork to feel and sense your body more is what you are trying to do. Sometimes just stopping to notice what is showing up in the body will help you get in touch with it. Let the feelings and senses build and come forth. They may not be pleasant, and they may be frightening. If you have a trusted friend or healer that you can do this with, it may be helpful to request their time. Make sure that they are someone that can help hold the space for you and allow this to come forth, not hinder and prevent it out of their fears or issues they struggle with in their life.

As you go into your body in a safe and comfortable room or a place without distractions, begin to allow yourself to focus on that which is coming up or causing immense anger. You might find that if you move your back, legs, or even your arms slightly in an observational manner, it might help kick things up. You might even find that you go further into the connection into your body that connects with your mind.

As the sensations or emotions build, you may feel the "fire" in your body getting more and more explosive. Allow it to come through as much as you can while keeping yourself safe. You may find that making a small sound or noise will help the fire energy to build through your vocal cords. As you do this, you might find that the automatic release of screaming happens naturally. In fact, this is more ideal than being forced because the more it can come from within you, the more powerfully connected it will be.

Sometimes just allowing yourself to make sounds such as ahhh or ohhh or whatever feels helpful will help bring forth the energy. It will build up into a scream. Let the scream come through and allow whatever feelings and emotions that appear to happen at that moment. If your body begins to shake or you feel other sensations, be an observer and watch them, notice them, and play with them. Use slow connected body movements to bring them through and help push the anger out of your body.

The scream or the body movements are not as important as how much you can connect them within your body. Your goal is to push the energy through, and not to get caught up in what it may be or how it shows up. When we analyze it, we're in the ego which is not helpful. Let go of the ego and be at one with it, playing like a toddler just discovering their body, movement, or the sounds they make.

Enteric Brain Work

Located in the abdomen is the enteric brain which often is referred to as a second brain. This region of your body does so much for your emotional and mental health. Many of the substances produced in this area of the body are like Valium or Xanax. While they may not be these specific substances, like them they help us deal with pain and stress. The enteric brain or gut-brain produces approximately 95% of these substances.

If your gut-brain is out of balance, it will impact so much in your life, not to mention your digestive system. We use the gut-brain or the enteric brain to do so much. Often, we refer to making decisions with our gut or listening to our gut. You can have a major influence on your emotional and mental health by learning how to work in this area. Of course, the more you can learn to connect internally in the body with this area, the more impact it will have.

Too many of us do not fully connect with the body. We give lip service that we do, and we know the jargon of saying the right words. However, the more you go into it and sense and feel, the more you will find that the body is a magical place of healing. Far too often we avoid feeling in the body, and we create all kinds of beliefs and rules and processes about what it means to feel in the body, rather than doing it. The process I have gone through in my life is about learning and teaching myself to go deep into the body. It is more than meditation. It is more than mindfulness.

Dr. Paul Canali taught me how to work through anger, and access the enteric brain, by using a fitness ball. Find one that is not very heavy. Even a two-pound fitness ball can be more than enough for you. Find a fitness ball that can easily fit within your hands, or one you can get your hands around. It should be large enough that you can work with it and not so firm that it feels uncomfortable. You need some pliability in it for it to move in the way that is effective.

Take the fitness ball and place it on your abdomen. With one hand (or even two hands), begin to move it around very slowly. You will want to vary the pressure and speed. You are using the fitness ball to observe and identify what is going on underneath the ball. Your goal is to feel what is happening below the spot where the ball is in your hands.

Movements in this work are very slow. Imagine that you are taking a magnifying glass or a microscope and attempting to see everything, through feeling, that lies underneath the fitness ball. If you think about the magnifying glass or microscope, you know that you need to move them slowly or you will not see much through the lens. As you move it around in your lower abdomen, feel for any areas that feel tight, tense, uncomfortable, or painful. You may need to vary the depth and pressure, but all of it is a sense of play in that area.

The first time you do this, you may not feel as much as subsequent times. Be patient with this technique. It will take you time to develop your senses and what you feel in your hands and through the fitness ball. Even if you do not think you're feeling very much, continued practice of it will help develop this language of connection between your mind and body.

Use your breath as you move it around and play with the depth and pressure and intensity. Breathwork helps amplify what is going on here. Make sure it is slower deep breaths, not rapid or shallow. You might want to play with the difference between the two types of breath, but the more slow, deep, and connected your breath is to what you are doing, the more power you have. Most humans breathe too little and too shallow, so anything that helps us connect to this is beneficial for the body.

When you find a place that is painful, tight, tense, or uncomfortable, try to hang out there for a few seconds, using your breath to connect to it. You can use your mind to help think about letting go or softening in this area. There is no need to analyze what is going on, as you need to be in the observer mode. Your goal is to connect and feel it, but not to the point where it is overwhelming.

If it gets too difficult to stay there, ease the ball off this area and feel the difference between the two moments. What did it feel like while you held the ball in that place and what does it feel like when you remove the ball from this area? You can play with putting it there and moving it away to help build up the healing language of connection.

Much of our healing comes when we sense and observe the stress in the body, and then when we let go or shift our place of focus and attention. You can always return to this place but make sure you don't force yourself into the discomfort. Allow it to happen, because by allowing it, you are observing. There is no judgment or ego at that moment, and the more we allow it, the more things can change and shift.

Play with the enteric brain work because if you do just a little bit every day, you'll be amazed at how this gets you to connect much deeper in your mind and body. It will also help you deal with stress, anger, mental, and physical issues. Don't overdo it because a little work in this area is a lot of work. The saying "less is more" is very key here. The key is not to solve every issue in one session, but to feel and sense as much as you can, allowing yourself to let go. Feeling and sensing help build awareness which brings a greater consciousness.

As you begin to learn how to work with the enteric brain, you may find that a two-pound ball will not be enough. Advance to a heavier ball and play around with how both of those feel. Also, you can also use your hand and fingers to do much of the same work, but use the ball to get a good feeling for it first. Get the technique of truly listening to the language of connection and sensing before going off in a million different directions.

There is so much more information available these days on the enteric brain. Much of it talks about what it is, but not much goes into the understanding of the deep body connection like I have learned. Play and experiment because the more you do, the more you will be rewarded. Knowledge is helpful, and the science behind it is crucial, but feeling and sensing in the body helps change our biology.

Large Fitness Ball

Sometimes when anger arises, I find myself just needing to pound things. Unfortunately, my anger sometimes comes out where those close to me witness it, and then it impacts them. I inadvertently hurt them without realizing it. One of the quick ways to lessen anger is to go and get one of those large fitness balls. I have one that I can put between my knees and that works perfectly for me.

I have a room where I can go and shut the door and get away from others in the house. I'll lay down on my back on my massage table and put this large fitness ball between my knees. I push in with my knees against the ball to hold it tight as I bend my knees and legs towards me.

While doing this, I begin pounding the daylights out of the fitness ball. If I can bring up sounds, tones, and screams, I engage those. I pound away as hard as I can, letting go of as much anger and frustration as I can at that moment.

By using the fitness ball held within my legs and drawing them towards me, I am engaging the body and the mind together. While this method is helpful to release some momentary anger, it does not go as far as some of the other techniques if I am by myself. However, with the right person assisting, you may be able to stay conscious and move much more energy out of the body.

Using the fitness ball is not the key here as much as getting in touch with the physical side of anger and allowing it to come out safely. Sometimes it just feels good to me to pound that ball. Generally, it doesn't take much time, but after it is over, I allow myself to rest. I feel and sense everything I can, and whatever happens in my body or whatever happens that I can feel, I allow to take place.

Massage

One of the things that has helped me the most is massage. Of course, not all bodywork out there is alike, and some methods are far more effective than others. Let me start on the topic of massage for anger and other body issues, since I am a licensed massage therapist.

Massage can help reduce anxiety and chronic pain from stress and issues in our emotional world. However, massage does not often go far enough, or the therapist does not sense or feel to the degree needed. Some therapists are good at holding the space, but I have found far too many unconsciously bring their agenda to the table, rather than holding the space. Often, it requires that a therapist has healed themselves deeply to be fully present with someone on the table.

Sometimes people think that the only thing that heals them or helps them is deep pressure. As a massage therapist, I've had so many people beg me to go deep into their body where it would push me beyond the safe point if I did. Most people cannot feel in their body like they think they do and I'm not referring to pain. I'm referring to feeling and observing what is within the body.

I'll never forget one massage practitioner I traded sessions with that wanted me to apply very deep pressure into his body. He was used to doing deep work on others and claimed he was fine with it on himself. As I started to work on him, I stopped at the point where I did not feel comfortable. He kept pushing me to go further, saying he was fine with it and he was guiding me. Like a fool, I listened to him. The next day he told me that he was bruised and sore. It is not a result you want. He finally admitted to me that he didn't realize just how deep I was going. I learned from that experience that if I don't feel comfortable, I stop no matter who the person is or what they say. It taught me a valuable lesson on how much we don't sense in the body, even when we think we do.

I am not saying there is no need for deep pressure, but often when that is all someone can feel, they are very numb in their body. I've seen it a million times. In these moments, a form of light pressure or light touch that brings the body into feeling can help them connect and move further than forcing your way into the body. It is all about the sense and touch, but when it comes to anger, you've got to reach the point where you go beneath the numbing and avoidance. Otherwise, you're just applying a Band-aid to a gushing wound and acting as if you have miraculously cured the body.

When the body is showing anger outwardly, there is a part of it that is numbing and avoiding what you cannot see. It hides the pain or experience below the anger, and the anger is the wall to keep you out. I've felt it in a body where the more you push into it, the resistance is almost saying "NO – STAY OUT." In cases like this, no one wins with deep pressure. If the body doesn't want you to go in, you're not doing yourself or the person any good. Anger is there for a reason and until you recognize that, it will lock you out. If you can get underneath it, past the layer that avoids and numbs the experiences generating the anger, you'll be far more effective than basking in numbing and unconsciousness.

The bodywork that is the most healing often is the work that helps you go in and sense and connect, then work to let it go and release it. Some techniques keep you feeling on the surface, but not deep within and so the results are only temporary. Learning to be grounded in your body and feel it from the innermost depths will bring about lasting change. Deep pressure may be required to help kick things up, but only when there is a connected point between the mind and body.

One of the things I use on myself is a form of deep pressure massage at my local mall. It took me a long time to be able to love that type of work. In the beginning, it was far too triggering and would only push the anger to the surface, but I didn't know how to deal with it. I also realize that not all deep pressure massage therapists are alike, just like with Swedish massage or any other modality. However, I found a therapist at the mall that I can connect with through my breathing, and I can push some major amounts of anger through my body because I can stay grounded to what he is doing.

In the past, I've used modalities like Trager® which can be helpful, but they often don't go far enough. They are good at helping to bring the body down, but not necessarily for moving through the emotional components. With many repeated treatments, they can help you achieve so much, but it is only half of the equation. If combined with more intense body-based techniques, the power is greatly enhanced.

This brings up a good point in dealing with anger. If you only bring it up to the surface, you are going to make the person's life miserable. If there is no way for them to move through it and find some relief, they are not going to love life in the least. Too many modalities and therapists do this, which almost cements trauma further in the mind body connection and results in little hope. Without hope that you can resolve this, you are setting the body and the mind up for failure. You're forcing the anger to go deeper and bury itself further, which makes it all the harder to heal and release.

Without taking the person into what is trying to come out, they will not find the deep peace that comes after that has happened. We all think we know what deep peace is, but it is much more than anyone realizes. When you experience this level of peace, your eyes will open in amazement. You will in no way want to come out of that peaceful place. I know very few people that can help bring me to this point. It is much deeper than meditation or mindfulness or relaxation.

Unified Therapy™ With Dr. Paul Canali

This entire topic could be a book, but so much of my experience and what I am sharing is a result of the work by Dr. Paul Canali. When I first found him, my body knew immediately and instinctively that he understood concepts I did not comprehend. I knew I needed his help.

In the beginning days, I did not realize just how much I had not healed. Each therapy session has been a progression to the next moment of healing and realization. It is like peeling an onion. Each layer removed gives a glimpse into what is below it.

The anger I have struggled with comes from the torture and trauma I endured. It also came from the fact that I never learned the skills to deal with what was going on in my life. Dr. Paul Canali, through his work, has helped me resolve so much of this trauma and torture. We still deal with the anger that I harbor deep within my body, but that is a continual process. With each session, we go a little further into the deeper layers of healing.

Often, we think that if we go in and do a little work, the healing part of life is over. I can tell you from firsthand experience that this is not the case. Healing is a progression of going in and feeling, confronting what is there and finding a way to move through it. As we do that, it is not an endpoint, but a moment of awareness and consciousness that gives rise to something deeper and more profound. If we stop there, we might gain a little of what we need, but if we use these moments to go deeper, we will discover truths, awareness, and consciousness that is beyond our wildest imagination.

The point we need to focus on with anger is how we go to the source and root of it in the body. The more we miss this key point, the more we will struggle. We end up chastising ourselves because the mind cannot stand up to the onslaught of energy from the anger.

Finding a therapist that allows you to go in and release the anger that is building up is valuable. I know very few that I can do this with that don't try to shame me or manipulate me into their way of thinking. Far too many want you to be happy because your anger and emotions often connect with unhealed parts within themselves. It makes them feel uncomfortable, even if they are not aware of this consciously, and it becomes too difficult for them to be in this space.

The more you tell people to think happy thoughts or just let go of their anger, the more harm you are inflicting upon them. Yes, they may need to do that, but without the tools and skills to do this, you're sentencing them to a life of internal torture. All the memes about anger that are spread online or spoken between people do far more damage than we realize.

If you're feeling angry, I say GO RIGHT AHEAD! Now I'm not saying direct that anger on to other people where it causes them damage and harm. Use that anger to help find your way through whatever emotional trigger or memory or energy blockage in your mind body is there. Use one of the methods I've described to let it out in a safe way.

Don't fear the anger, but instead use it to propel you forward. Use it to help enact the changes in your body and mind that you need to become more than you are. Anger impacts your relationships in all aspects of your life. The key is not to avoid and numb, but to feel and heal. The more we let go of it, the more we heal from it.

It is healthy to recognize anger and learn how to handle it appropriately. Hiding from it or ignoring it and hoping it will just go away is very unhealthy behavior that will only cause psychological and physical issues on down the road. Anger impacts us biologically, mentally, energetically, emotionally, and spiritually.

There are many ways to deal with anger and what may work for one person may not work for another. The important part is that you work to find healthy and appropriate ways to deal with the anger, rather than just letting it hide in the closets of your life. Learn the skills necessary for you to express anger in positive ways, not hold it in where it reaches the boiling point of harm to others.

Anger comes from within the body. The mind only translates what we feel inside. Before it reaches the mind, it has already sparked and set off from its origin in the body. Deep within is where we need to go in dealing with anger that is such an epidemic in the world. We have far too many pasting the smiles on their faces, rather than feeling in the body. I hope that we will reverse this course because if we don't, we are headed on a collision path that will bring us to calamity with the health of this world.

Try This Exercise

From the examples of dealing with anger in this chapter, see which one resonates with you and give it a try. If you don't succeed at first, give it another try and then write about the experience. Take note of how your body feels before and after. Pay special attention to how your body may shift during these exercises or if you notice something more significant.

Check out the companion CD to this book,

Mind Body Meditation Exercises.
The exercise on "Enteric Brain" corresponds to this chapter.
https://MindBodyMeditationExercises.com

18. Healing Is Hard Work

*"It (healing) involves the harmonious alignment of the physical, emotional, mental, and spiritual aspects of our being and how we relate to the world. The result is a greater experience of wholeness, wellness, and soundness." – **Dr. Donald M. Epstein, D.C.***

One of the reasons that healing doesn't go far enough with most people, I believe, is that it is hard work. You'd rather do other things than dig around in the skeletons of your life's closet.

I often find myself wishing for anything that would be better than going through the healing stuff. It is hard work and requires commitment and courage. In order to heal, it requires that you don't give up.

You didn't ask for it. You didn't ask to have to deal with all of this in life, or at least I don't recall that I did. It is something we were often forced into that made us into who we are at this moment. Well, okay, it is not necessarily the complete picture of who we are or all that we can be.

At times when I think back to the early days of healing, I can barely believe I made it this far. I didn't have a choice unless I wanted to stay paralyzed and struggling to do basic things for the rest of my life. I had to go into the healing to survive and get my life back. After all, the conversion disorder had robbed me of so much and had almost taken the last breath from me. There was no choosing to heal or not in my life, only how far I wanted to go. Conversion disorder and paralysis were big motivators for me.

I didn't even know in those early days what healing meant or where it would take me. I didn't know there was a journey or a path I would walk down into my own healing. It didn't dawn on me that healing was possible. In the early days, I didn't know if I wanted it or if I could even begin to do it.

I had no clue how to heal or get my life back. It was all too confusing and mind-boggling. I felt like someone who had no functioning brain who was somehow supposed to find their way back into life again. The first step to healing evaded me, and I was nothing more than a deer frozen in the headlights. No one gave me an instruction manual on how to heal my life or where to begin.

All I knew was I wanted to walk normally again. I wanted to move my hands and take care of myself again. I wanted to get my memory back, my speech back, and everything that I used to do. The odds were against me. The medical staff was not sure that I could return to normal. I badly wanted to prove them wrong! It was another powerful motivator in my life.

My energy level at the time stayed maxed out in exhaustion. My brain looked at things very slowly, and even that was a struggle of epic proportions. I understood very little. I didn't feel much physically. It was all a mystery that left me feeling like little more than roadkill along life's journey.

Back in 1991, there were no internet message boards and no social media to connect with other people struggling with the same thing. You were pretty much on your own, and while that was difficult, I didn't get indoctrinated into things that served very little usefulness. I had to sort through what I could find and understand in the limited resources I could access. More importantly, I had to listen to my body, my mind, and my gut reactions to things.

It turned out to be one of the best things, I believe, that helped me heal because it set me on the path where I needed to go. I could have easily stayed stuck in what my current situation was, and no one would have questioned me. People would have understood.

By not having the connection to other people who were suffering, it helped me turn inward to find where I needed to go. When I did that, I discovered that the healing I needed had to come from within my mind and my body.

No, I wasn't aware of all of this at that moment, and I had no idea what I needed to do, but now as I look back, my life was directed in the right direction. Far too often, we see the limits of our current moment, rather than what is beckoning us to a greater journey.

I Had To Be Willing To Try Things

I had to be willing to try things and venture outside of my comfort zone into anxiety, despair, agony, and depression. I had to give up what I knew and what made sense to see if I was going to find my way. I found that so much of what I thought was true in life was an illusion holding me back. It was keeping me captive in a world that prevented my healing. Many that are struggling do not grasp this key point in life.

In the early days of healing, I focused on putting one foot in front of the other. Because of the paralysis from the conversion disorder, normal movements that everyone takes for granted became a difficult but promising accomplishment in a day. Lifting my hand up and feeding myself was a big deal. So, figuratively and literally, I was learning how to put one foot in front of the other. The only way to do that was to try. Yes, I failed many times, but the more I failed, the more I learned what not to do. I learned through the difficult moments what things worked and what did not. The limitations were frustrating moments every day, but I learned how to accept what I could do and let go of that which I could not.

Being able to sit up in bed and roll over easy was like an all-time accomplishment in those days. In physical therapy, being able to take that first step as I held on to the walking bars for dear life, was like a child taking their first step. I had been able to do all these things not long before the paralysis of conversion disorder.

Walking to the bathroom from the hospital bed was the next major accomplishment. Then walking down to the end of the hallway in the hospital felt like I had once again found freedom. I learned that the little accomplishments helped me achieve greater things in my life. It was another motivating factor in my healing. We often forget that it is in the little successes that we find greater healing.

Yes, there would be many more of these difficult moments and accomplishments, but even though I did not realize it at the time, I was making major strides in my own healing. It didn't look like what I thought healing should be. It just felt like stuff that I had to do. Sometimes it felt like pure exhaustion and pain and difficulty that would never end. In those moments, it was laying the groundwork for moments where I could look back and realize how much I had healed my life.

Sometimes healing doesn't happen in the way we expect it to go, and it does not hold up a neon sign announcing we are healing. Often the brain doesn't allow us to see it as it critiques and criticizes our every move that we do. It is in those moments that we don't recognize we are hanging on, we are healing.

We must find the courage to tell the critical parts of our brains, fears, anxiety, and depression that we are healing. We must convince ourselves because what we tell ourselves and believe is what truly matters in our healing.

Many Things Will Try To Hold Us Back

There are plenty of things out there that will try their hardest to hold us back. Much of this comes from within the mind, more so than from anyone else. From the voices playing the old tapes over and over in the brain, to what our families say, to what society thinks, many may mean well but don't act in our best interest. We must not give in, but we must not close ourselves off from truths and discoveries that may help us.

Your wounded self will work its hardest to convince you that you cannot heal. It will tell you emphatically that you can't heal, and all of this is just too hard to do. It will tell you and try to convince you that you've already healed, and moving on is all you need to do.

While I was living a lie inside, it was easy to put on the happy face and convince everyone that knew me that I was okay. However, I had not moved on. Instead, I had numbed and disconnected. I had covered everything up. In my mind, I had myself believing things were not that bad because everyone else goes through stuff. I was not even in touch with the toxic poison buried deep within me.

We do our best to put on a good front to the world even though we are a mess inside and falling apart. I know I did that. All my friends thought I was the one that had it all together. I had them and myself so fooled. Thinking like this almost cost me my last breath.

Yes, we all know that stress and trauma affect the physical body. While we know it to be true or present, we ignore it. We flee from this as if it is a weird uncle talking crazy at a family dinner.

What happens in the physical body is a direct result of what is going on in the mind, in our emotions, and every other part of our being. The more we hide and numb the stuff, the more it builds up within the body. One day, the body will not be able to contain it, and that's when you'll come front and center with what stress and trauma have done to the mind and physical body.

These days, everyone is learning the mind-body jargon and will agree with many of the things I've stated, but very few have connected with it in the body. The body experience and connection are the crucial parts that are missing in our world and our healing. We know how to talk the talk, but not how to walk the walk.

We want to heal, but we are weary of thinking about the hard work that it will take. We don't completely believe that we are always worth it, or it is in our best interest. The wounded self tries to take control. Our words may say we want to heal, but our actions may be slow to unfold.

Unfortunately, our fears dropkick us right back into the hole of despair we find ourselves in every day.

Healing is by no means an easy task. It is challenging in the best of times and draining in the worst of times. Healing can be exhausting, paralyzing, and depressing. It shakes you to your core and shakes the foundation of your life upon which you stand. To reclaim your life and get back more of who you are, healing is the only way to move forward. You can try to circumvent it or escape it, but going into it is the only road I've found past what I have experienced.

It might sound like there is little hope in healing because it is too much. Some days it is easy to feel that way because it can be overwhelming. If you are like me, you've been there, done that, and gotten far too many t-shirts as souvenirs. However, know that the struggles you're now facing in life that may have brought you to this moment are the ones that most likely won't fade into the sunset without demanding attention.

Once these experiences are let out of the box, almost always they can no longer go back in the box. In many ways, you reach a point where it just becomes necessary to go forward in healing, even if you must keep dragging yourself kicking and screaming in the process.

For me, it became necessary to take these steps of healing. The more I started to take steps, the more I wanted to go forward. The more I went forward, the more I understood. It was not a quick and easy process. The words I write here evolved over many years. They come because of the pain and process that unfolded in what did not seem normal to me.

As I went along, I wondered if I was truly healing or going to get better. It felt at times like I was moving backward, rather than moving forward. It felt like I was at the end of my rope many times and I wondered if it was even worth it to continue healing. Many times I had no clue in those moments. I hung on to every small strand of the rope in hopes that I would find my footing at some point. Sometimes I hear people act as if hope is an illusion and it may be, but hope was the way I found possibility through the trauma.

Some days it felt like I was going nowhere. No matter how much courage I found or how much desire to heal I had, it sometimes felt like it wasn't enough. In those moments I felt like I would never get there, wherever there was. It felt like it was more than I could tackle. I questioned just how much of this I wanted to do.

I've learned over the years that I wasn't alone in all of this. I've seen it countless times, by so many, that I believe it is just part of the process of healing. I'm not saying it is a fun part, but it is part of it. Every day, people face these same moments, and it takes all the strength, courage, and determination to make it through the horrible times of healing.

In those moments, there is much more going on than we realize and understand or see. There are many neural pathways, I believe, that are beginning to rewire themselves and find different paths than what they have known. It is like a computer going in and reorganizing its complete file structure and doing clean up on files that are no longer necessary. It takes time.

Taking Care Of Ourselves

Sometimes in those moments, we need to remember to take care of ourselves. It is easy to head into the healing and become so motivated by healing everything all at once that we exhaust ourselves. We forget self-care. We forget that if we train the mind and body in all that helps us, we're going to progress in healing our lives. Sometimes by slowing down and taking a rest, we enable ourselves to grab on to more strength and power and courage that we will need in the next steps of healing.

It can be helpful to chart our course along the way, even with the things that we feel are so insignificant. As I did with my chart showing the little steps and recognizing the fears and boulders that held me back, it can be helpful in moments when it feels too difficult to take another step. Being able to go in and visually see that and reconnect with all these little steps can be so empowering. Whatever way works for you is essential. Record those little steps you take, no matter how unimportant they may feel.

Writing journals, blog posts, or creating poems can be helpful milestone markers to prove to yourself that you are making progress. I believe this was another big motivator in my healing because without these things, I focused on the misery and despair, not the possibility. As I found, don't underestimate the little things you do because they can empower and propel you further when it appears that all hope is gone.

Sometimes encouragement from those you trust is not enough. Sometimes you don't always want to listen to it. There are times you don't want to believe the encouragement that others are offering. Having these little moments to help give you proof that you're making it is like a shot of self-confidence, empowerment, and proving to yourself that you're doing it. You're kicking butt. You are healing!

For a long time on the front of my vehicle, I had a license plate sign that said, "Kicking Butt." It was my reminder that as I got in and drove and pushed forward in life, I was kicking butt in my own healing. I needed every reminder in those days that I was doing it because I worked so hard against my wounded self to prove that I was not.

These little things matter because they help make you stronger. The more you record them and the more you can go back and review them gives you strength. You can so easily see at a glance that "hey, I can do this," when all the demons in your mind are shouting that you cannot make it. I always kept my poster board (from Chapter 3) visible to me so that I could look at it every day. It was a reminder I needed.

Know that in the healing process, you will have good days and bad days. You will have gigantic steps of progress and some that are small steps. Some days you will take a couple of steps back, and that is okay. Other days you will take several steps forward. It is part of the process. I always figured that if I took three steps forward and then fell back two, I was still one step ahead. It helped me put all of this in perspective.

Often, we are just so hard on ourselves in healing, and we demand perfection. We demand complete adherence to everything that is supposed to be successful, and sometimes we miss that which is working.

We want everything to be healed and completed now, but again we're expecting gigantic miraculous feats from ourselves that no mere mortal could ever accomplish. We did not get this way overnight. Healing takes time. We will not heal overnight, but the more nights and days we work on healing, the more we will heal. It is a process that must unfold at the right time when we are ready, willing and able. If it happens too quickly, we will set ourselves back because we are not ready. If we try to supercharge it, we will most likely only exhaust ourselves causing further trauma and damage.

Healing happens when we allow it to take place and become more aware. When we've been traumatized and tortured, abused and stressed, we are blind to see what is present in our current moments. The mind tells us that we know what is going on, but our awareness and consciousness about what is truly happening is short-circuited.

It is in the process of letting it unfold that we heal and learn what we need to, so we can transform our lives from the inside out. Anything short of that is taking us away from true healing. We must become aware to see these parts of our lives and heal them from the root of where they come into existence.

You cannot get to the point of healing without trudging through the swamp and doing the work you need to do. You can't get to the high ground in the swamp without wading through it. It is through the little steps of healing that your life heals in ways you could never imagine at that moment.

It is the process that reveals so much to you through your awareness and consciousness. Without this part, you're only polishing the surface. While it may look pretty, it is what is inside that needs to be healed. The polished surface is only the outward manifestation of what happens internally. The surface is the outward manifestation of what is going on in the mind and the body.

I used to think that if I got to some arbitrary point in my healing that I would be finished. I would be complete. As I healed further and as I learned to walk again, talk again, and move again, I found out there was a world for me to experience beyond what I knew. It was not just an arrival point, but one that led me to a greater and deeper awareness of life, one that I had never seen before.

Healing takes us further into who we are and who we are meant to be. It is not a place of all that there is. While it might be for a moment, healing and growth continue to take us deeper and further if we allow them. I compare it to the peeling of an onion. You can't see the layer below until you peel off the upper layer. When you peel another layer, you see that there are more. Peeling one layer of the onion does not show the entire onion. Healing and awareness and growth are much the same way.

When the healing gets tough and hard, don't stop. Don't let yourself live an illusion thinking you have healed and your life is 100% magically better. Don't be fooled by those that claim this is true, because it is not.

Be careful not to fall into the trap that healing is what you are currently told and there is nothing beyond this moment. Medication, counseling, and therapy can take us to another level, but if we stop and embrace these things as our complete work of healing, we are short-changing possibility and potential. I did not think I would ever walk again, work again, or get major depression and anxiety under control. However, I found that there was a door beyond these points. Too many times we settle for the condition we find ourselves in rather than our total potential we cannot yet see.

Healing is about going further and not giving up. Healing is about becoming all that we truly are deep inside, not stopping because the journey gets tough. It is about shedding all those things that you believed were true in your life and seeing if they really are or if there is something better. It is about letting go of all those past experiences and hurts and pains, but realizing they brought you to the point where you are today.

We cannot deny where our journey began and how we arrived at this moment. To deny it makes us vulnerable to the voices that trick us into thinking that which is not true. Our life's journey is a part of us. Yes, it most likely was horrible if it was anything like what I experienced. However, it is now my choice to make of it what I wish to do, and it is my choice to set a new path for my life.

No matter what happened in the past or what I'm currently doing at this moment, it is still my choice and decision to move forward into healing and find all my life can be. I make that determination alone, even if my past influences what this current choice may be. It is up to me to learn and discover all I can about my life so that the choices I make are the best ones at this moment. I'm also at liberty to realize that maybe yesterday's choice was not the best, but now today I can make a new one. If I don't like today's choice, I can always make a different one tomorrow.

For years I beat myself up for things I thought I should have done or said. Little did I realize, my old self did not understand those moments the way my current self does. It was through my continued healing that I came to see the days before me in a different light than the moment I was living then. What we see as a child is not what we see as an adult and what we see as an adult is not what we see when we are a child. Even what we saw yesterday is not what we most likely will see today.

The only limits we place on our healing are what is happening in the mind and body at that moment. It is through awareness that leads to a new consciousness that we find continued healing and strength and courage. However, we must be willing to lose sight of the shore to journey into that space. We can choose to stay in the harbor if we want, but we will not discover new worlds in life if we do.

Realize that no matter what you've been through, there are others who also have experienced tremendous pain and hurt and trauma. You are not alone. Never let yourself think that you're the only one hurting, even though the depression, anxiety, and fear may work hard to get you to believe this is true.

There is a vast network of support out there these days, especially with social media and online forums. Yes, some of it is not the healthiest, but allow your gut and your mind and your body to help you find the way. Don't just listen to people because they can sound convincing. Check the support and resources out within your body and ask if it is true and helpful for you. What may be true today for your healing may change and shift as you reclaim those painful parts of your life.

Sometimes I ignore those that fail to see the big picture because it is not useful to my healing. I keep looking for the ways that resonate deep within me that show me the path forward in my life. The ways where I can see growth taking place are the points that I work further to discover and connect with in my healing. I look for the ways that help me become a better person from the inside out, not just something that polishes the surface.

We often ignore the signs within us. We're so desperately craving support and feeling like we belong that we avoid that which we feel inside and know to be true. Honor those parts of yourself and continue focusing on what works, but don't miss the healing moment because you weren't patient enough and moved on too quickly. Question everything with passion, but don't let your questioning stop you from healing.

No one knows as well as you do how to heal your life or how hard it is to heal. It is up to you and you alone to find that path. No one can tell you how to do it. They can offer advice and help illuminate the path with a flashlight, but at the end of the day, only you will know what to do. That is – if you follow what your mind and your body tell you. If you ignore those things, you will find yourself wandering as if you are lost in the fog. The hardest things I've had to learn are to listen to my body and trust my gut instincts. I often discount them because I don't trust myself enough. Healing takes place in the way that it needs to happen.

Just know that healing is something that you deserve, no matter how hard your path is or how difficult the pain was. We are much more than we currently think we are and what we see. We have much more potential than we realize. Within us, we have much more to offer our lives and others and the world than we might fathom at this moment. Never stop believing that you too will find out just how true this is and how sacred it is to connect with this in life.

Go the distance no matter how hard healing is for you. The reward is what you will gather as you continue along the path. Greater peace and joy are part of the human experience, even if that feels like a million light years away or something that hardly makes sense.

Don't stop healing. Keep taking those little steps, and soon you'll be walking further than you ever thought was possible.

Try This Exercise

Consider these questions on healing and find answers for them that fit your life.

Be as honest and conscious as you can, understanding that your ego, fears, anxiety, and insecurities will try to hide the truth from you.

Ponder the following questions.

- *What do you most want to heal?*
- *Are you ready to let go and heal it?*
- *Are you willing to do what it takes to heal?*
- *What are you covering up that prevents healing?*
- *What are your coping mechanisms?*
- *What would your life look like if it was healed?*

19. The Little Steps In Healing

"Healing leaves in its wake a sense of accomplishment, fulfillment, and empowerment. Healing involves surrendering control of our inner and outer experiences. Healing promotes wholeness... and unprovoked forgiveness." – Dr. Donald M. Epstein, D.C.

Sometimes in healing from childhood sexual abuse, trauma, or other challenges it feels like the mountain before us is too big to climb. In reality, it is the little steps that matter.

When I was facing the horrible moments of realizing all I had been through in my life, I wanted it over quickly. I wanted to be healed, and I wanted to forget. No part of it was fun or welcomed. It was pure torment and hell.

Not only did I have to live through all these horrible experiences of trauma and sexual abuse, but now in order to heal, I had to once again stare them in the face. It often felt to me as if it was a double whammy. I have known many others that felt the same way as I did.

Yes, I do want the big steps, but to get to them, I must experience the small ones. Small steps make the bigger steps.

When I was paralyzed, I wanted to walk again and, in my mind, I knew I could. I was not about to let the conversion disorder stop me in my tracks although I remember looking up at the hospital room ceiling and wondering if this was all my life would be.

The little steps to get walking included learning how to roll over and sit up. They included how to balance myself, how to get into a wheelchair, and how to use my arms to guide me so I could take a step. They included learning how to stand and hold myself up without support. Even after taking a few movements in walking, I had to learn how to go a few feet and then stop to rest. Next, I had to learn how to get to the bathroom in my hospital room which seemed like a million miles away at the time.

Soon, I was walking to the door of the room and then a few feet down the hall. The little steps I took were what got me to the point of walking regularly like I once did. There was no getting to the final result without going through the individual moments. These steps did not happen overnight, and it was a slow progression each day.

I freaked out, when I first started to have anxiety attacks. I didn't know what was happening to me, but I found myself hiding under a blanket on my couch. If I got very far outside the house, or around people, or to my job, I'd feel like I couldn't breathe. I would collapse and fall to the floor. My coworkers would lay me down on a couch at the office, and when I came to, they would take me home.

At first, the little steps included going on medication. I had no way to deal with anxiety, and so it was the only thing I could do to help get things under control. My little steps included allowing a friend to do some grocery shopping for me because being in a store more than five minutes meant I would faint and be on the floor.

The little steps included going into a store about five minutes before they closed, and the minute I felt like I could take no more, hurrying out the door. The little steps included going to therapy and group counseling to learn more how to deal with life. I limited sugar and caffeine and chocolate in my diet to help me in dealing with the anxiety, and I learned to take more time out for relaxation. Those were the small steps.

I learned to carry a small rock that was special to me in my pocket so when I felt anxious, I could grab ahold of it without anyone knowing and ground myself to it. While I didn't understand what grounding meant at the time, I knew that the rock felt safe to me. The little steps of learning that I was not going to die from an anxiety attack began to help me reframe how my mind saw these things. Without all these little steps and more, I would not have gotten to the point where I am today in my healing.

The little steps included finding someone to talk to that became one of the most beloved and helpful therapists I know. Other steps like writing and journaling helped me pour my heart out when I knew no one would see it. Meeting other survivors and getting involved in advocacy and support, plus helping to be there for others in online message boards were more of the little steps I took. Stepping up and staring FEAR down was part of my progress. There were so many little things I did, but the more I did the little stuff, I healed my life in bigger ways.

I think back to all the little steps I took and how they helped me, not forgetting the lessons they taught me. All those little steps helped give me the tools to continue my healing and become more than I thought I could be. The little steps became the tools in my toolbox.

It took many years and a lot of little steps to get to the point where I am today. However, sometimes I still have moments where the memories try to take me down. The memories of the past are horrible and the body memories are much worse. I've woken up screaming in the night. I've lost many nights of sleep and felt like a zombie most of the day because of the memories. There were moments where I would have given up my life if I thought they would end. In fact, I did try to end my life and it never helped.

In those dark moments of my attempts at suicide, I didn't believe there was a way out. I thought all was lost and nothing could change to make it any better. I didn't care if it could be better in those moments because it did not feel that way. There were many attempts and somehow, there was something that didn't allow me to succeed. My heart aches for all that have struggled with suicide and the pain for those left behind.

I Had To Let Others Be There For Me

I also had to learn to let others be there for me in those moments I could not be there for myself. It was not easy to do! There were many little steps in trying to help me see that others loved me, and sometimes to this day I still struggle with this issue. When you have faced a life of torment and trauma and abandonment, it feels like you can trust no one in your life. However, the more you push people away, the less support there is for your life.

There was a little step which turned into a big one where a friend of mine shared how her son's suicide impacted her life. It was a lightbulb moment for me because I was like, "How could I do that to the ones that love me?" If I took my life through suicide, it would cause them so much pain, and I could not do that to them. Others may see this differently but it helped me wake up and see things in a new way.

Little moments included being able to let someone hold me while I cried, not expecting me to have to open up with them about what I was facing. They looked at me through eyes of love, with no judgment, and through that experience, I realized that there was more for my life.

The little steps of being able to tell a doctor-therapist friend of mine that I struggle with these dark moments and not having judgment, but pure love and acceptance, meant the world to me. It helped me to know that if my brain started to focus on this, I could call him. He was there for me.

The little steps seem so little at times, but that's how we get to the bigger steps. Healing isn't a one-time event. Healing is not about getting there as quickly as you can. It is about doing the things to build the foundation of your life, so you can truly discover all parts of yourself.

Yes, when you're in the midst of the torment and horror, it isn't fun. It is normal to want to escape that and get past it. While you're in the middle of that process you're building up the strength and the tools you need which helps to heal the layers. It is where we begin to let go of the pain while finding the life that we were meant to live.

It is far too easy to want to bypass that and just go to the pretty rainbow after the storm. Unfortunately, a storm has the rain and wind come through before we see the rainbow. Leaving out the middle part is something that would rob us of so much of the experience.

The Little Steps Give Us Strength

I believe it is in the little steps where we find the strength to go forward and discover the way to heal. It is not an easy process for anyone, and at times I've felt like the mountains are higher than I can climb. If I think that I can only climb the mountain in one step, I'll give up before I start. If I realize that I can climb a few steps every day, it makes it much easier to accomplish.

So often, though, we miss the little steps because we are so focused on the big moment of healing. They pass us by as if they didn't exist. Years later I realized that some little moment happened. I didn't even see it at the time. It was there without me being aware of it.

Give yourself time, love, self-care, and be patient in allowing yourself to go through the little moments. I'm not going to say these times are easy because I know they are not. I will say, though, that they lay the foundation for things to come together and to get the tools you need to become more in your life.

Healing is about discovering ourselves, but it is in the little steps where we find the way to heal. It is what brings us into the answers for our lives. It is the building blocks of the foundation of the true and authentic self that was hidden when we went through the trauma and abuse.

Try This Exercise

Each day, take note of every little step you have taken in your healing. They may almost appear as if they are insignificant, but if you look for them, you will see them. Look over these weekly so you'll keep the momentum going. When you get discouraged, it will help you see your progress. Make a note of the physical issues you have, and bonus points if you can connect them to your healing progress. If we challenge the mind to see these things, we will most likely be surprised at what we might have missed.

20. What Has Worked For Me

*"Always, in order to change, we have to come to a new understanding of self and the world so that we can embrace new knowledge and have new experiences." - **Dr. Joe Dispenza, D.C.***

Often in my own healing, I've had people compare their paths to mine and exclaim, "You had it much worse than me. Your trauma is much worse than mine." While sometimes that may have been true, at the end of the day, trauma is trauma.

No matter what you've experienced or dealt with in your own life, it is your experience. It is what you know. It is for you to work through and heal, and find a way to rise above it.

Your path is different than my path or anyone else's. It makes us human and makes us unique in many ways. It becomes our struggle and our path of learning and awareness.

No one can tell you how to heal on your path. No one can tell you what it feels like because they do not walk in your same shoes. It is your path and your path alone.

However, many have walked horrible and traumatic paths that were so intense that they did not think they would make it through it. So, while we don't know what your path is like, we do know what similar things are and just how difficult they can be to overcome.

The key is not so much in sharing the exact experiences and healing paths, but having compassion and love for one another. When we do this, we offer strength and support on the parts of our journey where we connect. When we heal, we can be there more for others.

It is through the journey of the connection with one another that together we become stronger and our lives rise to new levels of awareness and consciousness. We are not as strong on our own as we are when we connect with others that help us walk through the fires of life.

There have been so many people who walked alongside me that I didn't fully appreciate until many years later. Many were there for me in small ways and big ways, but often they just seemed like another friend or acquaintance. I didn't recognize them at the time for what they were because it was just what I needed at that moment. It did not seem like anything out of the ordinary.

I'll be forever grateful to every one of these people, knowing how they provided so much support, love, friendship, and help to me even when I didn't know it. I believe they were angels walking beside me. Many were lending an ear or a hand of support through little moments that meant the world to me.

From the days when I first could hardly walk to the days when I was working hard to reclaim my body and my mind, each person has played a special and unique role in my life. I marvel at how they came into my life at the exact moments I needed them.

It is often too easy for us to miss these folks. Sometimes we shun others and push them away. Sometimes we get in our own little mindset of how things should be, and we miss the important moments of support.

We Close Our Ears And Minds

There are times when we discard things we hear and see in others because it doesn't fit our mold of what healing should be. It doesn't fit our beliefs and opinions on what should be helpful to us. We discount it as if it is hogwash. We close our ears and mind to it.

While this is part of being human and walking our own paths, we must be careful that we are not discarding something so crucial that will propel us forward. If we ignore that which can help us, how will we find the healing and support and help that we need? You cannot look away from that which is in front of you and still expect to see it.

Often there are things that I have found that have shown up in my life for a reason and sometimes I have struggled to let them in my life. Sometimes I have slammed the door on them. Later, I found out that they had something to offer me, but I was not ready for them. Sometimes those moments lay the groundwork for us to be ready for them to appear. You cannot build the house unless you lay the proper foundation first.

I'll never forget the girl who was in a wheelchair who I was trying to help at a concert. I was trying hard to be respectful, but I knew she needed help. No, I did not attempt to help her out of pity. She looked at me with scornful eyes and said, "You don't know what it is like to be in a wheelchair!"

My heart had a lump in it at that moment, and I replied back to her, "Oh but I do. I was in a wheelchair not long ago." Her eyes wanted to hide, and as they welled up with tears, she said, "Oh, I'm so sorry." Her heart melted a little that day, and I'll never forget her. We push people who are helping us away far too easily. I know, because I've done the very same thing.

Yes, some people have ulterior agendas, but some of us want to be there as much as we can for others. Some of us help from the point of compassion coming from deep within our hearts. Be careful about pushing others away too quickly because you might be making your healing that much harder.

Be careful in thinking others don't understand you, because they might see more than you can at this moment. I saw something the other day where a person was lashing out so hard at people who they thought did not understand what it was like to deal with their issues. Instead of trying to help someone else understand or maybe give new possibility to their paradigm, they slammed the door. In this case, the person wished that someone else would experience the same pain so they would understand. My heart was saddened when I saw that because I would never wish my experiences on anyone.

It is easy to give up. It is easy to crawl in our little cave and hide, keeping the world at arm's length, but in those moments, we are making our own lives much more difficult. Sometimes we want to give up, but sometimes, other people are there right when we need them. Treasure them as gifts, not as something to scorn.

As you've read through this book, you most likely understood that no matter what, I did not give up. I could have given up so many times in my life and throughout my healing. You've read about some of the moments when I almost gave up and nearly did not make it.

There are moments when I am angry for all that I endured, but somehow deep inside of me, I know there is more to the story than I even understand at this moment that I am writing. At one time, you could not have convinced me of this, and I would have laughed in your face. However, now I see that the more I heal my life and share that with the world, the more I'm touching others and helping them heal.

Challenge Your Beliefs To The Core

It is too easy to go through life wrapped in our beliefs and opinions and views of how everything should function. I'm not telling you to discard those completely, but I am begging you to challenge them to the core. Some are worthy of your life, and some need to be reworked until they are.

We are taught so much from the day we are born, and much of it is not helpful to how we endure life and how we find our way through the difficult moments. It doesn't necessarily mean we should blame our parents, but we must recognize that they weren't taught either and so they taught us what they knew – good or bad. It has been a tough lesson for me to begin understanding. I'm not letting them off the hook for what they did to me, but I realize that I now must teach the little child within what was not taught to me. It is up to me to do this, and no one else can do this for me.

Often our consciousness and awareness prevent us from learning and seeing and discovering all that is out there. We use it to hide behind, rather than to challenge ourselves to heal. It is easier that way, of course, because if you don't confront anything in your life, you can just keep presenting the pasted-on smile to everyone you meet. We are often masters of fooling ourselves and others.

Unfortunately, the more we stay stuck in who we have always been, the more we limit what we can be. When we limit what we can be, we limit what we offer the world, and we hold the world back. I firmly believe that our lives impact the entire world more than we realize. It is either positively or negatively and sometimes that shifts from day to day.

To uncover and unearth our lives is to find so much that not only helps us grow and heal but puts us in touch with who we are and all that we can be. If we keep our eyes closed, there is no more that we can discover. We end up existing at that moment as if this is all life will be.

It took me a long time to put together what the mind and body connection meant for my life. The physical paralysis of the conversion disorder and the way it unfolded in the early days showed me this without a doubt. I know that taking my first step and making the conscious decision to talk to someone, asking for help, was no coincidence. You can no longer convince me that it was.

If I had not begun to make the connection to all that I had been through with what was happening in my body, I would not have made it this far. Even in those early days, I didn't connect the entire breadth of what I had experienced. I just knew I had been through stuff, but I could not articulate it.

Don't Stand In The Way Of Discovery

The thing is, I did not stand in the way of discovery. I did not stop myself from becoming aware of it no matter how hard it was. It was extremely difficult in the early days. I remember looking up at the ceiling of my hospital room wondering if, at 26 years of age, this was all I could expect for the rest of my life. You want to talk about being confronted with the depths of what it means to be in a human body, try being at this moment. It is an eye-opener.

If you want to have life smack you hard up against the head, put yourself in the position I was in during the conversion disorder. Life was coming to an end. My body was shutting down, and no one knew how to bring me back. It wasn't up to anyone to bring me back. I had to make the conscious choice that I wanted to come back.

There was no roadmap to healing for me. There was no one telling me how to heal and what to do and how to do it. In those early days, there was no internet support group for what I was experiencing. I found very few knowledgeable and enlightened people that could provide the light along the dark path I was walking.

I had to pick up every rock along my path and see what it held underneath. Some of the rocks were meaningful, and some were not. Most were heavy to lift. People were saying many different things, and some were helpful, but others took me into a moment of chasing pretty rainbows.

I learned throughout all my healing to judge in my body what was helpful and what was not. Long before I met Dr. Paul Canali, I learned to evaluate things, and if they had a lasting body effect upon me, I knew there was something to them. I pursued those with my eyes looking ahead to what they might connect me to in life.

Each moment led me to the next moment. Each new insight provided a piece to build upon for the future. The ones that didn't offer much in the way of impacting deep healing within my physical body, I would thank for showing up and allow to move on.

No matter what, I did not stop searching. No matter what, I didn't give up. I kept looking and discovering as I kept my eyes open. I tried hard to recognize when my own beliefs and concepts that I had been taught were getting in my way.

Sometimes I sat down and rested for a while. Sometimes I traveled at breakneck speed, and sometimes I sat in confusion and despair and hopelessness. At some point, even in the moments when I felt like I was getting nowhere, I would find some rock to grasp on to in my path. Maybe I had missed a rock that I thought was not there previously.

Maybe the storms had not washed the dirt off the path enough for me to see a stone right before my eyes.

We sometimes are our own worst enemies, holding us back from healing, growth, and awareness. We think that we must have all the answers immediately. We think we need to be able to solve every issue in one moment. Patience is not something we long for at times.

Healing is not a step one, two, three process that unfolds in seven day's time. It is a process of discovery and healing, followed by peace and often moments of struggle which lead to further healing and discovery. It is an ebb and flow situation where we go into things and where we pull back. It is a process that unfolds with time.

The more we discover, the more we become aware. The more aware we become, the more we discover. It is through learning how to open our eyes to see all that is before us, that we begin to see more.

The physical realities of the trauma that I have been through still haunt me at times. They are ghosts that lurk in the dark shadows waiting for the opportune time to strike, when I feel the most vulnerable. If I get lost in the pretty rainbows, rather than going in and feeling the trauma that I've been through in a very physical way, then I've sentenced my life to more pain.

If I can go in and shake hands with all the trauma that haunts me in my mind and MY BODY, then I have the opportunity to reclaim the energy it has robbed from me. I have the possibility of learning from it so that on my next leg of the journey, I can go further and farther. Please note the emphasis on the body part of this equation because it is lacking in our healing modalities, methods, procedures, and beliefs.

It is not something we only do from the mind. The mind is very critical in healing from trauma, but without the body engaged, it is like sitting on a chair with only two legs. You might be able to balance it, but without all four present, you're going to struggle to sit upright.

I did not understand how important the physical body and felt sense were in my healing until I met Dr. Paul Canali. He has taught me so much, and through all my healing sessions with him, I now understand that the cells remember much more than we often accept in life. We turn our awareness and consciousness off to this by putting our own Band-aids of our beliefs over the wounds and pains. We must expose what is there with the light of truth, not the ignorance of our beliefs and opinions.

Even as we find healing from the most difficult situations, we will soon discover that there are layers to healing. Once you peel back one layer, you'll see another. You can't see that layer until you've peeled the outer layer off first. You know it is there because it gives substance to your life, but you can't see it until you peel it.

Healing is not a one-time event. It is not a level you reach. It is not a place where you say, "I'm all done, and that is that." At least in my view, it does not happen that way. It is a process of going in and discovering more, and through that discovery, you see further.

After going through the trauma that I did as a kid, I often despise it and hate it, and it angers me. Anyone would feel the same way, most likely. However, now in my life, I am beginning to see what a gift it was and through that gift, I see the world in a way that many don't. I see beyond the physical pain of others and connect with that which is impacting their own mind and body connection.

No, I don't wish trauma on anyone, but I know that for my life I have discovered it has helped me connect with compassion to so many. It has helped me be there for others when they felt like there was no one else. It has helped me have an awareness of what is possible, and not just saying it as words, but knowing it deep within me.

I cannot tell you what will work for you in your healing and life that will bring about greater awareness. What has worked for me is a lot of little things coming together, challenging me and my beliefs until I let go and discovered so much more.

I can tell you that the sum total of all that we know in this world to heal trauma and change our lives is just beginning to come into view. People such as Dr. Paul Canali, Dr. Peter Levine, Dr. John Sarno, Dr. Joe Dispenza, Dr. Bessel Van Der Kolk, and Mike Lew have all played important roles in helping me see what I have seen.

Many have part of the process figured out, but there are some, as mentioned above, who demonstrate through their work that they are truly helping change lives. The life-changing work they do is not just mind oriented but from the deep core of the body. I cannot emphasize enough the body part of healing and overcoming challenges.

Too many will give every excuse and chase pretty rainbows to heal, but true healing comes from going deep into your body and connecting to all that is there. It requires no judgment, but pure openness and allowing it to show up. As you move that energy through, and out of your body that has been trapped by trauma and life's experiences, you become alive and vibrant. You become the possibility of so much more.

I hope that as you have read this book, you take everything I learned and have experienced and see if you can find a way to apply it to your own life. Don't stop at what I have discovered. Take what I've learned and push it to the limits. Challenge your beliefs and awareness in the context of what I have discovered. Push it further and farther than you think is possible.

The world depends upon each one of us to be all that we can be. The more we hold ourselves back, the more we allow darkness to flourish in this world, causing more pain and trauma. It is through each one of us opening our eyes to the light of truth that makes it much harder for the darkness of trauma to exist.

My heart goes out to every person that reads this book. I know the struggle of overcoming challenges, trauma, and pain in life. I also know that there is healing and hope and a life that reaches far beyond this moment.

The inhabitants of our world are hurting deeply. There has been pain and evil inflicted upon the innocent in ways that are almost too difficult to share. I write this book to help be a light in the darkness, and I hope that you will keep pushing your life into healing so that you too are a light in the darkness.

Together we are stronger when we go inside and confront the shame, darkness, and pain we have experienced. Let us find that deeper connection to healing through the body and the mind, and in the process help the world overcome challenges it faces.

The journey continues.

Try This Exercise

Now, it is time to share your story. Feel free to contact me and share what you've done to heal your life. With permission, I'll gladly post it on my website. By helping others, we help ourselves. When we share what has worked for us, we offer valuable help to others. I have found, though, it is far too easy to preach to others, but what is powerful is when we share our vulnerability in our experiences. The experiences are like gold to others struggling to find their way.

www.OvercomingAMysteriousCondition.com

Can You Help Me?

Thank you for taking the time to read Overcoming A Mysterious Condition. If you enjoyed it, please consider telling your friends or posting a short review. Word of mouth is an author's best friend and I appreciate it so much.

Thank you.
Don Shetterly

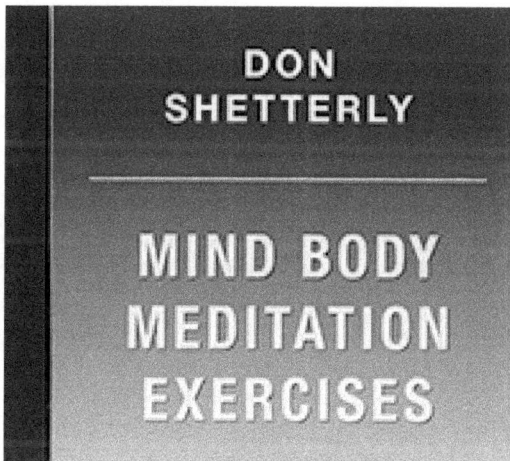

Please check out the companion CD to this book,

Mind Body Meditation Exercises.

For More Information, go to
https://MindBodyMeditationExercises.com

Additional Resources

- **Companion CD**
  Mind Body Meditation Exercises – Companion CD to this book.
  https://MindBodyMeditationExercises.com

- **Mind Body Thoughts**
  Website – Learn more about mind-body healing, awareness, and consciousness. Created by Don Shetterly.
  https://MindBodyThoughts.com

- **Evolutionary Healing Institute**
  Website of Dr. Paul Canali on Unified Therapy™, a new model for healing pain disorders, anxiety, PTSD, and sports injuries.
  http://www.EvolutionaryHealingInstitute.com

- **Integrative Bodywork**
  Website of Jim Fazio, LMT, CSI, UTP. – A wealth of information on trauma, pain, and anxiety as Jim incorporates Unified Therapy™ into his healing practice.
  http://www.JimFazioIb.com

- **The Courage To Heal**
  Book By Ellen Bass - One of the first books I read when I started dealing with child abuse. I was fortunate to hear her speak at a VOICES conference. ISBN 0-06-096931-8

- **Victims No Longer**
  Book By Mike Lew - His book helped me as a male survivor of child sexual abuse. I was fortunate to be able to interview him for a VOICES newsletter article. (Victims Of Incest Can Emerge Survi-vors). Check out his other books. ISBN 0-06-097300-5

- **Waking The Tiger**
  Book By Dr. Peter Levine - I was introduced by Dr. Paul Canali to Dr. Peter Levine's work and this book. It is an excellent resource for healing trauma in the body. ISBN 1-55643-233-X

- **The Body Keeps The Score**
  Book By Dr. Bessel Van Der Kolk - Many of the things he writes about in the book help me make sense of the experiences I have been through. ISBN 978-0-670-78593-3

- **Breaking The Habit Of Being Yourself**
  Book By Dr. Joe Dispenza - I love the books by Dr. Joe Dispenza because they helped me see that we can rewrite and change who we are. ISBN 978-1-4019-3808-6

- **All The Rage**
  Documentary by Michael Galinsky - I was introduced to Dr. John Sarno's concepts through Dr. Paul Canali. This documentary tells the story of Dr. Sarno and the story of pain. http://AllTheRageDoc.com

- **The Fear Poem**
  Poem By Joy Harjo - One of the best poems I know that has helped my healing journey in ways that are hard to describe. http://joyharjo.com

- **Songs For The Inner Child**
  CD By Shaina Noll - I used these songs to help me convince myself that I was more than I could see. https://www.shainanoll.com

- **Adverse Childhood Experiences**
  (ACE Study) from the Centers For Disease Control (CDC). https://www.cdc.gov/violenceprevention/acestudy/index.html

Please check out the following page for more resources.

https://OvercomingAMysteriousCondition.com/resources

Index

Abundance 191
Abuse 17·20·37·39·51·66·
73·76·77·78·80·81·
114·122·237·240·
253
Abused 19·20·24·37·72·
169·171·173·231
ACE study 254
Adverse Childhood Expe-
riences 254
Advice ii·43·51·92·159·
163·190·234
Alcohol 29·73·145·157·
160
All The Rage 159·167·254
Ambulance 42
Andy Griffith Show, The
160
Anger 2·21·29·30·55·68·
77·84·95·125·174·
184·199·200·201·
202·203·204·205·
206·207·208·209·
210·211·213·214·
215·216·218·219·
220·221·222·223
Anxiety 1·3·19·20·22·26·
28·31·32·38·39·50·
75·80·81·94·108·
112·120·128·131·
134·147·172·179·
187·189·219·226·
227·232·234·235·
238·253
Anxiety attacks 19·120·
128·238
Apologize 24·25·26
Appetite 46
Avoidance 68·139·143·
145·146·147·148·
171·172·173·174·
175·220
Avoiding 9·32·37·63·79·
82·83·139·143·145·
147·148·149·150·

151·154·155·161·
169·170·171·172·
173·174·175·177·
178·181·184·194·
204·209·216·220·
222·234
Awareness 1·3·6·9·10·11·
12·14·50·51·53·60·
63·64·67·72·73·75·
78·89·90·94·98·
102·108·109·111·
112·113·116·123·
126·135·136·137·
139·142·144·147·
149·152·153·154·
155·162·182·183·
184·185·195·196·
197·206·207·218·
222·231·232·233·
243·246·248·249·
250·253
Balanced 93·96
Baptist Counseling Center
32·37
Baptist Health Medical
Center 54
Bass, Ellen 38·253
Baths 188·210
Beliefs 14·51·60·96·97·98·
100·102·109·124·
127·130·131·193·
196·199·216·244·
245·247·248·249·
250
Bible 124·135·153·163·
187·199
Biological 76·78·110·111·
121·122·143·154·
187·195·213
Blog 230
Body 5·9·10·11·12·13·14·
17·19·30·33·39·40·
41·44·45·46·47·49·
50·51·53·54·55·56·
57·58·59·60·61·63·
64·65·66·67·68·69·
70·71·72·73·74·75·
76·77·78·79·81·82·
84·85·86·87·88·89·

92·93·94·98·99·
100·102·103·105·
106·107·108·109·
110·111·112·113·
114·116·117·121·
124·125·131·134·
135·136·137·139·
140·141·142·143·
144·145·147·150·
151·152·153·154·
155·157·158·159·
160·161·162·163·
164·165·166·167·
170·171·172·173·
174·175·182·183·
184·185·186·188·
189·195·196·197·
200·201·203·204·
205·206·207·208·
209·210·211·212·
213·214·215·216·
217·218·219·220·
221·222·223·226·
228·230·232·233·
234·239·244·246·
247·248·249·250·
253
Body Keeps The Score, The
254
Bodywork 14·59·67·109·
117·118·166·170·
171·219·220
Brain 5·10·12·13·17·46·47·
49·50·58·59·65·72·
73·74·78·84·88·89·
106·109·111·122·
124·134·137·149·
180·199·205·207·
216·218·225·226·
227·228·239
Brainwashed 19·37
Breaking The Habit Of
Being Yourself 13·
254
Breath 17·58·59·60·64·88·
106·107·141·142·
172·174·175·210·
217·225·228
Breathe 15·19·112·217·238

Breathing 12·15·21·57·58·
    61·93·107·122·131·
    137·142·154·174·
    175·197·205·212·
    214·221
Breathwork 74·213·215
Brother 25·26·165·190·202
Canali, Dr. Paul 12·13·64·
    72·75·87·133·140·
    143·171·203·216·
    221·247·248·249·
    253·254
Caplan, Dr. Rochelle 68
Caregivers 153·187·192·
    204·207
CD 15·74·212·213·223·
    251·253·254
CDC 254
Challenges 1·3·4·5·7·11·
    40·61·63·67·69·71·
    72·80·84·86·94·
    116·117·122·127·
    133·138·147·167·
    184·189·192·194·
    237·249·250
Chiropractor 115·151
Christmas 31·77
Chronic pain 73·208·219
Church 17·18·37·54·55·75·
    187·188
Cold water 210·211·212
Conscious 1·3·5·9·12·13·
    43·46·50·58·65·85·
    89·108·109·110·
    121·128·130·133·
    134·136·137·140·
    141·143·144·145·
    149·154·158·163·
    170·173·177·181·
    182·194·205·207·
    210·219·235·246·
    247
Consciousness 3·6·9·10·
    11·12·14·50·51·60·
    64·65·67·73·78·88·
    102·111·112·116·
    123·125·126·128·
    133·142·144·149·
    153·154·182·183·

184·185·193·195·
    196·197·199·203·
    206·207·218·222·
    231·232·233·243·
    246·248·253
Conversion disorder 1·2·
    3·4·5·10·12·14·17·
    22·41·53·67·68·69·
    75·88·116·120·127·
    135·136·151·153·
    157·158·163·171·
    196·225·227·237·
    246·247
Coping 20·80·81·82·86·
    235
Courage 22·38·45·46·47·
    48·83·92·129·130·
    148·158·180·182·
    191·195·196·225·
    227·229·230·233·
    253
Courage To Heal, The 38·
    253
Cry 28·30·42·201
Dad 18·24·25·26·29·30·
    113·159·188·190·
    201·202
Darkness 20·21·121·250
Depression 3·20·24·30·31·
    32·39·50·75·80·81·
    94·95·120·128·131·
    172·189·226·227·
    232·234
Determination 46·47·48·
    51·129·130·180·
    182·208·230·233
Die 30·31·43·211·238
Disconnect 2·9·17·65·67·
    69·73·75·78·84·85·
    88·105·108·109·
    110·111·116·123·
    124·135·139·143·
    147·148·151·152·
    153·155·157·158·
    161·172·174·185·
    189
Disconnected 2·5·10·12·
    14·39·41·56·59·65·
    66·67·69·71·72·75·

85·87·89·125·134·
    141·142·143·144·
    152·153·155·157·
    158·171·172·228
Dispenza, Dr. Joe 13·169·
    243·249·254
Doctor 3·19·41·42·44·45·
    46·48·49·55·56·
    105·115·117·120·
    145·157·159·163·
    165·166·239
Doctors 150
Dog 96·161·164·201
Dyer, Dr. Wayne 177
Easy fix 164
Emma's Blue Pills 160
Emotion 10·26·57·59·60·
    65·68·134·136·155·
    159·166·167·171·
    181·184·192·201·
    212·215·222·228
Emotional release 65·166
Encouragement 42·230
Energy 13·41·47·49·51·59·
    60·78·87·88·89·92·
    99·112·113·122·
    124·125·129·135·
    142·145·148·151·
    155·167·172·180·
    185·187·194·203·
    205·211·212·213·
    214·215·216·219·
    222·226·248·249
Enteric brain 111·205·216·
    218·223
Epstein, Dr. Donald 225·
    237
Escape 1·29·42·43·44·68·
    83·88·90·107·128·
    179·202·229·240
Evolutionary Healing
    Institute 13·253
Family 17·18·19·21·22·24·
    25·26·28·29·34·40·
    66·76·106·115·126·
    127·159·187·193·
    195·228
Family secrets 18·21·26
Father 19·27·29·68·77·114·

116·126·191·202
Fazio, Jim 253
Fear 12·18·19·21·22·27·
28·33·39·42·63·64·
65·73·78·83·87·91·
100·109·110·119·
120·121·122·123·
124·125·126·127·
128·129·130·131·
154·155·159·161·
170·171·173·185·
189·191·192·196·
197·212·222·234
Fear Poem, The 254
Feel 3·9·10·11·13·21·25·
29·33·36·37·38·42·
43·47·48·50·55·57·
58·59·60·61·63·65·
67·68·69·70·71·72·
73·74·75·76·77·78·
80·84·85·88·96·98·
99·100·105·106·
107·109·110·112·
117·122·125·129·
130·131·134·135·
136·137·140·141·
142·144·146·147·
151·153·154·155·
157·160·162·171·
172·174·175·177·
178·186·187·188·
189·190·204·205·
206·209·210·211·
212·213·214·215·
216·217·218·219·
220·222·223·226·
229·230·234·238·
239·248·249·250
Feelings 10·11·19·26·57·
84·85·113·134·135·
136·140·155·171·
192·215
Felt sense 9·13·14·85·134·
135·136·137·139·
140·141·142·143·
155·157·161·162·
163·166·182·183·
186·206·248
Galinsky, Michael 254

Gay 19
Gendlin, Dr. Eugene 63
Gershon, Dr. Michael 111
God 17·19·20·29·37·40·43·
163·199·202
Goliath 124·153
Grandfather 21·165·166
Grounded 90·96·125·220·
221
Growth 6·12·91·96·109·
110·131·138·154·
184·185·232·234·
248
Guided relaxation 54·56·
162
Gut-brain 216
Harjo, Joy 131·254
Hate 89·90·106·124·126·
179·189·207·249
Heal 1·2·3·4·5·10·26·30·
35·38·40·45·46·48·
49·50·51·60·65·66·
75·84·85·91·92·94·
97·98·102·116·127·
143·148·153·158·
159·164·165·169·
171·173·174·175·
183·184·185·189·
195·196·200·205·
208·210·221·222·
225·226·228·229·
231·232·234·235·
237·240·243·245·
246·247·249·250
Healing iii·1·4·5·6·12·13·
14·20·23·25·26·27·
33·35·37·38·39·40·
46·47·48·49·50·51·
52·53·63·64·65·66·
72·73·75·80·85·90·
91·92·93·94·96·97·
98·99·101·102·103·
110·112·119·126·
133·139·143·149·
154·159·160·161·
162·164·166·167·
169·170·171·172·
173·174·175·177·
178·182·183·184·

185·193·195·200·
204·212·213·214·
216·217·218·220·
221·222·225·226·
227·228·229·230·
231·232·233·234·
235·237·238·239·
240·241·243·244·
245·247·248·249·
250·253·254
Health ii·56·58·66·72·88·
93·97·101·112·120·
124·125·128·131·
134·140·169·178·
190·200·214·216·
223
Health treatments 120
Healthy 9·59·60·63·80·90·
96·121·158·203·
204·206·223
Healthy behavior 60
Heart iii·4·10·12·20·21·
28·34·39·43·57·79·
93·94·121·140·191·
196·208·238·239·
244·245·250
High school 55·114·163·
187·193
Holidays 31
Hope 2·3·6·14·24·25·29·
39·40·43·51·74·78·
81·85·86·88·96·98·
101·123·125·155·
158·174·179·183·
197·221·223·229·
230·250
Horsey 21
Hospital 17·20·42·43·48·
53·54·55·56·57·67·
84·88·127·157·161·
163·227·237·247
Hot And Cold Baths 210
How Could Anyone 38·
197
Ice 27·108·211·212·213·
214
Ice bath 212·214
Insecurity 187·188·189·
190·191·193·194·

196

Inspirational thoughts 55

Journal 134·230

Journaling 238

Journey 1·2·4·6·35·44·48· 52·53·56·57·61·70· 72·83·85·92·102· 103·126·136·138· 148·149·163·164· 173·196·197·204· 225·226·233·243· 248·250·254

Joy 3·58·70·72·76·80·85· 87·89·90·94·120· 149·155·174·175· 178·214·235

Kill myself 32·34

Kittens 115

Labels 47·49·50·52·153

Letters 19·20·24·26·195

Letting go 4·11·24·39·56· 58·59·60·65·66·85· 87·88·122·123·127· 128·129·130·138· 140·158·166·178· 182·185·192·193· 195·196·205·207· 209·213·217·218· 219·222·227·233· 235·240·249

Levine, Dr. Peter 9·64·119· 206·249·253

Lew, Mike 38·249·253

Love iii·2·19·20·25·26·33· 38·42·44·47·48·52· 59·79·80·85·87·89· 90·93·94·122·155· 173·177·184·220· 221·239·240·243· 244·254

Magic pill 160·161·166· 167

Maladaptive 68·69

Maladaptive problem solving 68

Mantras 2·5·59·88·90·175

Massage 59·67·97·117·118· 133·164·170·171· 218·219·220

Massage - deep pressure 67·219·220

Massage therapist 97·170· 219

Medical condition 127

Medical procedures 126· 158·165

Meditation 15·54·70·74· 141·157·205·216· 221·223·251·253

Meditation Exercises 15· 74·223·251·253

Memes 1·203·222

Memories 206

Memory 10·20·22·30·33· 123·149·187·222· 226

Mental health issues 66· 200

Mind 3·5·6·9·10·11·12·13· 14·17·18·19·21·22· 23·27·28·29·30·31· 32·33·37·42·43·44· 45·48·51·52·53·54· 56·57·58·59·60·61· 63·64·65·66·67·71· 72·73·74·75·76·77· 79·81·82·84·85·87· 89·92·93·94·98·99· 100·102·105·106· 107·109·110·112· 114·115·116·121· 124·125·126·128· 129·133·134·135· 136·137·138·139· 140·141·142·143· 144·145·147·148· 149·150·151·152· 153·154·155·157· 158·159·161·162· 163·164·165·166· 167·170·171·172· 174·177·178·179· 180·183·185·186· 187·189·190·192· 197·200·205·206· 207·208·210·211· 212·213·214·215· 217·218·219·220·

221·222·223·225· 226·228·230·231· 232·233·234·237· 238·241·244·246· 248·249·250·253

Mind body 9·10·11·12·13· 14·53·59·61·63·64· 66·77·135·141·142· 144·151·152·164· 167·183·205·207· 213·221·222

Mind Body Prescription, The 159

Molested 19·157·171·184

Mom 19·24·25·26·29·34· 55·77·153·165·166· 190

Monsters 28·29·33·55·124· 128

Movement 65·130·142· 194·206·215·216· 227·237

Multiple sclerosis 42

Negative pleasure 140·147· 177·178·179·180· 181·182·183·184· 185·186

Nervous stomach 55·114· 163

Nervous system 5·10·80· 111·117·142·151· 152·174·210·213· 214

Neural pathway 149·150· 151·153·186·189· 195·230

New age 14·56·60·97·107· 112·143

Nightmare 24·27·28·31·32· 35·92·94·98·125· 194·202

Noll, Shaina 38·197·254

Notice 6·10·12·13·15·41· 59·61·63·69·70·71· 72·74·79·89·90· 100·105·112·135· 138·139·141·143· 144·152·155·170· 174·175·186·197·

207·208·210·214·
215·223
Numb 2·5·12·17·56·57·
59·60·63·65·67·68·
69·72·73·75·82·87·
105·108·109·134·
143·145·147·148·
150·151·152·153·
154·155·157·158·
161·174·185·212·
213·220·222·228
Numbing 1·2·57·60·67·69·
74·82·85·109·110·
111·116·133·135·
139·143·145·147·
148·150·151·152·
153·154·155·171·
175·194·203·209·
220
Nurses 44·45
NutriBullet 213
Oatmeal 213·214
Observe 13·15·59·61·112·
119·141·142·143·
155·167·181·195·
208·217·218
Onion 148·221·232
Opinions 51·96·102·109·
124·127·193·196·
199·244·245·248
Overwhelm 63
Overwhelming 17·31·44·
63·85·88·95·109·
114·122·129·136·
147·149·150·151·
154·155·172·205·
217·229
Pain iii·1·2·3·6·9·12·13·27·
28·29·30·31·32·33·
34·36·40·50·52·60·
65·67·69·72·73·75·
78·81·88·89·92·94·
96·98·108·111·112·
114·115·117·122·
125·126·131·134·
135·139·142·143·
144·145·146·147·
149·150·151·152·
153·154·155·159·

160·165·166·167·
172·173·178·179·
194·197·199·200·
201·204·205·206·
208·209·214·216·
219·220·227·229·
233·234·239·240·
245·248·249·250·
253·254
Paralysis 3·12·14·17·41·
48·64·65·89·115·
116·151·183·225·
227·246
Paralyzed 2·10·49·51·53·
67·75·84·92·120·
123·183·225·237
Paralyzing 121·229
Parents 17·19·20·23·24·
25·26·30·37·42·47·
55·68·187·192·193·
195·203·246
Past 2·4·7·17·25·37·39·
52·59·64·66·70·73·
75·79·87·88·90·93·
100·101·109·110·
111·112·113·114·
116·123·125·130·
139·140·150·151·
152·153·155·161·
172·184·189·191·
194·205·212·220·
221·229·233·239·
240
Past experiences 59·75·79·
101·109·110·111·
112·139·140·150·
153·191·233
Peace 3·23·24·36·39·53·54·
56·57·58·59·60·61·
70·72·76·77·80·85·
92·94·107·113·120·
122·142·147·148·
149·155·162·175·
214·221·235·248
Pendulation 64·65
Perfectionist 54
Pets 18·31·33·69·201
Physical ailments 56·66·
116

Physical therapy 45·46·
227
Piano 55·190
Placebo effect 166
Placebos 165
Platitudes 1·2·9·92
Poem 35·38·230·254
Poster board 35·131·231
Prayers 2·43·59·92·163
Prescription 160·165·166
Primack, Jeff 212
Primal screams 215
Process 1·6·11·14·25·31·
46·48·64·71·72·89·
90·91·106·109·110·
112·126·133·142·
152·163·164·173·
174·182·183·184·
185·193·194·195·
202·205·206·207·
211·212·213·214·
216·222·229·230·
231·232·240·248·
249·250
Pseudoseizures 41·42
Psychiatrist 31·32·45·163
Psychologist 37
Punishment 18·19·31
Purple 27·30·32
Qigong 205·212
Raped 30·157·184
Rash 140·154·210·211·
213·214
Relaxation 53·54·55·56·
57·58·59·60·61·69·
70·99·114·122·161·
162·163·214·221·
238
Religious 18·145·193·196
Resources 253
Rewire 74·230
Rewiring the brain 65
Sadness 30·68·204
Safe word 205
Sapolsky, Dr. Robert 105·
157
Sarno, Dr. John 159·199·
249·254
Screaming 12·21·22·27·

55·67·108·111·115·
190·201·202·212·
213·215·229·239
Seizures 116
Self-confidence 47·231
Self-pity 178
Sense 1·9·10·13·14·22·27·
28·30·45·48·63·67·
70·71·72·74·75·78·
80·85·108·134·135·
136·137·139·140·
141·142·143·144·
155·157·158·159·
161·162·163·166·
171·174·181·182·
183·186·190·202·
206·215·216·217·
218·219·220·226·
235·237·248·254
Sexual abuse 17·81·237·
253
Showers 188
Show Me Your Face 35
Sleep 32
Sleep difficulties 125
Somatization 12
Songs For The Inner Child
254
Strength 24·28·31·38·39·
46·47·48·65·69·72·
89·92·122·129·130·
142·148·173·179·
193·194·195·212·
230·231·233·240·
243
Stress 29·44·55·59·66·69·
72·73·74·75·76·77·
78·79·80·82·93·94·
105·106·108·109·
110·111·112·113·
114·115·116·117·
118·120·121·122·
134·135·139·143·
147·151·157·158·
163·171·172·174·
177·194·199·205·
211·214·216·218·
219·228
Stressful events 65

Stressors 12·61·67·68·69·
72·110·117
Suffering 52·67·70·72·75·
76·122·127·149·
165·167·183·226
Suicidal thoughts 20
Suicide 39·120·128·179·
180·239
Suicide attempts 179
Support 26·39·42·73·85·
157·234·237·238·
239·243·244·247
Suppress anger 208
Survival 12·14·23·28·70·
73·75·76·77·78·79·
80·82·83·84·85·86·
87·88·89·90·91·92·
93·94·95·96·98·99·
101·102·109·121·
122·123·126·128·
130·131·137·140·
157·161·162·166·
167·175
Survival mode 70·73·75·
76·77·78·79·80·82·
83·84·85·86·87·88·
89·90·91·92·93·94·
95·96·98·101·102·
121·122·123·126·
128·130·131·140·
161·162·166·167·
175
Survive 25·68·78·79·81·84·
123·126·131·148·
158·159·169·225
Swamp 232
Thanksgiving 28·29
Therapies 158
Therapist 33·34·35·37·46·
47·50·54·81·97·
169·170·219·220·
222·239
Therapists 157·169·219·
220·221·238
Therapy 20·31·34·45·46·
72·134·140·153·
162·164·170·171·
203·206·221·227·
232·238

Thoughts and prayers 43
Threats 18·75·76·77·79·82·
83·84·85·122
Tiger 79·80·82·83·92·93·
121·122·128·140·
173
Tolle, Eckhart 133·145
Toxic 19·33·55·59·66·76·
79·82·122·139·140·
150·172·193·195·
200·205·228
Toxic stress 59·66·76·79·
82·122·139·172·
205
Traffic cop 207
Trauma 3·6·17·40·41·65·
66·69·70·73·74·76·
78·79·80·82·84·88·
93·95·109·122·135·
139·143·151·158·
166·170·171·172·
177·221·228·229·
231·233·237·239·
240·243·248·249·
250·253
Traumatic experiences 51
Trigger 123·130·170·205·
222
Unconscious 47·66·94·
121·125·133·134·
135·136·137·138·
139·140·142·143·
144·147·150·154·
160·194·203·204·
208·209
Valium 216
Van Der Kolk, Dr. Bessel
17·41·64·187·249·
254
Victims No Longer 253
VOICES 37·38·39·253
Waking The Tiger 253
Walked 1·32·33·49·52·55·
115·195·243
Wallace, Emma 33·81
White light 44·45·47·48
Wounded self 228·231
Writing 230
Xanax 216

Chapter Quote Sources

1. Hope And Possibility Through Trauma, Don Shetterly
2. Freedom From Pain, Dr. Peter A. Levine, Ph.D.
3. The Body Keeps The Score, Dr. Bessel van der Kolk, M.D.
4. The Body Keeps The Score, Dr. Bessel van der Kolk, M.D.
5. Hope And Possibility Through Trauma, Don Shetterly
6. Focusing, Dr. Eugene T. Gendlin, Ph.D.
7. Dr. Paul Canali, Evolutionary Healing Institute
8. Dr. Paul Canali, Evolutionary Healing Institute
9. Why Zebras Don't Get Ulcers, Dr. Robert M. Sapolsky, Ph.D.
10. Freedom From Pain, Dr. Peter A. Levine, Ph.D.
11. The Power Of Now, Eckhart Tolle
12. Huffington Post Article written by Eckhart Tolle
13. Wired.com Article on Dr. Robert Sapolsky, Ph.D.
14. You Are The Placebo, Dr. Joe Dispenza, D.C.
15. Quote from Dr. Wayne Dyer's Facebook Page
16. The Body Keeps The Score, Dr. Bessel van der Kolk, M.D.
17. Freedom From Pain, Dr. Peter A. Levine, Ph.D.
18. The 12 Stages Of Healing, Dr. Donald M. Epstein, D.C.
19. The 12 Stages Of Healing, Dr. Donald M. Epstein, D.C.
20. Breaking The Habit Of Being Yourself, Dr. Joe Dispenza, D.C.

About The Author

In 1991, Don Shetterly suffered from a mysterious condition called conversion disorder, also known as a somatoform disorder. He experienced paralysis, pseudo seizures, anxiety, depression, and suicide attempts as a result of being tortured, abused, and molested as a child.

Don graduated in 2003 from Educating Hands School Of Massage and is currently a licensed massage therapist. He trained under Dr. Paul Canali, a pioneer in trauma healing, beginning in 2004.

He is a prolific writer and blogger. He has also released several relaxing piano music CD's since 2002 and is the author of Hope and Possibility Through Trauma, published in 2010.

In 2010, Don was part of the 200 Male Survivors episode on Oprah and in 2012, he was a guest on the Dr. Drew Show.

Don enjoys conducting workshops on the topics of relaxation and the mind body connection.

Residing in Central Florida, Don enjoys being outside in nature and taking photographs. He is extremely creative and loves to travel.

https://OvercomingAMysteriousCondition.com

www.ingramcontent.com/pod-product-compliance
Lightning Source LLC
Chambersburg PA
CBHW071412090426

42737CB00011B/1433